COLONISED MINDS

T0244328

COLONISED MINDS

Narratives that
Shape Psychology

Akira O'Connor
Erin Robbins

1 Oliver's Yard
55 City Road
London EC1Y 1SP

2455 Teller Road
Thousand Oaks
California 91320

Unit No 323-333, Third Floor, F-Block
International Trade Tower
Nehru Place, New Delhi – 110 019

8 Marina View Suite 43-053
Asia Square Tower 1
Singapore 018960

Editor: Janka Romero
Assistant editor: Emma Yuan
Production editor: Martin Fox
Copyeditor: Elaine Leek
Proofreader: Tom Bedford
Indexer: Charmian Parkin
Marketing manager: Camille Richmond
Cover design: Shaun Mercier
Typeset by: C&M Digitals (P) Ltd, Chennai, India
Printed and bound by CPI Group (UK) Ltd, Croydon, CR0 4YY

Library of Congress Control Number: 2023946090

British Library Cataloguing in Publication data

A catalogue record for this book is available from the British Library

ISBN 978-1-5297-9180-8
ISBN 978-1-5297-9179-2 (pbk)

CONTENTS

PREFACE
POSITIONALITY STATEMENT

This book is our attempt to understand the modern canon of psychology as it may be encountered at universities in the English-speaking Global North. The authors have spent time studying and working in the USA, but have written this book as academics employed at the University of St Andrews in Scotland. Our context informs our approach. We are situated in an academic environment that is part of the British higher education system, but that is also heavily influenced by North American research, discourse and culture. The research, narratives and historical context we use bleeds across these English-speaking worlds, as it does across these pages.

In the context of our discipline, the use of the term canon—a set of works that it is considered essential to study, and a readily accepted way of teaching them— may seem confusing. Disciplines such as English literature and art history lend themselves to intuitively being thought of as teaching a canon, but this seems less descriptive of psychology. Scratch beneath the surface of any undergraduate curriculum though, and you will find a set of commonalities in the assumptions we make, the ideas and analytic tools we use and the perspectives that underpin our teaching. This is the canon that we are trying to understand.

The book has its origins in a series of short segments included in statistics lectures given as part of a compulsory Introduction to Psychology undergraduate module. These segments focused on the people behind the statistics being taught, and were intended as a change of pace, mid-way through each lecture. After a few years, they were worked into a series of well-received departmental talks, and then a talk given to the heads of all UK university psychology departments. As sector-wide interest in decolonising and diversifying curricula grew, the focus of the talks shifted from the historic figures themselves, to the systems of inequality they strengthened with their work. As the focus on systems became clearer, it became apparent that this approach could be applied to many subdisciplines within psychology and neuroscience. 'I can't diversify my teaching, because I teach only the most influential work' stopped being a reason not to engage and became a reason to explore why work is considered influential, and what the systems are that perpetuate this influence. And so the rationale for the book, as a text exploring the origins of a broad range of subdisciplines of psychology, became clear.

WHERE DO WE KNOW FROM?

We are not decolonial scholars. Rather, we are researchers in memory and developmental psychology who have attempted to find ways to acknowledge the origins of our discipline. For this reason, there will be passages, whole chapters even, where the paths we have taken to this understanding seem clumsy, where we have missed key issues or figures, or where our interpretation does not align with yours. On the whole though, we hope that our approach is accessible and interesting. Most importantly, we intend to give you guideposts for understanding the subdisciplines we have covered, and to make you inquisitive enough to find routes to understanding those we have not.

Akira O'Connor is a Senior Lecturer who received his undergraduate and postgraduate education at the University of Leeds (England). He spent two and a half years working at Washington University in St Louis (USA), before taking up a permanent lecturing position at the University of St Andrews (Scotland). Akira researches memory, memory decision-making and memory phenomena such as déjà vu. His parents are Irish and Japanese, and he grew up in North-West London—not British, but a mixed-race Londoner. He is a trade union member and serves as the Race Equality Charter Chair at the university, coordinating an institutional bid for a Race Equality Charter award.

Erin Robbins is a Lecturer from the South of the United States. She completed her undergraduate education at Birmingham-Southern College in Alabama (USA) and her postgraduate training at Emory University in Atlanta, Georgia (USA). In-between she worked in a number of different jobs, from technical writer to conservationist. Her primary interest is in the role of culture in cognition and development which led her to pursue field work, primarily in Samoa and Vanuatu. She is queer, a trade union member and serves as the Director of Equality, Diversity and Inclusion for her department.

Our personal and professional experiences continually shape and reshape how we think about psychology. Despite our critique of this approach in Chapter 5, Akira has published neuroimaging work using functional magnetic resonance imaging (fMRI) and presented thresholded statistical maps that show areas of brain 'activity' and 'inactivity'. Despite what we write in Chapter 2, Akira spent the majority of his career so far at St Andrews teaching statistics in a way that did not make the eugenic origins of the discipline clear. Erin has used cross-cultural methods extensively in her own research, but in Chapter 8, we discuss the philosophical and ethical issues with such approaches when it comes to making psychology a more representative and inclusive science. We hope you do not take these contradictions as evidence of our willing hypocrisy but understand our previous experiences as starting points for the development of our thoughts in these areas. We do not propose that our current intellectual positions are the 'right' ones, nor that the path we have taken to them should become canonical. Once again, we hope that our own development—from positions minimally critical of the canon to positions that are more engaged in thinking about *why* we teach and research in the way that we do, and *what alternatives* there might be—serves as an example of how this change can be pursued. We think our accounts provide examples of how colleagues can engage in critical discussions about our discipline, and how self-reflection can be incorporated into scholarship.

Returning to our positions within canonised institutions, we have spent our careers at English-speaking universities in the Global North and are now permanent employees of the University of St Andrews. Ours is a 600-year-old institution steeped in privilege, and with a worldwide reputation for academic excellence. Given the narratives within this book, there is temptation to distance ourselves from privilege, emphasising instead the minoritised facets of our identities. But this would be disingenuous. We have been able to publish this book because we ourselves hold privilege, our employers hold privilege, and these combined privileges allow us to contribute to an aspect of the canon. Whilst we have benefitted from aspects of our identities and positions within structures that confer privilege, what we hope becomes evident is that we also 'know from' a range of experiences that are not canonical (Zuroski, 2020).

THE BOOK

The Title – Colonised Minds: Narratives that Shape Psychology

An important realisation we made early in the writing process was that there is no single story about how psychology came to be. There are many narratives because the power structures that shape our discipline are also multiple. This book is not a decolonial project, though elements of our thinking are certainly informed by decolonial work. The way we do our scholarship—even the fact that we are publishing a book with an established publisher—is all positioned within an institutional framework that is the legacy of colonialism. We cannot escape this fact, nor should we minimise it. Ours is therefore a critical approach—one that seeks to illuminate how the study of minds (ours included) has been shaped by this history.

Content

This book comprises a series of interlinking narratives that we use to highlight how a range of power structures have influenced the discipline of psychology. In deciding which subdisciplines to focus on, we initially thought about structuring the book to have a chapter for each of the British Psychological Society's key teaching areas. In exploring the literature further to follow narratives that explain canonical thought to their origins, we moved away from this structure and towards one that gives each chapter the most compelling and congruent narratives. This is why we have chapters that amalgamate a range of the British Psychological Society's teaching areas—e.g. those on technology (Chapter 5), women and race (Chapters 6 and 7), culture (Chapter 8) and universities (Chapter 9)—alongside chapters that are much more focused on specific teaching areas—e.g. conceptual and historical issues (Chapter 1), research methods (Chapter 2) and developmental psychology (Chapter 3). This structure is intended to make the book as engaging as possible to those with a passing interest in psychology but who do not have knowledge of its subdisciplinary divisions, as well as to scholars and students who hold full awareness of them.

Terminology

The language we have written here mirrors the dominant reality of academia in the English-speaking Global North. Nonetheless, we have tried to be deliberate and mindful of the preferences of those being described in the terminology we have used to characterise people and their origins. In some instances, we use the same terminology as authors we cite as a way to honour terms that have been reclaimed by minoritised communities (e.g. 'queer' rather than 'LGBTQIA+'; Riggs & Walker, 2006). There are instances where our deliberate use of language gives way to less preferred language drawn from our sources. For example, there are times when we use 'Western' for consistency with our sources, when we would prefer to use 'from the Global North'. We have also quoted language that is now considered offensive from sources who either did or did not consider it so at the time. We apologise if this is shocking but believe that there is value in presenting language as it was originally written.

We have chosen to capitalise 'Black' and to lowercase 'white' when these terms are used in racial, ethnic or cultural senses. This choice mirrors Associated Press style, but deviates from others, including American Psychological Association style, which capitalises both. Our decision to capitalise Black was straightforward. In doing so, we recognise the shared experiences that exist for Black people, including historic and current discrimination and marginalisation. By capitalising Black, we push back against 'colourblind' arguments that skin colour, particularly Blackness, is not important to people's experiences of the world. Our decision not to capitalise white was harder. Whilst arguments for capitalising white include consistency with our approach to Black, and making issues of race, ethnicity and culture in psychology more relevant to white people, we ultimately decided that there were stronger arguments against doing so. First, white people do not share seismic historic or current experiences of discrimination based solely on the colour of their skin, especially in the contexts about which we are writing. Second, we saw no need to draw attention to whiteness in how we write about it because, as we will present throughout this book, so much of psychology has always been influenced by and centered on it.

In writing a document to be printed and made into an ebook, we recognise that preferred language will change over time, whilst this text will not. We also recognise that, despite our intentions, we will not always have made the right choices. We will learn from the mistakes we have made.

Illustrations

A message central to the book is that psychology is not in the shape it is in because of the actions of comic book heroes and villains. No one individual has ever wielded enough power to single-handedly push the discipline in any specific direction. Systems and communities have always carried far more influence. With this in mind, it perhaps seems strange that we have nonetheless highlighted the contributions of specific people in the text and with portraits. We made the decision to feature portraits to celebrate the work of minoritised scholars because we decided that this visibility was potentially valuable. There is undoubtedly room for more diversity within the characteristics of those we chose to feature, but we hope that what we have done in this book adds to the growing body of work that seeks to make more visible the work of historically minoritised people.

In commissioning the portraits—from Gaby Guilarte at Nudos lab[1]—we gave consideration to the stylised representation of people of colour. In many ways, portraying all contributors to psychology with black outlines bordering light skin is the perfect representation of white supremacy—a re-imagining of the canon in which we the authors depict Black scholars with light skin. But, the constraints of copyright licensing and black-and-white printing imposed on us meant that we had little choice but to proceed with stylised original portraits, should we wish to print portraits at all. Once again, we decided that the visibility gained by including portraits was important, and so made the choice to include portraits, albeit breaking from the black/white binary with the choice of grey for the outline. There will be people who disagree with this choice. In any case, we would like you to know that we reflected on this, and asked others to give us their thoughts on this. We made these choices after a great deal of consideration.

---

[1]See https://www.instagram.com/nudos_lab/ for more of the artist's work.

Further Reading and Discussion

We finish each chapter with recommendations for further reading. These materials were, in many cases, seminal in the formulation of our narratives, and we think are worthy of your attention. In some cases though, they were popular media—magazine articles or television shows—that provided an interesting or neat distillation of some of the key issues covered in that chapter. Adam Curtis' television series *Can't Get You Out of My Head* (2021) is an example of the latter sort of recommendation. We recommend that programme at the end of this statement because it illustrates a sort of historical story-telling that excited us about how we might write this book.

If at all possible, we also recommend that book chapters be discussed in small groups. During our time at St Andrews, we have found that regular meetings to discuss issues of equality, diversity and inclusion (EDI) are often most stimulating and productive when they are presented for discussion as topics of interest in their own right. An activity that has worked well in our experience is to approach EDI issues through the lens of culture, as in the example of informal reading groups[2] that engage with popular media (magazine articles, film, television, podcasts) as an interesting and accessible way to introduce big ideas about equality, diversity, ethics and governance to a broad audience. We find that this approach invites deeper discussion and greater participation, particularly from colleagues and students who ordinarily avoid engaging with EDI activities. EDI encompasses many issues of societal and scientific importance, yet its abbreviation into three sterile letters suggests a uniformity and proceduralism that leads many to avoid those discussions where they can. We hope that situating what are essentially EDI issues in the canon of psychology leads those who might typically avoid them to reconsider and engage in discussion.

FINAL REMARKS

It is crucial to recognise that, whilst many of the power structures we discuss have colonial roots, we do not advance a plan to decolonise the curriculum in this work. Our advocacy for an antiracist, antisexist curriculum that acknowledges its colonial origins does not equate to decolonization in the sense of radical, disruptive practices that would dismantle the system entirely (Tuck & Yang, 2012). The steps we propose in the **What Next?** sections of each chapter remain within the bounds of existing power structures. We understand that this gradual approach

---

[2]Culture Club (https://cultureclub.wp.st-andrews.ac.uk/)

will not instantaneously dismantle these structures and may fall short for those eager to witness immediate, transformative change. There are others, whose expertise and deep insights derived from academic inquiry and the raw truths of lived experience, who are better positioned to spearhead a systemic revolution. Nonetheless, our approach prompts an essential question: What good might come from adopting our gradual approach, even within the existing system? We believe the merit of our work rests in its ability to cultivate connections that could, in time, pave the way for new, more just systems of creating, sharing and ultimately, applying knowledge.

FURTHER READING

hooks, b. (1994). *Teaching to Transgress*. Routledge. [book]

A powerful and prescient presentation of the importance of critical thinking, politics and passion in the university classroom. Whilst not cited in this chapter, hooks' collection of essays explores the critical approach that has heavily influenced our own work, and would be an ideal starting point for someone looking to do the same in theirs.

Zuroski, E. (2020). 'Where do you know from?': An exercise in placing ourselves together in the classroom. https://maifeminism.com/where-do-you-know-from-an-exercise-in-placing-ourselves-together-in-the-classroom/ [website]

An 'ice-breaker' exercise that situates participants in the value of many forms of knowledge.

Curtis, A. (2021) *Can't get you out of my head*. BBC. [TV series]

A documentary written by Adam Curtis that explores the ways in which today's societies have been shaped by now-forgotten historical narratives.

ACKNOWLEDGEMENTS

Writing a book is not possible without others. Whether they know it or not, many people inspired, bolstered and carried us through this process.

To the good people of Drimnin, Ardfern, Dundee, London, and the various towns and villages across Fife where we wrote: thank you for your hospitality.

To Scotland, our adopted nation: Thank you for opening your arms to us. Here in your natural beauty, in small pubs and winding streets we found courage, kindness and community.

Thank you to public libraries, coffee shops, supermarket cafes. You are glorious!

Gratitude to our colleagues, now and in the past, whose engagement opened a world of ideas to us: Chris, Bentley, Tanya, Philippe, Elena, Sapi, Edgar, Fischer, Paul, David, Tom.

Appreciation to our friends, family and communities whose constancy provided support and solidarity: Lorna, Libby and Sarah, Des and Yoko and Kenji, Rick and Barb, Douglas and Karen, Rachel and Carrie, Sam, Matt, Anna, Robert, Dave, Liz, Jackie, Anne, Richard, Catherine, Prabs, Amritesh, Dharini, Shruti, Jasmin.

Our thanks to the University of St Andrews for providing us with time and resource to write this book. To our publishers and editors—Janka, Emma, the team at Sage and Donna—we must extend our deepest appreciation for their patience, enthusiastic support and curiosity in taking on this project with us.

To our children: how wondrous and bittersweet it is to encounter this world anew with you.

1

INTRODUCTION

THE CANON AND SYSTEMS OF THOUGHT

> Disrupting Western canons of scholarship requires alternatives to the single narrative that infuses current epistemological, methodological, and teaching approaches. The alternative must include knowledge systems that value multiple realities ... the Western knowledge system is one of many knowledge systems in the world and cannot claim monopoly over knowledge production. (Canham et al., 2021, p. 195)

Psychology as a discipline is a colonial project. What we mean by this is that psychological science is rooted in ways of thinking, observing, feeling and relating that stem directly from British, European and North American global domination (Adams et al., 2018). *Coloniality* describes the particular forms of knowledge and ways of being that arise from this history. It refers to ideas, values and cultural practices that were imposed across the world in the past and that continue to influence psychology in the present (Adams et al., 2018; Bhatia & Priya, 2021). We are at a moment in time when it is no longer morally defensible or feasible to pretend that this colonial past was benevolent, or that it is irrelevant to current practice. Understanding our colonised psychology requires us to reflect on how our beliefs about the mind first emerged and then cemented themselves in our way of doing scholarship.

We have approached this book and its content as a series of stories. Some of these are origin stories, tracing the roots of an idea or movement and explaining how that history influences contemporary practice. Some of these are detective stories, bringing to light names and notions that may have been lost to memory. Some of these are speculative stories, imagining what the history and future of the discipline could look like in different philosophical and cultural contexts.

This chapter is a creation story. It attempts to identify and describe the cultural frameworks and philosophical systems that are foundational to psychology. In what follows we explore this notion of a 'psychological canon'. We then identify some of the canonical persons, perspectives and processes that we believe have shaped the field of psychology as we know it. Throughout the chapter, what we contribute to the topic is a fourth consideration, power, which is not typically included when we talk about the origins and history of our field. Power structures implicitly and explicitly shape the way a discipline develops by determining access to resources and by establishing what topics, modes of inquiry and kinds of scholars get to participate in the system. By exploring how these themes bear out in the psychology of the English-speaking Global North, particularly in the UK and USA, we seek to better understand the kinds of stories we tell, who is allowed to tell them and how.

WHAT IS A CANON?

A canon is a set of essential works or ideas that define a field. It serves the important function of 'anchoring' a discipline by contributing to the conservation and stability of knowledge and techniques (Gordon, 1992). In short, a canon represents a set of beliefs that are commonly taken to be true and that guide our understanding of the proper way to share and expand on that knowledge.

When ideas are described as canonical, they tend to be widely known and endorsed by members of a given community (Canham et al., 2021). Consensus is important because it gives canonical beliefs gravity—a sense that they must represent 'the truth' about a field. We who are familiar with the canon can talk about canonical figures who are central to the discipline—for example, we can point to Sigmund Freud as the founder of psychoanalysis. We can also think of ideas and practices as being canonical, in the sense that they are considered essential pieces of knowledge and indispensable ways of doing things. Describing psychology as the scientific study of the mind and behaviour provides an insight into both a canonical belief and canonical practice. As practitioners we believe that ours is an empirical, experimental discipline, meaning we practise scholarship in a way that emphasises objectivity and tests evidentiary claims.

The establishment of a canon is a complex interplay of philosophical, cultural and financial forces. The kinds of questions a society deems appropriate topics of investigation may be shaped by *epistemology*—beliefs about the origins, scope and importance of knowledge. Such beliefs then drive the cultural practices that determine who produces, exercises and controls knowledge. People, institutions and texts may all become repositories not just of the knowledge itself, but of 'the way things are done.' For this reason, canons are inherently political: they are a powerful force for social cohesion and meaning-making (Bruner, 1991). Taken uncritically, however, a canon can generate the false impression that there is a single, universal way of doing things, and a single, universal history that represents everyone (Costall, 2006). Tensions arise when a canon becomes too rigid to accommodate change in the form of new technology, information, or perspectives. We are arguably living in such a moment now, when the stories that many see as foundational and central to our field are being challenged by those of us who have felt excluded and marginalised by systems of power. This is not to say that what we think of as our foundational stories are unimportant, or that the values and knowledge they espouse are wrong. Without question, they have shaped the way we think about and practise our discipline. But our storytelling is often incomplete.

The psychological canon of the English-speaking Global North is a legacy of European and American colonialism. It developed in the larger framework of a system that privileged the values, knowledge and politics of whiteness. Many of the concepts and methods in our modern, scientific arsenal developed in response to the beliefs and needs of colonial systems whose survival depended on the prediction and control of behaviour (Linstrum, 2016). As a field, psychology has often reinforced coloniality while simultaneously presenting itself as an impartial and value-neutral enterprise. It generated and celebrated knowledge about an idealised, abstract, universal 'mind' while systematically devaluing and minimising the knowledge and lived experience of the minoritised persons who contributed to that body of work. We cannot speak for all the persons whose stories have been supressed or erased from the canon. Instead, our aim is to explore this psychological canon, identifying the threads of power that enabled this story to develop over the countless others that could have taken root.

WHAT CHARACTERISES THE PSYCHOLOGICAL CANON?

We can think of a canon as comprising three Ps: people, perspectives and processes. The **people** who are canonical to our field are the 'big names' and 'founding fathers.' In some cases, these identities are so well known they lend their name to a set of findings or apparatuses. For example, Freud is famous for his theories about the unconscious mind, enough so that we speak of 'Freudian slips' when we make a particular linguistic mistake. Psychology students may encounter Skinner boxes (enclosed containers that deliver a reinforcement or punishment to an organism in response to their behaviour, a nod to B.F. Skinner's work on operant conditioning) and may describe automatic responses as Pavlovian (a reference to the classical conditioning work of Ivan Pavlov).

Similarly, what we mean by canonical **perspectives** are those values, theories and findings that are so core to the field as to be considered established fact. We have already seen one such example (a description of psychology as the scientific study of the mind and behaviour, presented earlier in the chapter). Other examples might include the idea that the brain is the seat of thought, or that the nervous system comprises individual cells called neurons. Canonical beliefs have tremendous staying-power. We think of them as self-evident, yet rarely examine our basis for doing so.

Finally, **processes**: there is a corresponding set of canonical methods that psychologists have used to generate knowledge about the mind, as well as accepted practices about how this knowledge should be documented and disseminated.

What we advocate in this chapter is that consideration of these three Ps is incomplete without an additional consideration: **power**. A critical approach to psychology involves questioning and analysing the underlying power structures of our discipline. This may include institutional sources of power, such as the universities, academic bodies and professional organisations that all play a role in shaping the direction and application of psychological research. It may include cultural or societal influences that impact interpersonal decision-making. Power may also be economic, as in the example of funding sources or market forces that impact research priorities.

Canonical people, perspectives and processes are those that have generated substantial debate and interest over a long period of time. Note that this does not mean that canonical figures or ideas are necessarily accurate—we can certainly think of famous thinkers who got it wrong. Rather, canonical works and individuals have endurance and shape the direction, development and thinking of future scholars. In this way they consolidate power and influence. As a result, canonical works, persons and processes enjoy a high degree of acceptance, consensus and recognition amongst experts and potentially the broader public. In the next section, we explore this last point in more detail, examining how the idea of public scholarship and engagement relates to the development of the psychological canon.

CANONICAL PEOPLE

Canonical figures in psychology are often described as eminent, meaning they are persons who are well known and well regarded within the field. Historically, the people we celebrate as eminent scholars in psychology often came from privileged backgrounds. For the most part they were white, male, affluent and classically educated. They benefitted from access to elite networks, and often they occupied central positions in these networks which positioned them to collaborate with and train other psychologists (David & Hayden, 2012; Linstrum, 2016). In this section, we unpack the idea of canon as people. We first discuss the idea of eminence and how it explains the centrality some figures have had in the field. We then turn our attention to the question of how it is that canonical figures achieve the status that they do.

Pop Culture and Psychology

A canon of foundational texts is inherently intertwined with the history and stories of the figures whose scholarship comprises those works. These influential scholars serve as symbolic representatives of the field's core principles and historical trajectory. Their names are synonymous with theories or concepts and their ideas have enduring impact, shaping research and discourse long after their active scholarship. Their work often becomes a touchstone for understanding the field's evolution, both within and outwith the discipline. Following this logic, if we want to characterise the psychological canon, one intuitive way is to identify the thinkers who are known and celebrated outside psychology, either in other disciplines or in pop culture more broadly. Ideas, concepts and names that originate within the academic canon often trickle into mainstream media, impacting how people perceive and discuss psychological concepts in their everyday lives.

Terminology from the theories of Sigmund Freud, for example, populate our everyday speech. We may describe a particularly fussy colleague as *anal retentive* or talk about the way a friend might be in denial about their habit of *projecting* their personal problems onto other people. From *ego* to *libido*, these concepts all trace their origins or popularity to Freud's psychoanalytic movement (Kelly, 2014). Beyond English vernacular, psychoanalytic principles developed by Freud explicitly informed cinematic thrillers and melodramas of the 1930s and 1940s (see Alfred Hitchcock's *Spellbound* for a particularly illuminating example) and show up in paintings and sculptures by Salvador Dali as well as in novels by Virginia Woolf. Freud himself has even been immortalised in media ranging from *Looney Tunes* to *Bill and Ted's Excellent Adventure*.

An article published in *Smithsonian Magazine* also illustrates this point nicely. The article explores the theories and motivations of B.F. Skinner, lauded as a 'leading 20th century psychologist' who theorised that all behaviour is a response to external factors rather than internal drives (such as thoughts or emotions; Koren, 2013, para 1). The article observes that Skinner 'was a controversial figure in a field that tends to attract controversial figures. In a realm of science that has given us Sigmund Freud, Carl Jung and Jean Piaget, Skinner stands out by sheer quirkiness.

Afterall, he is the scientist who trained rats to pull levers and push buttons and taught pigeons to read and play ping-pong' (Koren, 2013, para 1). From this quote we make two important observations. First, there is a set or pantheon of influential and widely known psychologists—a canon—of which Skinner is a member. Second, this group of thinkers are known for their genius as well as their personal attitudes and behaviours. In other words, they cannot be reduced to their ideas; their canonicity hints at some cultural as well as scientific importance.

Psychologists with cultural cachet are likely to be influential because they engage with the public. Skinner, for example, published a novel entitled *Walden Two* (1948) which presented his vision of a utopian society, one in which social justice and well-being are made possible through the application of behaviourist principles. Or consider the case of another famous pair of behaviourists, John B. Watson and his wife, Rosalie Rayner. The two are probably best known today for their studies of Little Albert, a 9-month-old infant who was conditioned to become fearful of white rats (Beck et al., 2009; Harris, 1979). However, during the 1920s, Watson was also influential for his popular science writing. Watson's conviction about his behaviourist theories was so strong that he published *Psychological Care of Infant and Child* (1928) as a self-help manual for parents. The manual drew from Watson's experiments and provided step-by-step guidance on how to cultivate independence and eliminate invalidism in children; a contemporaneous review of the book celebrated Watson's ideas, boldly stating that his knowledge 'may prove of greater value to the human race than even Faraday' (Jensen, 1928, p. 284). To put the magnitude of that appraisal into context, Michael Faraday discovered electromagnetic induction, and his invention of the Faraday cage fundamentally transformed how we use electricity.

These examples highlight the reciprocal relationship between an academic canon and popular culture. Scientists that we think of as influential may be so because they successfully made their ideas accessible to a broad audience. Chapter 9 explores this idea in more depth, investigating how impact is one amongst many metrics currently used to measure and rank academic productivity and quality. The examples shared here also underscore the ways in which foundational ideas from academic disciplines like psychology can shape the way we think, talk and interact with the world around us, even if the original theories themselves are often simplified or adapted for consumption in popular culture.

Scientific Eminence

Tracing the popular legacy and reception of a researcher is one way to establish their centrality to the field. Quantifying their contributions to the field is another. Some academics are included in the canon because of a magnum opus that redefines the field. Other researchers are more expansive, publishing at high volumes or in high visibility outlets. Doing the latter can increase the odds that a researcher's ideas will spread; their work will be referenced in other studies, and as a result they may be invited into prestigious societies. One way of quantifying fame or eminence is therefore to examine the number of citations and awards an academic accrues in their working lifetime.

An early example of this methodology appears in a study by Dennis (1954), who counted the number of pages dedicated to researchers featured in two popular psychology texts at the time, Boring's (1929) *A History of Experimental Psychology* and Murphy's (1929) *An Historical Introduction to Modern Psychology*. Seventeen names appeared with high frequency across the two texts (some of which appear throughout this book). Nearly fifty years later, similar methodology points to the enduring legacy of these same influential scholars. Haggbloom and colleagues (2002) measured eminence by counting citations and induction into honorary societies and attainment of major disciplinary awards. They also invited over 1700 members of the American Psychological Society to nominate the individuals they perceived as the greatest psychological scholars of the 20th century. Behaviourist B.F. Skinner (1904–1990), developmental psychologist Jean Piaget (1896–1980) and Sigmund Freud (1856–1939) ranked highest in eminence out of the 219 scholars identified. The paper by Haggbloom and colleagues (2002) is also noteworthy for the names and identities that were *not* identified as part of the psychological canon.[1] No women appeared in the list of top 25 scholars, and only six women appeared in the top 100. We can see evidence of this trend replicate across the various factors that comprised the eminence scores for the study. For example, only one woman (memory researcher Elizabeth Loftus) appeared in the top 25 scholars cited in psychology textbooks. The surveyed members of the American Psychological Association (APA) consistently identified just one woman eminent enough to appear in the top 25 peer nominations (developmentalist Mary Ainsworth), and the top 25 names for journal citations included no women at all.

Another way to think about the relative eminence of a researcher is to consider the density and size of their scientific network. Prolific and influential scientists may be more likely to collaborate with other academics, and to mentor their students in ways that ensure their protégés are also professionally successful. We can therefore examine the academic lineage of a researcher to better understand their prominence in the field. An academic genealogy captures the lineage of a scholar

---

[1]Though this is made more difficult by the fact that data on other characteristics like race or sexual orientation were not included in the analysis.

by representing their own supervisors and mentees as part of a family tree.[2] By examining the academic lineage of a researcher, we can gain a sense of the size of their immediate scientific network and the extent to which their 'family' is integrated with other research groups.

Consider the academic lineage and career of G. Stanley Hall (1844–1924), the first elected president of the American Psychological Association (Albee, 1996). Hall is not a household name like Freud or Skinner, yet he regularly appears in analyses of historical eminence (e.g. Dennis, 1954; Haggbloom et al., 2002). One factor underlying his eminence (at least amongst other psychologists) may be his connection to other luminaries in the field. Hall studied under two men who were eminent in their own right: William James (1842–1910), widely considered to be the founder of North American psychology, and Wilhelm Wundt (1832–1920), frequently cited as the founder of experimental psychology. Hall apprenticed directly under Wundt at his laboratory in Leipzig and imported Wundt's model of lab culture to the USA. In 1833, Hall founded the first American psychology laboratory at Johns Hopkins University; estimates suggest that approximately 12% of experimental psychologists working in the USA between 1883 and 1900 received their training under Hall (Benjamin, 2000).[3] Using the metaphor of the family tree, we can see how the number of Hall's academic 'children' (he supervised at least 16 PhD students) ensured his legacy. Of relevance to this book, Hall supervised James Cattell (1860–1944), Henry Goddard (1866–1957) and Lewis Terman (1877–1956), all of whom were eugenicists who contributed to the development of intelligence testing in the USA (see Chapter 3). One of Hall's academic 'siblings' who also trained under Wundt was Edward Titchener (1867–1927). Titchener in turn trained Edwin Boring (1886–1968), who wrote extensively about his academic forefathers in *History of Experimental Psychology* (1929)—the aforementioned text that served as an introductory textbook to several generations of North American undergraduate students (Danziger, 2006). Titchener, Hall and Boring are collectively responsible for enacting policies within the APA and other organisations that stymied the progress of professional women in psychology (Chapter 6). They enjoyed enormous control over who got to participate in the field and how.

---

[2]The family tree is an intuitive metaphor that represents one's lineage based on PhD supervisor and lab-group, and prompts such pride and curiosity that it is documented in online resources such as Neurotree: https://neurotree.org/neurotree/

[3]An additional 27% of American psychologists at the time studied with Wundt or split their time between the labs of their academic 'father' (Hall) and 'grandfather' (Wundt; Benjamin, 2000). That is an astonishing figure—nearly 40% of the earliest American psychologists could trace their academic genealogy to the same figure!

Hall occupied a place of centrality in North American psychology, and these connections ensured that his ideas (if not his name) lived on in the accomplishments and collaborations he forged with his academic kin.

Quantitative analysis of the scientific networks of eminent psychologists reveals a similar pattern of elitism and exclusion. For example, Diener and colleagues (2014) examined the scientific networks of 348 psychologists judged to be eminent on the basis of their citation metrics, major awards and coverage in psychology textbooks. A small number of exclusive doctoral training programmes disproportionately contributed to the education of the eminent psychologists—for example, 13% of the psychologists on the list earned their PhDs at Harvard. Although there are more than 258 accredited graduate courses for psychology in the USA, nearly 40% of the eminent figures attended just one of five programmes (Harvard University, University of Michigan, Yale University, Stanford University and the University of Pennsylvania; Diener et al., 2014). Based on these findings, it becomes easy to see how seats of power establish the canonicity of a figure and, conversely, how eminent figures help concentrate influence within institutions.

In the next section, we turn our attention from canonical persons to the canonical perspectives that are foundational to psychology. As we shall see, the same power structures that determine the eminence of a researcher also shape which perspectives gain prominence and which remain marginalised.

CANONICAL PERSPECTIVES

Certain ideas have more tractability than others. This is in part because of their veracity—their perceived ability to speak truth to nature—but also because socio-cultural conditions give that truth currency. Simply put, some ideas are more valuable than others because we mutually agree that they are more useful. In this section we argue that just as there are central figures who are canonical to psychology, so too do certain ideas achieve a level of endorsement that makes them foundational to the field. In this section we first address some of the core ideas that define psychology as a science. We then identify several themes that run throughout psychological research, framing these as dualities that fundamentally define how we practise research and teaching.

What Makes Psychology a Science?

Psychologists often trace the origin of the discipline to Greek philosophers like Plato and Aristotle who attributed behavioural phenomena to natural (as opposed to supernatural) causes and advocated for systematic ways of making naturalistic observations (Smith, 1974). According to this canonical perspective, however, it was not until Wundt established his research lab at the University of Leipzig that psychology formalised as a distinct scientific discipline (Benjamin, 2000; Capshew, 1992). Wundt's emphasis on using empirical methods and rigorous experimentation to understand internal mental states differentiated him from philosophers who were also interested in the origins and limitations of sensation and perception (Ashmore et al., 2005). This emphasis on empirical experimentation was vital to the psychologists of the 1800s who worried that the field was associated with occultism, paranormal activity and spirituality (Benjamin, 2000). Lab science and experimentation made psychology credible in the eyes of the lay public and other scientists.

At this point, it is probably useful to take a step back and reflect on what, exactly, makes something a science. Open any introductory psychology textbook and authors routinely refer to objectivity as one of three key qualities (alongside reliability and validity) that class methods as scientific. These qualities allow for the independence and reproducibility of empirical findings. In qualifying psychology as a science, the APA (American Psychological Association, 2023) contrasts objectivity to subjectivity. Objective interpretations and judgements are those that stem from external data rather than internal beliefs or states. Objectivity is important because it means that scientific progress and growth result from increasingly accurate theories and refined methods; they reflect a system that, through the application of experimental methods, comes closer and closer to understanding 'the truth' about the natural world. According to Harding (1995), science has embraced objectivity as a way to justify its legitimacy and importance in society. Objective methods or facts are those stripped of personal context or individual perspective that might otherwise influence or bias the value of that information. In this sense, objectivity allows for a universal understanding of a phenomenon that cannot be reduced to a single perspective; it is therefore associated with neutrality, impartiality, fairness and standardisation. However, this kind of value-neutral, *aperspective* science is a relatively recent convention, a reaction to increased automaticity, internationalisation, depersonalisation and marketisation of intellectual work (Costall, 2006). It is a safeguard against bias, particularly when the complex, highly specialised and often sprawling nature of contemporary scientific collaborations makes it difficult to vouch for the trustworthiness of each component part of a project.

As a science, psychology is framed as involving the objective, dispassionate and replicable observation and measurement of behavioural phenomena (Bills, 1938). As we shall see next, this framing predisposes the field to certain dualisms—tensions between contrasting ways of thinking about the mind and the best way to study it.

Psychology Is a Science About Dualism

Think about some of the fundamental questions in psychology: What is a mind and how does it relate to the body? What is the relationship between thinking (rationality) and feeling (subjective sensation)? Is gender multiple or binary? Are human cultures more collectivistic or individualistic? What these questions share is an emphasis on duality. There are countless dualities that could characterise science; here we highlight a few that have helped to define psychology as a specific discipline (Demertzi et al., 2009; Pérez-Álvarez, 2018).

Many of the dualisms identified below stem from a single assumption that defines the field: the fundamental unit of analysis in psychology is the individual. Psychology is therefore the study of the *individualised* mind, of the relationship between the mental states of an agent and their own behaviour. We can think about individuals embedded into more complex systems, but ultimately these collectives are comprised of and reducible to singular agents. This has had profound implications for how we conceive of the relationship between mind and matter as well as the nature of selfhood. This single assumption has given rise to several dualities within psychology, including mind–body dualism, rationalism vs empiricism and individualism vs collectivism.

At the risk of oversimplification, **mind–body dualism** has been one of the most enduring legacies of psychology in the English-speaking Global North. First proposed by Rene Descartes during the 17th century, the concept refers to the observation that our minds interact with the external world but are largely unknowable and inaccessible to us. We can also think of this in more concrete terms: our (physical) bodies are controlled by an (abstract) mind that we cannot directly perceive. One way in which psychology tries to sidestep the issue of mind–body dualism is to focus on behaviour, rather than the totality of the individual producing the behaviour. A benefit of this emphasis on behaviour is that it translates well across subdisciplines—it is a unit of analysis that works for complex systems like neurons, flocks of birds and cultures. But, of course, there is a trade-off: the emphasis on individuality frames agents as abstracted from their larger physical, environmental, social or cultural context (Adams et al., 2018). As a result, psychology does not usually adopt a holistic approach to studying behavioural phenomena.

Closely related to the issue of mind–body dualism is the contrast between **rationalism and empiricism**. These contrasting positions promote different understandings about the relationship between internal, subjective experience and an external, ostensibly objective reality (Christopher & Hickinbottom, 2008). In the early days of the discipline, European philosophers (Spinoza, Leibniz, Kant) developed theories of mind and psychological functioning that heavily emphasised rationality. According to this view, there must be innate cognitive structures that allow us to deduce and reason about the world; some knowledge must be independent of experience. In contrast, British Empiricists (Hume, Locke, Berkeley) argued for an experiential basis of psychology grounded in the senses. From the senses we can deduce the laws that govern behaviour. Subjective experiences are informative about the content of mind, not unreliable signals to be ignored. In other words, mind–body dualism has profoundly influenced what psychology considers to be the origin of mind. Chapter 3 explores how this tension plays out in developmental psychology as part of the so-called 'nature versus nurture' debate.

These distinctions about the nature of mind may seem gratuitous until you realise they raise profound questions about ethics and selfhood. If mind is an emergent property of the physical interactions going on in our bodies at all times, for example, is it even appropriate to think of a central 'self' around which all our experiences are organised? Can collectives that demonstrate complex behaviour be said to have a mind, and if so, how should we confer rights and responsibilities onto such entities? These questions point to a tension between **individualistic and collectivistic** ways of understanding the self (Wilson, 1995). The psychological canon largely maintains an individualistic view of the mind as something that possesses agency, autonomy and self-determination. In contrast, other systems of thought—including those outside the Global North—do not view such independence as universal or self-evident (Christopher & Hickinbottom, 2008). Instead, in other cultural contexts and historical traditions, minds are characterised by *inter*dependence (Costall, 2006). This has generated competing understandings of what constitutes 'the good life': individualistic cultures tend to prioritise individual fulfilment and self-determination whereas more collectivistic cultures view selfhood in relational, inclusive and extended terms (Christopher & Hickinbottom, 2008).

Dualities are often interconnected. They assign meaning to complex phenomena in ways that provide conceptual clarity, though perhaps at the cost of oversimplification. Consider, for example, how the contrast between objectivity and subjectivity is framed in discussions of race, gender, sexuality and ability. Throughout the psychological canon, the experiences of individuals who are not white, male, able-bodied or heterosexual have been linked to irrationality and pathology (Chapter 4). Certain subdisciplines may err more towards one end of the continuum than the other, but as a general observation, the psychology of the English-speaking Global North tends to favour theories and methodological approaches that emphasise objectivity and individuality and de-emphasise contextual factors and subjective ways of knowing.

CANONICAL PROCESSES

How do people and ideas achieve the lasting level of prominence that ensures their entry into the psychological canon? We address that question here by examining the processes that make people and perspectives central to the discipline. In particular, we highlight how the adoption of technology and textbooks define for the field what science and scientists should look like.

Psychology and Technophilia

Part of what formalised psychology as a unique discipline was a shared understanding amongst researchers about the importance of using tools that could provide objective and reliable measures of mind. Researchers employed a variety of methods and tools borrowed from other fields to study psychological phenomena. These tools conferred prestige on the new discipline and helped cement its reputation for being technical and experimental. Consider reaction time—psychophysicists like Weber, Helmholtz and Fechner borrowed the concept from physics and used chronoscopes to quantify physiological responses to internal mental states. Its application canonised judgements about how to reliably assess internal mental properties using externalised behaviour (Benschop, 1998; Schoenherr, 2017). Methods and tools also reflect and reinforce normative definitions of objectivity. In the case of chronometers, the ability to record responses with millisecond accuracy, and to do so repeatedly, aligned with a cultural understanding of the time that equated objectivity with automaticity and mechanical rigour (Daston & Galison, 2007).

Instrumentation and statistics helped forge the identity of psychology as a scientific discipline distinct from other branches of natural science. The earliest psychology labs researching psychophysics were organised around instruments (like the chronoscope) whose use established a collective identity for psychologists as technical and analytical scholars (Schoenherr, 2017). As we will see in Chapters 2 and 5, the incorporation of statistical methods and neuroimaging into psychology research methodology later accomplished a similar goal. These tools and methods reflected a 'cult of empiricism' that emphasised how the methods of psychological science were value-neutral, replicable and objective.

The early application of standardised measurements to psychological questions helped to establish the perceived legitimacy of psychology as a discipline, and the technophilia that came to define psychology granted it authority and credibility in the public domain. However, the emphasis the field often places on technology is not without consequences. Uncritical, mass adoption of a methodology may confer trustworthiness on study findings even when the technology in question is inappropriate or misapplied. An uncritical adoption of technology also effectively hides the colonial roots of many approaches we use in contemporary psychological science. Chapter 2 explores how the popularisation of statistical methods obscured the eugenic origins of many of the approaches taken to understanding data. Chapter 4 documents how the application of diagnostic instruments concentrated power in the hands of clinicians who often used this authority to influence or reinforce social norms about gender and sexuality, or to suppress the ability of enslaved persons to protest their subjugation. And in Chapter 8 we examine how cross-cultural methodologies codified certain ways of thinking about variability that devalued the experiences of Indigenous persons. What is the responsibility of the researcher in addressing the historical legacy of some of our theories and tools? This is a question we will return to again and again throughout this book.

Textbooks and the Codifying of Scientific Practice

Textbooks and laboratory manuals are the instruction manuals and record-keepers that tell the story of a particular subject or discipline. Their homogenisation is part of what gives them staying power—the topics, format and even stylistic conventions are prescriptive, focusing our attention to certain ideas and ways of thinking. They codify the canon and the stories that are considered foundational to the field.

Prior to the 1850s, most universities classified psychology as a subdiscipline of philosophy, physiology or physics (Schwarz & Pfister, 2016). Lab manuals detailing psychological experiments became the first textbooks for the field and carved out an identity for psychology as a distinct discipline (Smyth, 2001). Those labs who documented their methods—and whose politics aligned with the governing forces of the universities at the time—were therefore critical in defining what constituted valid questions and approaches in psychology. The content of a textbook similarly reveals the knowledge, values and practices perceived as relevant or essential to the discipline. A great strength of textbooks is their ability to distil a body of findings into a central, coherent story. This requires the prioritisation of some content and the excising of others. As a result, textbooks often omit information about how discoveries were made: description of the informal meetings, networks of associations, dependence on resources and negative findings may be culled from the record as extraneous content that adds no actual knowledge (Smyth, 2001). As a result, the forces that shape the canon are often rendered invisible, leading to the erroneous impression that certain findings were inevitable—they are presented as stemming from the strength of the underlying theories alone (Tauber, 2022). As the remainder of this book makes clear, there are reasons to doubt such a linear, decontextualised account of science.

As part of the editorial process, textbooks create canon by highlighting the contributions of a selection of scholars. For example, consider the language that appeared on the dustjacket for a 1963 text by Watson titled *The Great Psychologists: Aristotle to Freud*: 'This book tells the story of psychology in terms of the *men* who made it great' (emphasis ours). Amongst others, the book identifies Plato, Aristotle, Descartes, Locke, Wundt, Galton, Binet, Hall, Titchener, Watson and Freud as canonical figures. Considerable evidence suggests that this tendency to emphasise male contributors to the canon is not an isolated occurrence. Analysis of citation metrics demonstrates that there is significantly more textbook coverage dedicated to white men compared to any other demographic group (Cramblet Alvarez et al., 2019; Hogben & Waterman, 1997). White male perspectives may be overrepresented in textbooks because minoritised scholars (or scholars writing on issues pertaining to minoritised people) are often encouraged to publish in niche, specialist publications that do not typically receive wide readership, a point we return to in Chapter 8. Textbooks also tend to focus on theoretical developments in psychology (often the purview of white male scholars) rather than on the application of psychological theories (topics that are more commonly pursued by women and racially minoritised people; Cramblet Alvarez et al., 2019). As a result, readership often fails to recognise non-white, non-male contributors to the field (Cramblet Alvarez et al., 2019; see Focus Box 1.1). Various political and financial motives also influence the editorial choices that go into the content selection for a textbook. As is often true with research funding, publishers may face pressure to support the ideas and products most likely to appeal to a wide audience. Resources to support new ideas and pedagogy may be limited, or access to them highly competitive. In this way, market forces also cement and perpetuate a particular canonical understanding of a discipline (see Chapter 9).

Focus Box 1.1

Mamie Phipps Clark

When Mamie Phipps Clark (1917-1983) earned her PhD in psychology in 1943 from Columbia University, she was the first Black woman and only the second Black person to do so (Goode, 2023). As a scholar and civil rights activist, she was influential for developing novel ways of studying racial identity in children. However, despite these notable achievements, many of Clark's accomplishments are either attributed solely to her husband, psychologist Kenneth B. Clark, or omitted from psychology textbooks (Cramblet Alvarez et al., 2019). Clark's story—and her minimisation in the discipline—reveals much about the way that power shapes the psychological canon.

As an undergraduate, Clark intended to study mathematics but found the sexist attitude towards female students aversive and so enrolled in a psychology course (Goode, 2023). It was during her psychology degree that she met Kenneth Clark who became her long-time collaborator and husband. After briefly working for the National Association for the Advancement of Colored People (NAACP) Clark pursued a PhD, initiating her doctoral studies against the backdrop of scientific racism that suffused psychology in the 1930s. Yet despite her training and experience, Clark was blocked from university appointments. She coined this the 'silent challenge' for Black women in psychology (McNeill, 2017). The experience of being barred from lectureships because of her gender and race motivated Clark to study identity in her research.

(Continued)

Figure 1.1 Mamie Phipps Clark

In 1950, the Clarks jointly developed a new methodology for studying racial awareness in children. The 'doll study' presented 3- to 7-year-old Black children with two dolls, one brown and one white. Children answered a series of forced choice questions about the dolls, including which they preferred and which most resembled them. The Clarks compared the responses of children attending racially integrated and racially segregated schools. In all schools, the majority of Black children preferred the white doll and were much more likely to assign it positive attributes compared to the brown doll (Clark & Clark, 1950). Black children attending racially segregated schools explicitly mentioned the race of the dolls when justifying their choices. When asked why they rejected the brown doll, children from segregated schools explained that it was ugly, dirty and a 'n*gger', and that therefore the white doll was preferable (Clark & Clark, 1950, p. 347). In comparison, when asked questions about which doll they most resembled, Black children often froze, unwilling to speak. The research pointed to a grim conclusion—that as members of a racially minoritised community, Black children suffered negative self-perception in ways that white children who comprised the cultural majority group did not. 'It is clear', Clark and Clark wrote, 'that the Negro child, by the age of five is aware of the fact that to be colored in contemporary American society is a mark of inferior status' (1950, p. 347). The Clarks cautioned that this conflict between racial self-identity and negative social evaluation harmed the mental health of developing children, and they advocated for better educational programmes and counselling as a remedy.

The implications of the Clark and Clark doll study reverberated through legal circles in the USA. The couple were asked to provide evidence in several school segregation court cases, including one that pitted the Clarks against Mamie's former doctoral supervisor, Henry Garrett. Eugenic scientists like Garrett argued that because racial differences were innate, educational segregation was a reasonable and responsible policy (McNeill, 2017). The Clarks systematically dismantled this position in case after case, culminating in their testimony before the US Supreme Court during the 1954 *Brown* vs *Topeka Board of Education* hearing (Goode, 2023). At stake was a precedent that established 'separate but equal' provision of state educational resources based on race. Drawing from their doll study, the Clarks explained how segregation resulted in internalised racism that psychologically damaged the children with whom they worked. Their evidence contributed to the court's decision to repeal the law, which paved the way for the racial integration of the public school system in the USA (McNeill, 2017). In Chapter 7 we explore a similar story about the legacy of racism in British schools and how psychology both legitimised and challenged policies that segregated racially minoritised children based on intelligence test scores.

Where do things stand today? The racist educational policies of the Jim Crow era may have been abolished but underlying cultural attitudes towards race and imbalances of power remain problematic. Early childhood education in the USA remains more racially segregated than any other level of schooling (Goode, 2023). Schools with a high proportion of racially minoritised students receive significantly less funding than majority-white schools (Spatig-Amerikaner, 2012; UNCF, 2023). In schools where there is a significant presence of students from racial minority backgrounds, resources are directed more toward enforcing disciplinary measures rather than supporting education or mental health. According to some calculations, around 1.6 million children in the USA are enrolled in schools where law enforcement officers are present, but no counsellors are employed (UNCF, 2023; US Department of Education CRDC, 2016). These educational inequalities may have contributed to recent replications of the Clark and Clark (1950) doll study: over 70 years later, the same persistent bias for white versus brown dolls characterises Black preschool children in the USA (Gibson et al., 2015).

In the story of Mamie Phipps Clark we can see how experiences of privilege and disprivilege are interlocking and complex. Even after years in the public eye, the prominence and visibility of her research never secured Mamie Clark an academic appointment. Kenneth Clark was disadvantaged by racism throughout his personal and professional life, and at the same time, his gender enabled him to obtain university lectureships (Brame, 2021). Perhaps as a result, he is the better-known member of the Clark and Clark collaborative team, and by some estimates Kenneth Clark receives five times more citations for their joint work on racial identity than does Mamie (Cramblet Alvarez et al., 2019). The end result is an entry into the psychological canon that feels definitive but that tells only part of the story.

WHAT NEXT?

Each chapter in this book provides a critical lens to major topics in the field of psychology. In each of these stories we attempt to identify the persons, perspectives, processes and power structures that allowed some ideas to flourish while others were suppressed, censored or left behind.

One theme that runs throughout the book is the relationship between psychology and coloniality. Many of the stories we highlight occur at an important historical junction—the height of British and American colonial expansion and the establishment of psychology as a distinct discipline. As a result, many of the chapters address the persistent Eurocentric cultural biases apparent in the psychology of the Global North. Another commonality is the way in which dominant norms were imposed on other cultures, often without sufficient consideration of their relevance or applicability to Indigenous knowledge systems. As part of this analysis, we also trace how psychological studies were used to support and legitimise policies depicting colonised populations and minoritised groups as inferior, irrational and primitive. This research was used to develop methods of social control and surveillance that further reinforced power imbalances between groups. As we will demonstrate throughout the book, questions about the who and why of psychology are not trivial. The answers to these questions influence what we collectively agree is worthy of investigation, who is worthy of doing the investigation and in what manner.

FURTHER READING

Clark, K. B., & Clark, M. P. (1950). Emotional factors in racial identification and preference in Negro children. *Journal of Negro Education*, *19*, 341–350. [article]

The landmark research study that informed the desegregation of the American public school system.

Linstrum, E. (2016). *Ruling Minds: Psychology in the British Empire*. Harvard University Press. [book]

A nuanced investigation of the relationship between psychology and British colonialism.

Daston, L., & Galison, P. (2007). *Objectivity*. Zone Books. [book]

A colossal and fascinating tracing of the history of objectivity.

2

THE EUGENICS PROBLEM

THE ROTTEN IDEALS UNDERPINNING TODAY'S STATISTICAL TESTS

STATISTICS AS A TOOL FOR 'HARDENING' PSYCHOLOGY

Few of us are drawn to study psychology because we want to learn statistics. For most, statistical tests are a formalised way of understanding our data. A necessary evil. Those viewed as proficient in statistics are regarded in a manner similar to those who know how to use power-tools, or repair cars. This view of statistics as a technical, even mechanical discipline, strips it of the personal context that runs through the rest of psychology. Whilst there are still a whole host of researchers' names associated with statistical tests (indeed they are unavoidable when selecting between competing statistical procedures), we don't cite Pearson (1896) to lend intellectual heft to a correlation analysis, nor do we reference Fisher (1925) to let others know exactly how we have conducted an analysis of variance (ANOVA). This decontextualization strips these tools of their origins in a way that is somewhat unique within psychology. It has done as much to hide their origins as any wilful cover-up ever could.

Before we discuss these hidden origins, it is worth focusing on *why* statistics has attained this decontextualised status, and why psychology has embraced statistical analyses to the extent that it has. Psychology is a discipline largely devoid of 'laws' (Teigen, 2002). It is difficult to identify inalienable psychological truths, meaning that even the concepts we seek to measure are inexact. Not only are our observations messy, so too are the psychological states we measure. For example, measuring someone's attitudes via questionnaire depends on the individual questions used, but also the participant's state of mind when they are doing it. Contrast this with an astronomical measurement of an asteroid's velocity. The observation may be influenced by a number of sources of atmospheric and instrument noise, but the state being measured is exact. An asteroid can't decide to have a different velocity depending on who is measuring it! The end-result is that our experimental analyses require complex tools specifically designed to deal with uncertainty, which identify differences evident only in the averaged measurements of many participants.

The inexact nature of psychological data confronts us with some challenges. Full understanding of the analytic tools we use lies beyond most of our interests, and therefore our training and expertise. It was researchers with mathematical and not psychological training who formalised even the most basic statistical tests. And yet, despite our ignorance of how they work, we are dependent on these tools to reveal and communicate our findings. Given that we would be reluctant to rely so blindly on psychological tools we don't understand, why do we make an exception for statistical tools? Perhaps it is *because* statistical tools are alien to psychology—alien in a way that lends objectivity and credibility to the discipline. This is perhaps because psychology still has something of a public relations problem when it comes to being considered a legitimate science. Given that statistics has been described as the discipline 'most frequently employed to "harden" the "soft" sciences' (MacKenzie, 1981, p. 1), it makes sense for psychologists who want their work to be taken as seriously as that of biologists, physicists and chemists to employ statistics to do this.

There is some debate about the extent to which scientists should embrace the perception of objectivity, and therefore the legitimacy, that statistics affords psychology. For example, John Platt's (1964) *strong inference* proposes a scientific method with a 'resistance to analytical methodology' (p. 348), in which experiments are designed to generate qualitatively distinct outcomes according to the hypotheses proposed, i.e. results that are obvious to the naked eye. Such alternative approaches have, however, largely been ignored (though see Focus Box 2.1). Erasing citations from statistical analyses is the icing on the cake of our collective ignorance. We deceive ourselves into believing that these tests we don't understand are timeless mathematical truths, like the formula for the circumference of a circle. In fact, they are anything but. The statistical tests we use today were developed in a specific socio-political context, and in some cases, developed to further the goals of movements we now find abhorrent.

In what follows, we will discuss the origins of the most widely used statistical analyses in psychology. We will then explore how we might best deal with and advance from this position. Given the extent to which we psychologists use statistics in our work, this is perhaps one of the most universal chapters in this book. Given the extent to which we obfuscate the origins of these statistical tools, it is perhaps one of the most important. The first step is to give names to those whose work we are using.

THE 'GREAT MEN' OF STATISTICS

Francis Galton, Karl Pearson, William Sealy Gosset and Ronald Aylmer Fisher developed the statistical tools that form the key quantitative analytic techniques used in psychological research today. Their work emerged from rapid acceleration of statistical advancement in the early 20th century, and was a product of their close relationships, both good and bad. Here we take a closer look at who they were and how they shaped statistics.

Francis Galton (1822–1911) was Charles Darwin's half-cousin through grandfather Erasmus Darwin. This fact provides revealing context for Galton's academic interests. He was obsessed with the idea of hereditary genius, publishing studies of men of great reputation (he did not examine women, stating that his argument was 'so overpoweringly strong, that I am able to prove my point without having recourse to this class of evidence'; Galton, 1869, p. 3) and men of science (Galton, 1874). Faced with the conundrum of measuring precisely what made these men great, Cambridge-educated Galton developed and named the fields of psychometrics, anthropometrics and biometrics—the formalised measurement of psychological, human and biological properties.

Though the study of heredity did not begin with Galton, he brought to it an approach that may be familiar to psychologists today. He used big data. Similar to the model used by modern consumer-facing genetic testing companies, Galton charged the public for the privilege of being measured at his Anthropometric Laboratory, and did so extremely successfully. At the 1885 International Health Exhibition in London, more than 9000 people paid 3d (approximately £1.50 in modern currency) to give him their data (Galton, 1885). Amassing these records allowed Galton to develop new statistical tools to quantify the relationships between these anthropometric observations. To understand his results, Galton developed the ideas of correlation (Galton, 1888) and regression to the mean (which he termed 'regression towards mediocrity'; Galton, 1886).

Darwin's scientific standing was a consequence of his proposal of *natural selection* (Darwin, 1859). This theory, that organisms with qualities that maximise their likelihood of reproducing will be more likely to pass these qualities on to future generations, was vital in shaping Galton's work. In thinking about how selection could be applied to human society, Galton developed and named the discipline of *eugenics* (from the Greek *eugenes* – good in stock). He defined it as the investigation of 'the conditions under which men of a high type are produced' (Galton, 1883, p. 44). In doing so, he made plain the proposal that humans could be selected for qualities of 'civic worth' in their own breeding. So exciting were these ideas to scholars of the time, that University College London (UCL) incorporated the Galton Eugenics Laboratory into its organisation in 1907, and used funds bequeathed by Galton to appoint its first Professor in Eugenics in 1911. Taking these interests together—the study of inherited qualities, and the desire to better society through selective breeding—we begin to see why Galton and his work have been re-evaluated far less favourably since his death.

Karl Pearson (1857–1936) took a circuitous route to dominating the field of statistics. Following an undergraduate degree in Mathematics at Cambridge University, he moved to Germany, where he gained reputation as a scholar of German language and literature. He also became an admirer of Karl Marx to the extent that he changed the spelling of his own name from Carl to Karl (Salsburg, 2002). On returning to England, he studied Law before coming full circle to Mathematics by appointment to various professorial positions in London (Filon et al., 1934). It was in London that he was introduced to Galton and proposed many of the statistical tools we use today. His achievements include formulating the chi-square test (Pearson, 1900), developing Galton's idea of correlation into the correlation coefficient (Pearson, 1895), and generalising Galton's biological concept of regression to the mean into regression analysis (Pearson, 1903). On Galton's death, Pearson took over his laboratory, becoming the first Professor in Eugenics at UCL.

Pearson's interests aligned closely with Galton's. He was an ardent eugenicist, following the same path in studying biometry and heredity with the goal of bettering society. Such was the interest in these areas at the time, that specialist terms defined by Pearson have made their way into everyday language. Examples include *sibling*—its definition narrowed from a much looser meaning closer to *kin*, to children of common parents—and *histogram* (David, 2009; MacKenzie, 1981). As a place to publish the many biometric observations that formed the basis of the statistical advances they were making, Pearson, Galton and the man who had introduced the two to each other, Raphael Weldon, founded the scientific journal *Biometrika* in 1901 (Cox, 2001). Alongside biometric curiosities including the variation in the shapes of chicken combs and termites (Pearl & Pearl, 1909; Warren, 1909), the journal's anthropometric output included Pearson's own work on the skin colour of 'the crosses between negro and white' (Pearson, 1909, p. 348), and the patterns of penile albinism in people of Malawi (Stannus, 1913). It was well funded enough to include in its articles both photographs and complex equations, which were unusual in journals of the time due to their cost. This remarkable link between biometrics and statistics was such that by Pearson's death in 1936, the journal had become one of the most prestigious periodicals for theoretical statistics, a specialism it maintains to this day.

William Sealy Gosset (1876–1937) graduated from Oxford University with a degree in Mathematics and Natural Sciences. He was hired by Guinness, who assumed his expertise in chemistry would be beneficial to their brewing process, and spent his entire career with the company, rising to the rank of Chief Brewer (Pearson et al., 1990). At the Guinness Storehouse in Dublin, there is a shabby, easily missed plaque commemorating Gosset's time with Guinness, with the inscription *Student 't' test*. These three words give some clue as to why Gosset is not celebrated more prominently by the company for whom he worked for nearly four decades.

Contrary to their expectations, Gosset's pioneering work in statistics was to benefit Guinness far more than his background in Chemistry. He was particularly interested in how well buyers could use small samples of data (e.g. the quality of a handful of hops assessed at market) to draw conclusions about the population from which it was drawn (e.g. the properties of the whole batch that Guinness would buy to brew their stout; Ziliak, 2008). Gosset identified that small samples produced sampling distributions (distributions of means from lots of experiments) that deviated slightly from the bell-curve-shaped Normal distributions they had previously been assumed to produce. He took a secondment to Pearson's laboratory at UCL, where he used the resources there to develop what we now know as the *t* distribution and the *t* test (MacKenzie, 1981; Student, 1908).

Readers familiar with these statistics may, at this point, be questioning why we refer to these ideas as *Student's t* distribution and test. The answer is that Gosset developed these tools for a company that prized the scientific approach taken by its experimental brewers, and considered their work its intellectual property. Believing his work to be of huge importance to statistics, Gosset secretly published under the tongue-in-cheek pseudonym 'Student'. The story goes that Guinness were unaware of the twenty-plus papers published by Student until they were approached to fund publication of Gosset's collected works after his death (Gosset, 1947; Salsburg, 2002).

Finally, Ronald Aylmer Fisher (1890–1962) graduated with a degree in Mathematics from Cambridge University. Like Gosset, he took employment as an applied mathematician, in Fisher's case at the Rothamsted Experimental Station agricultural research facility north of London (Box, 1978). Here, he applied his considerable mathematical ability to making sense of decades of detailed observations on the influences of crop yield. The messy nature of these data—that multiple potential factors could have affected outcomes in the observed data—led

Fisher to develop a new set of statistical tools capable of mathematically disentangling the various effects acting on the variables being measured. These ideas would be formalised as analysis of variance or ANOVA (which uses the F distribution and F statistic, with the initial chosen in homage to Fisher; Fisher, 1918, 1925; Snedecor, 1934).

In spite of his fabled mathematical genius—he was apparently capable of intuitively thinking in many mathematical dimensions (Salsburg, 2002)—Fisher published a handbook, *Statistical Methods for Research Workers*, in which he made his methods accessible to those without extensive training (Fisher, 1925). This modern-day 'impact' has been massively influential, not only in statistics, but in genetics and evolutionary biology (Bodmer et al., 2021). Given these fields of influence, it is perhaps unsurprising to learn that Fisher was, like Pearson, fascinated by heredity and eugenics (Fisher, 1930). He used his academic authority to campaign for a number of eugenic social policies, including the voluntary sterilisation of the 'feeble-minded', and in the late 1940s attempted to arrange a visit to Britain for Nazi sympathising geneticist Otmar Freiherr von Verschuer (Bodmer et al., 2021).

The overlap of Fisher's academic and socio-political interests with Pearson's did not lead to close links between the scholars. Pearson was fiercely critical of Fisher's work and used his influence as the foremost statistician of the time to limit Fisher's professional opportunities (Pearson et al., 1994). Under Pearson's editorship, Fisher published only twice in *Biometrika*, on both occasions whilst he was still early in his career. Gosset, who was on good terms with both, attempted to mediate a reconciliation between them, but was unsuccessful (Salsburg, 2002). Fisher's mathematical brilliance eventually won out, aided by the timeline of their respective careers. Following Pearson's retirement in 1933, Fisher ascended to the position of Galton Professor of Eugenics at UCL.

SOCIETY AND EUGENICS

Eugenics found fertile ground in early 20th century Western society against a background of moral panic about the urban poor, known as the 'residuum' (MacKenzie, 1981; White, 1885). Indeed it was the same panic that found a political outlet in the beginnings of Britain's welfare state, starting with the provision of free school meals in 1906, and culminating in post-war reforms of the 1940s, including the foundation of the National Health Service in 1946. Many scientists though viewed welfare-based parliamentary reform as treating the symptoms rather than the causes of society's problems. They wanted to use the newly popular Darwinian understanding of natural selection, but in a manner more deliberately guided by an end goal—the improvement of society. They argued for eugenic reforms that would maximise individual 'civic worth' through selective breeding (both positive—incentivising those with desirable heritable qualities to have more children, and negative—discouraging and prohibiting those with undesirable qualities from having children). By the time eugenics had taken hold of the scientific community, it was not a fringe argument for Pearson to be praising Hitler's newly enacted 'race hygiene' policy (Filon et al., 1934):

> [The culmination of Galton's preaching of Eugenics lies] in the future, perhaps with Reichskanzler Hitler and his proposals to regenerate the German people. In Germany a vast experiment is in hand, and some of you may live to see its results. If it fails it will not be for want of enthusiasm, but rather because the Germans are only just starting the study of mathematical statistics in the modern sense! (p. 23)

From its origins as an idea that had struggled to gain favour by the end of Galton's life (Galton, 1907), within another decade eugenics had taken hold of the scientific community. So overwhelming was the consensus that almost all biologists were eugenicists, and so too were scholars in many other domains (Louçã, 2009). Opposition was thin on the ground, and came largely from those outside the scientific community, including writer G.K. Chesterton (Chesterton, 1922), politician Josiah Wedgewood IV and various church bodies (MacKenzie, 1981).

So why had eugenics taken hold so comprehensively? First, it was not presented as a politically loaded idea, but a scientifically objective one. Much as we command politicians of all leanings to follow the scientific evidence today, in the early 20th century eugenic policies were lobbied for by the scientific community, and were largely accepted by politicians. As a demonstration of this support across the political spectrum, the post-World War II association between eugenics and the political right is muddied by support from Marxists like Pearson and the leftist economist John Maynard Keynes (Freeden, 1979; Keynes, 1937).

The second reason for its popularity within the academic community is that eugenics was proposed as meritocratic. The fundamental goal of meritocracy is that opportunity and reward should flow to those who deserve it—typically, those whose combination of innate ability and work ethic led to them excelling in a civically worthy domain such as their learning or their profession. Eugenicists looked to the professional middle class as the stratum of society in which merit was already best rewarded (Fisher, 1917). If you worked hard, you got promoted. If you worked harder still, you became a manager. And so on. Just as merit could be linked to earnings and middle-class status, the eugenicist saw the linking of reproductive rights to merit as a natural extension of this widely accepted ideal.

Within this framework, it was difficult to apply these principles to the lower classes, who were not given opportunities to excel, or the upper classes, who inherited wealth and so did not have to excel. These groups, then, were largely left out of eugenic thought (MacKenzie, 1981). But, far from being perceived as a weakness, this class myopia was presented as a strength. In excluding the lower classes, eugenics actively dealt with the 'residuum'. In excluding the upper classes, it became a revolutionary engine of social mobility!

Of course, this eugenic engine of social mobility required expert operators. For each generation to be improved, decisions about an individual's value to society needed to be made by those who understood the principles and goals best. Who better in the scientists' eyes to do this than the scientist himself (and it was invariably gendered this way). Indeed, Galton wrote a science fiction novel about a utopian state, *Kantsaywhere*, in which eugenic policies had been fully realised (Galton, c. 1910). Replacing the government in the novel is the Eugenic College, whose relation with the populace is 'like that between the Fellows of a College and the undergraduates' (p. 17). Modelled so closely on the academic environment that scholars of the day controlled, it is no surprise that scientists saw themselves in the driving seat of a rational brave new world.

THE EUGENIC ORIGINS OF STATISTICS

Statistical theory, and the tools that follow from it, was informed by data collected by eugenicists to understand the heritability of a person's value to society. So, to what extent was the discipline of statistics shaped by eugenics? Put another way, would modern-day statistics be different if it had been developed by engineers interested in ballistics, or physicists interested in radioactive decay?

Academic and societal interest converged in the early 20th century to accelerate the development of statistics as a discipline. One of the most straightforward ways in which this happened was through the channelling of money that buys space and time. Space, in the form of research departments, allows people with similar interest to work in close proximity to one another, to meet by arrangement or by chance, and holds the resources they need to allow them to work efficiently. Time from influential thinkers, alone and in collaboration, allows for the concentration of intellectual effort on a set of questions. Time from those they train and employ allows for vital but repetitive tasks (e.g. calculations on hand-cranked mechanical calculators) to be out-sourced, giving more of it back to the superiors.

Galton's death in 1911 led to a number of donations to his former employer, UCL. These donations bought space in the form of the Biometric and Eugenic Laboratories (MacKenzie, 1981). They also funded Pearson's time by establishing the Galton Professor of Eugenics, allowing Pearson to give up his teaching duties and focus solely on his research. The Department of Applied Statistics, as the laboratories would go on to be known (again demonstrating how close the disciplines of eugenics and statistics were), was the first university department in Britain devoted to advanced teaching and research in statistics. It was from here that Pearson oversaw his team, edited *Biometrika* and collaborated with his colleagues. The importance of this sort of space and time is seen in the timeline of the *t* test. Gosset started working for Guinness in 1899, amassing experience that informed his statistical outlook. However, it was only in 1906, after his employer allowed him to travel to London to work with Pearson at UCL, that this work came to fruition (MacKenzie, 1981). Gosset (under his pen-name Student) published 'The Probable Error of a Mean'—the paper that laid out the theory underpinning the *t* test—in *Biometrika* in 1908.

To what extent then, was statistics developed as a set of eugenic tools? The answer to this question depends on whether we consider the situations in which statistics is needed to be narrow—making eugenics the only context to which statistics is *applied*, or broad—making eugenics one of many contexts to which statistics is *applicable*. The statistics we learn during our psychology training was formalised by proving how data that contain natural variation, or *error*, behave. We use tools developed using biometric, brewing and agricultural data because these data contain error in the form of natural variation. Psychological data are exactly the same. Statistics gives us ways of understanding all of these many varieties of messy, noisy, complicated data. The fact that there are many sorts of data with many applications tells us that, although statistics has its origins in eugenics, it is not a narrowly applied discipline, but a broadly applicable one.

In spite of this, statistics would not have provided such a coherent set of mathematical tools were it not for the umbrella of eugenics under which it was developed. We can take as an example the insight that the amount of error in related observations is likely to be linked—an idea that paved the way for understanding correlation. In the mid-19th century, Dutch scholar Charles Schols demonstrated that errors in one variable were not independent from the errors in a second, related variable (MacKenzie, 1981; Seal, 1967). An example Schols used was that, when firing artillery, if one overshot or undershot a target, one was also likely to miss to the left or right. What he did not do though, was formalise how one would quantify the degree of dependence between the two errors. Schols had done the work to show that dependence was present, but had not extended this to quantifying the degree of dependence that existed. Galton and Pearson were interested in precisely how much error there was in the transmission of a heritable characteristic from parent to child. They therefore made it their mission to understand how errors related to each other and formalised this understanding in the formulae for regression and correlation. Because the study of heritability places error at its core, the eugenicists had expanded scientific understanding of correlation and regression in a way that their predecessors had not even thought to.

Another example relates to the statistical tools we apply to nonparametric data. In quantifying the value of a person to society, Galton decided that their civic worth was far better to rank relative to other people (a nonparametric measurement) than it was to measure in absolute terms (a parametric measurement; Galton, 1889; MacKenzie, 1981). Consequently, he described descriptive statistics better suited to rank-ordered data, including the median, and the inter-quartile range. A method for calculating correlations of rank-ordered data was described by Charles Spearman (another statistician and eugenicist who would go on to work at UCL; Spearman, 1904). He referenced Galton's biometric data before illustrating his method using an example of hereditary civic worth, 'conscientiousness' in brothers. These statistics, then, clearly all have eugenic origins. Even statistical terms that we use so often that their meanings have become obscured are rooted in eugenics. The term 'population', now used for the entire set of observations that could be made, has its origins in literal populations of people who were to be differentiated. The word 'sample', i.e. the data we collect, is in the vernacular as a term to describe biomedical matter or tissue taken for examination, making clear its link to biometry. Even the seemingly innocuous 'factor', an independent variable manipulated by an experimenter (as in factorial ANOVA), was chosen by Fisher as a reference to Mendelian factors—the smallest unit of genetic variation that Gregor Mendel described in his study of sweetpeas (Fisher, 1918). The links between the statistics we assume to be an objective, value-free system for making sense of data, and the troubling eugenic ideals of race and class purity, are hiding in plain sight.

THE MANY LAYERS OF PRIVILEGE

The mythos of the rivalry between Pearson and Fisher lends itself to a fascination with their feuds and conflicting, prickly personalities. Fellow statistician William Kruskal described Fisher's life as 'a sequence of scientific fights, often several at a time, at scientific meetings and in scientific papers' (1980, p. 1026). Science writer Sharon Bertsch McGrayne wrote that Pearson 'introduced two generations of applied mathematicians to the kind of feuding and professional bullying generally seen only on middle school playgrounds' (McGrayne, 2011, p. 45). So real were the consequences of their rivalry, that Fisher was effectively excluded from statistical publishing circles until Pearson's retirement, at which point he rose to prominence and even started a fresh rivalry with Karl Pearson's son, Egon!

Focusing on the Pearson–Fisher rivalry, however, suggests there was more ideological and professional difference between these statisticians than there actually was. Sociologist Donald MacKenzie, is his brilliant book on the eugenic origins of statistics in Britain, wrote that their conflict 'obscured a fundamental fact about Fisher: the extent to which his work was in continuity with that of Karl Pearson, and with that of Galton before him' (MacKenzie, 1981, p. 183). One of those lines of continuity was that both regarded the introduction of eugenic policies as necessary for the advancement of society, and their expertise and authority as academic leaders as appropriate levers by which to engineer such change. A more obvious conclusion from the freezing out of the educationally privileged, highly intelligent Fisher, is that there were many, many layers of privilege in operation in early 20th century academia, as there still are now. If Fisher, with his Harrow and Cambridge education, his mathematical brilliance and his ideological overlap with Pearson, had nonetheless been denied the opportunity to advance in his field, just imagine the impossibility of someone of a lower educational standing, let alone a member of the lower-class 'residuum', being given the training and opportunity to develop to their intellectual potential. Even as we consider these issues of class and race equality as paramount to today's educational experience, we would do well to consider how petty historic squabbles can blind us to the far more egregious absences from the canon—absences from the work we read and the tools we use that resulted from the highly unequal society that originated the field of statistics. Moreover, we should consider how the scientists who developed these tools used their professional prominence alongside the tools themselves to attempt to cement that societal inequality through political means.

WHAT NEXT?

It is undeniable that the founders of statistics were brilliant mathematicians. It is also undeniable that their association with eugenics was not merely a coincidence, but a systemic, cultural enmeshment that shaped their attempts to carve humanity in a new image. Even as they were lobbying for eugenic policies, they anticipated the devastation they would cause, and invoked arguments of collective, rather than individual benefit (Daston & Galison, 2007). Of course, this was a benefit that would accrue only to the collective of civically worthy white people with which they identified. In justifying the colonisation of North America, and the genocide perpetrated against the Native American peoples, Pearson wrote the following in his scientific compendium *The Grammar of Science* (1892):

> The feeling of European to Red Indian is hardly the same as that of European to European. The philosopher may tell us it 'ought' to be, but the fact that it is not is the important element in history. (p. 437)

Men like Pearson believed it was their responsibility to use their reputations to educate others on societal morality and social policy. In doing so, they both invoked and disregarded arguments of collective solidarity as and when it suited them. In an environment that now seeks to right past wrongs and engage more genuinely in collective and inclusive practice, what should we do with their knowledge? What should we do with their statistics?

The first thing we must do is acknowledge that these men were not comic-book villains who used statistics to covertly promote eugenics. Their papers, published in journals with names as transparent as *Biometrika*, are so reliant on eugenic examples that this is not in question. Galton, Pearson, Gosset and Fisher were simply scientists doing, with more or less zeal, what they could to support the scientific trends of the day. The fact that knowledge of their links with eugenics may be news to many of us is the result of a distillation of ideas that has occurred over decades, leaving behind the examples that are no longer palatable, and carrying forward only those that have endured. Statistics as a field has been stripped of its eugenic context because this background no longer resonates with modern audiences.

Of course, some of this decontextualization has been pursued more actively than others. Salsburg (2002), whose scholarship would undoubtedly have made him aware of the entirety of their views, nonetheless argued that Pearson used statistics to make a clear-sighted argument against Nazism, and that Fisher was a fascist. Whilst there is evidence in isolation for each of these statements, they present Pearson and Fisher as incomplete caricatures. Arguments like this lure us into the false view that one of these men was good and the other, bad. They also stop us having to confront the far more uncomfortable truth that almost all scientists of the day held beliefs that we now find abhorrent. It is vital that we do not fall into the traps of ignoring the origins of statistics, or of caricaturing their originators, such that we turn them into pantomime heroes and villains. Once we have avoided these traps, our next responsibility as students and teachers who care about collective and inclusive practice is to decide what we do with our new-found knowledge.

One course of action is to abandon these statistics altogether. Alternatives to the practice of null hypothesis significance testing—the statistical system the tools described above have grown into—include methods commonly referred to as *the new statistics* (Cumming, 2014). The new statistics includes effect-size-based estimation, interpretation of confidence intervals and Bayesian statistics. Whilst the arguments for this shift are compelling on the basis of the different theoretical assumptions that these statistics make, to do so because of the eugenic origins of statistics requires each of us to make choices about how we choose to use, or not use, knowledge. Moreover, it requires us to update our choices as new information emerges, or as our opinions change. Whilst many of us attempt to apply such ethical principles to our day-to-day consumerism, were we to undertake a similarly rigorous examination of the originators of the new statistics it is likely that we would not have any formal statistical tests to use at all (see Focus Box 2.1).

Another course of action is to continue using these statistical tools, but change how we refer to them. Just as organisations such as the baseball franchise the Cleveland Guardians (formerly the Cleveland Indians) have chosen to distance themselves from their offensive colonial references, we could similarly remove mention of Pearson from the correlation coefficient, or Fisher's initial from the ANOVA F statistic. This solution would be prone to the same vetting problems that apply to abandoning the statistical tests altogether. It would also obfuscate the origins of statistics even further—an out-of-sight-out-of-mind solution that alleviates the guilt of those who enact it, but thereafter does nothing to educate people about the foundations of the tools they continue to use and benefit from.

As might be expected from the authors of a book such as this, we propose a course of action that emphasises understanding of the origins of the statistical tools we use. Within this proposal, these statistical tools should continue to be taught. Importantly though, we propose embedding the history of statistics into its teaching, so that when we do conduct a correlation analysis or an ANOVA, we have an understanding of what its privileged and exclusionary origins are. We could even use antiracist examples and datasets in our teaching, to subvert the ideologies infused into these tools. Another vital addition to the curriculum that we propose is to discuss the work of scholars whose legacies may be as important as those of Galton, Pearson, Gosset and Fisher, but whose contributions have not made their way into the canon (see Focus Box 2.1). In doing this, we can play an active role in expanding what we teach to include a more diverse array of people and ideas. Whilst the new scholars and scholarship we learn about will all be products of varying degrees of privilege, breaking from the Oxbridge-educated white men of the late 19th and early 20th centuries will, at the very least, highlight that the particularly British, Imperial privilege that these men held is worthy of comment. In having these conversations, we will better understand that all knowledge, even the most objective-seeming mathematical formula, has a context.

What we propose does not deal with knowledge we find uncomfortable by regressing to ignorance. Instead, it acknowledges that science, like all historic artefact, has a socio-cultural origin that tells a story of privilege. In understanding the eugenic origins of statistics, we reckon with the violence of eugenic practices that incentivised the civically worthy to have children, and disincentivised the unworthy from doing this same. For some of us, this reckoning will open our eyes to analogous violences that persist today. The systematic exclusion and 'othering' of minoritised groups, and the negative eugenic policies that still exist, for example in state benefit caps, are both injustices whose foundations are laid bare by this particular origin story. The fuller a picture we have of the past, the better equipped we are to understand the present.

─Focus Box 2.1─

Diversifying Statistics

One of the few anti-eugenicists contemporary to Pearson and Fisher was the Cambridge-educated Lancelot Hogben (1895–1975). Hogben was an experimental zoologist and biostatistician whose work in South Africa resulted in the discovery that female African clawed frogs are so sensitive to pregnancy hormones that, if injected with urine from pregnant oxen, they extrude eggs (Hogben et al., 1931). This formed the basis of the Hogben test, a human pregnancy test carried out using live frogs, that was the medical gold-standard until it was overtaken by chemical testing in the 1960s (Yong, 2017). Hogben's active resistance to the racist politics of South Africa eventually led him to leave for London (Anker, 2004). Prior to leaving, he had objected to the eugenic policies promoted by contemporary biologists. Hogben's argument was that eugenics was flawed because it could not be enacted fairly— 'social bias will enter into the actual selection and interpretation of data' (Hogben, 1919, pp. 155–156). He is acknowledged as the only British biologist active in the 1920s to campaign *against* eugenics (Werskey, 1979).

Other influential statisticians managed to steer clear of eugenics by pre-dating it altogether. One of the cornerstones of the new statistics, Bayesian statistics is, it turns out, not so new at all. The Reverend Thomas Bayes (1701–1761), who attended the University of Edinburgh rather than Oxford or Cambridge, developed what we know as Bayes theorem with the ambitious goal of proving the existence of God (Bayes & Price, 1763). Pierre-Simon Laplace (1749–1827), whose working life was spent in France, formalised this theorem for a different purpose, that of understanding the movements of celestial bodies (McGrayne, 2011). Whereas we have seen how eugenics acted as a common thread to the statistical tools we routinely use in psychology, Bayes and Laplace demonstrate that common threads are not inevitable. Whilst Bayes was concerned with godliness, the theologically trained Laplace had rejected his training and was a committed atheist. Indeed, he is said to have responded to Napoleon's questioning on God with 'I had no need of that hypothesis'. Laplace's worked examples catered to one of France's primary interests of the time, gambling.

Despite using Bayes theorem initially, Fisher took against it, and by developing the tools that would lead to the widespread adoption of null hypothesis significance testing, can be credited with largely extinguishing Bayesian statistics from psychological teaching until recent times (McGrayne, 2011). Fisher's preoccupation with mathematically rigorous data interpretation also did a great deal to marginalise what to many is a far more intuitive method for drawing inference from data–graphical presentation. Many of us will know of Florence Nightingale (1820-1910) as the founder of modern nursing. Perhaps less widely known about Nightingale is that she was also the first woman to be elected to the Royal Statistical Society for her pioneering work in what we would now describe as infographics. Following Nightingale's initial experience of working in a military hospital during the Crimean war–an environment so dire that that the risk of death from disease was greater than in London during the bubonic plague of 1665 (Cohen, 1984)–Nightingale instituted a range of hygiene improvements and successfully reduced mortality rates by an order of magnitude. Most importantly for her contribution to statistics, she kept detailed records, and used them to construct a number of annotated graphs to illustrate the dramatic effects of her hygiene interventions. No statistical tests were necessary to interpret her figures, which demonstrated the sort of blindingly obvious result that Platt (1964) would call for a century later in his call to reform the design of experiments. The measure of any statistical method lies in how well it communicates the underlying data. Nightingale's data visualisations were so compelling, that they were included in a Royal Commission report that led to the implementation of hygiene reform at all military and public hospitals within the British Empire.

Figure 2.1 W.E.B. Du Bois

W.E.B. Du Bois (1868-1963) was a Black sociologist and writer born into a free family in Massachusetts. He was a founder member of the National Association for the Advancement of Colored People (NAACP) and the first African American

(Continued)

to earn a doctorate at Harvard. Unlike the white scholars driving the eugenic movement, Du Bois recognised the effects that the biometric study of racial difference were having in justifying scientific racism, and often (though not always—see Chapter 7) railed against what he viewed as a new form of slavery (Battle-Baptiste & Rusert, 2018). His contribution to statistics was similar to Nightingale's, though he was faced with the formidable task of having to show not only that there were inequities detrimentally affecting Black Americans, but also that these inequities could be attributed to systemic societal racism and not deficiencies of character. He did all this whilst celebrating the flourishing of a people in spite of these challenges, and on the grandest stage, the 1900 Paris Exposition. He presented a series of hand-drawn and coloured infographics that stun in their beauty and capacity to communicate his message. It is notable that Du Bois is best remembered in this statistical context, for collecting and presenting data to show the mostly white attendees at the exhibition that Black citizens deserved to be able to navigate society as easily as them. It is an injustice that over a century later, at every university at which this book is read, there remain students and staff of colour who are still having to continue this effort.

FURTHER READING

MacKenzie, D. A. (1981). *Statistics in Britain, 1865–1930: The social construction of scientific knowledge*. Edinburgh University Press. [book]

A detailed but readable history of the origins of modern statistics.

Yong, E. (2017). How a frog became the first mainstream pregnancy test. *The Atlantic*. https://www.theatlantic.com/science/archive/2017/05/how-a-frog-became-the-first-mainstream-pregnancy-test/525285/ [magazine article]

A short history of Hogben's pregnancy test.

Mansky, J. (2018). W.E.B. Du Bois' visionary infographics come together for the first time in full color. https://www.smithsonianmag.com/history/first-time-together-and-color-book-displays-web-du-bois-visionary-infographics-180970826/ [web page] or Battle-Baptiste, W., & Rusert, B. (2018). *W. E. B. Du Bois's data portraits: Visualising Black America*. Princeton Architectural Press. [book]

The website provides a description of Du Bois' Paris Exposition alongside a small selection of his infographics, whilst the book presents them all.

Cohen, I. B. (1984). Florence Nightingale. *Scientific American, 250*(3), 128–137. http://www.jstor.org/stable/24969329 [magazine article]

An account of Nightingale's contribution to statistics, including a selection of her infographics.

3

THE IDENTIFICATION OF THE 'FEEBLE-MINDED'

HOW PSYCHOLOGICAL TESTING AND SEGREGATION GO HAND-IN-HAND

What are the most important characteristics of the unfolding of mental life? How far is it conditioned by heredity, and how far by education? What are the outstanding features of the process by which the mind comes into conscious possession of itself and clear recognition of its autonomy? (Tracy & Stimpfl, 1909, p. ix)

Abstraction of universals from particulars can be seen in market terms as a currency of the intellect that strips individual thoughts of their singularity and makes everything in nature repeatable and commodity-like. Commodification of thought met with commodification of time and labour ... thus abstracting of intelligence has become one of the currencies in which we exchange values about each other. (Goodey, 2011, p. 283)

The motivation to understand human development has often accompanied a desire to shape its trajectory. Nowhere is this more apparent than in the history of intelligence testing. Intelligence testing holds a controversial spot in the history of developmental psychology. It emerged in the late 1800s in response to eugenic concerns about the relative malleability or fixedness of an individual's life circumstances. This chapter traces the history of the first standardised intelligence test: the Stanford–Binet Intelligence Scale. In what follows, we aim to demonstrate how the Victorian preoccupation with intelligence testing reflected changing views about children, their role in society and their utility as scientific subjects. The use of intelligence testing in educational research was intended to provide an objective rationale for how resources should be apportioned to support pupils and facilitate social mobility. Its apparent success in classing students as either capable or 'feeble-minded' inspired the development of an industry devoted to the standardised assessment of human aptitude and performance. Yet a century later, we argue that the most enduring legacy of intelligence testing has been the further entrenchment of inequalities within schools and the larger communities in which they are embedded (Coard, 1971/2021).

The rapid industrialisation of Britain in the late 19th century resulted in appalling living and work conditions for members of the labouring class. Social mobility was negligible, and the use of child labour was widespread; sending children to school represented a significant loss of income for many families. At the same time, the popularity of evolutionary theory and eugenic ideals meant that 'pauperism' was viewed both as a personal shortcoming and a heritable trait rather than the foreseeable consequence of an economic system stacked against the 'residuum'—the urban poor. Poverty implied a form of moral degeneracy, and 'feeble-minded' became a descriptor applied to the most disruptive and least capable members of society. Controlling the feeble-minded first required their identification. For the elite, it became paramount to find a way to systematically measure the qualities of the populace, and to class people according to this knowledge (Burman, 1994; Rose, 1985). Intelligence testing met this need by providing a seemingly objective, scientific way of discriminating between individuals.

Intelligence is a sticky concept, and there is no singular, universally accepted definition for intellectual ability or disability. Intelligence and intellectual ability are historically contingent notions, and thus the tests we use to measure them are also products of their time and place (Goodey, 2011). For the purposes of this chapter, when we talk about intelligence testing, we are referring to any formal assessment that attempts to measure an individual's ability to acquire, manipulate and apply knowledge. Such assessments typically tap into an individual's capacity for self-awareness, spatial reasoning, linguistic comprehension, abstraction and logical inference, critical thinking, planning and problem-solving. A core feature of the intelligence tests we discuss in this chapter is that they were designed to categorise and compare individuals. The individual's results can only be interpreted in relation to a standard or group norm.

To appreciate how and why the first intelligence tests were devised, we must first understand the socio-cultural context in which developmental research was embedded at the turn of the century. In the first part of this chapter, we discuss the rise of child studies in the 19th century. We link changes in cultural attitudes toward childhood to educational reform movements in the USA and the UK. Some early proponents of intelligence testing viewed it as a tool for ensuring provision of education to all children. Others viewed intelligence testing as an efficient, objective method for segregating children (and later adults) according to perceived ability. We trace the origin of the first formal intelligence test (the Binet–Simon Intelligence Scale) and describe how the tool was adopted for use outside educational contexts. We then identify the impact of intelligence testing on the field of psychology, and in particular how use of the tool helped canonise certain assumptions about development and individual differences. In the closing this chapter, we examine the legacy of intelligence testing in contemporary educational contexts. Throughout the chapter we will see examples of how intelligence testing—and by extension, the field of psychology—served as a tool for maintaining and reinforcing inequalities of opportunity and outcome.

THEORETICAL AND CULTURAL ORIGINS OF INTELLIGENCE TESTING

The widespread adoption of intelligence testing would not have been possible without shifts in how the scientific community—and Western culture more broadly—viewed children. Implicit in the development of intelligence testing was the assumption that children had individual minds that could be measured and understood. However, as we demonstrate below, this was not always a shared belief, and concepts about children and childhood changed markedly over the course of Western European history. We trace this evolution below to understand the scientific and cultural context that made intelligence testing possible.

Childhood as a 'Sensitive Period' in Human Development

What does it mean to be a child, and what do we mean when we talk about 'childhood' as a phase of life? Numerous anthropological investigations suggest that childhood is a social construction reflecting various religious, legal, ethical and biological understandings of the role young people play in society. What we recognise as 'childhood' likely emerged as a shared understanding at the end of the 17th century. John Locke's 1690 'Essay Concerning Human Understanding' put into circulation the notion of *tabula rasa*, or the mind as a blank slate. In the view of Locke and other empiricists, individuals are born without concepts or other cognitive architecture to organise experience; the structures required to process information are formed through sensory experience alone. This meant that the environment—rather than any inherited traits—determined the kinds of beliefs and abilities possessed by children. It painted a picture of the self as something unconstrained and self-determined.

Another pivotal moment was the publication of '*Émile, ou de l' Éducation*' (translated from French as *Émile, or On Education'*) by Jean-Jacques Rousseau in 1762. Rousseau was influenced by the writings of Locke, and his philosophy reflects a similar emphasis on the value of individualism. The novel portrays the relationship between the titular Émile and his tutor. In exploring Émile's develop-ment from young boy to man, Rousseau advocates a radical reframing of education. He explicitly identifies infancy, childhood and adolescence as three distinct phases of life characterised by different needs, abilities and challenges. Across these stages, the unifying story of development is one of self-determinism: Rousseau argues that man is imbued with free will and through his own self-exploration derives the knowledge and values that enable him to become a social, moral and rational member of society. According to Rousseau, formal education hinders this development and corrodes the natural, pedagogical relationship between parents and their children (Vanpée, 1990). Rousseau's work was not well received by the French ruling class. The book explicitly repositioned the seat of scientific and moral authority in the individual and the family unit rather than in the church or state. Vanpée (1990) documents how, within one week of publica-tion, copies of *Émile* were seized and burned, leading to Rousseau's exile from France for the next eight years. Despite this censorship, Rousseau's ideas circulated widely throughout Europe and the UK and his writings were often cited in pam-phlets advocating educational reform.

Rousseau's emphasis on pedagogy, coupled with Locke's belief in the nascent mind as a *tabula rasa*, generated a cultural understanding of childhood as a sensi-tive period in which the child is most open to the influence of their environment. Children were vulnerable, both physically and mentally. Their inner lives were not like those of adults; their thoughts, emotions and motivations were immature and required guidance. We can see evidence of this cultural shift in the art of the time; a burgeoning middle class possessed the means (and interest) to depict children for their own sake. Victorian artists romanticised the innocence of childhood, portray-ing children in pastel colours and decorative clothes and often with a dreamy, other-worldly expression (Smidt, 2006). New to these portrayals was a sense of lei-sure, curiosity and play—children engaging in games, often with toys. These images circulated widely in ad campaigns, encouraging middle-class parents to treat their children as a new class of consumers (Hudson, 2017). However, this idealised notion of childhood applied only to a small minority of the populace. Heywood (2001) suggests that the modern concept of childhood is a direct reaction to the inequitable societal conditions that allowed child labour to flourish. Working-class children were often exposed to messages about their sinful and degenerate nature. Hannah More, founder of the Sunday School movement, argued that formal education was the only means by which the delinquent character of labouring youth could be corrected (Smidt, 2006). Pauperism denied childhood to those children and adolescents working as domestic servants or on factory floors.

If romanticised paintings obscured class distinctions, the invention of photography made undeniable the unequal life conditions of children in Victorian Britain. With unsentimental detail, photographs chronicled children working in squalid and unsafe conditions. As a result, a series of legislative acts curtailed child labour practices: in the UK, the Factory Act (1833) and Mines Act (1842) banned children younger than nine from employment and limited the hours that older children could work. At the same time, the late 1800s witnessed the rise of compulsory education throughout Britain, Europe and the USA (Burman, 1994). Public debates about how children should be disciplined, educated and nurtured raised important questions about the role of formal education and the provision of state resources to schools.

The Rise of Child Studies

Infants and children were largely excluded from the psychological canon until the end of the 19th century. Until that point, there were no widespread or systematic efforts to understand mind through the study of children, or indeed to study children for their own sake. At a practical level, children were often excluded from research studies on the basis that their physiologies and temperaments did not lend themselves to the sorts of tedious experiments favoured by psychophysicists. Psychophysics experiments often entailed sustained periods of attention to sets of stimuli that were considered by many to be repetitive and dull. As a result, researchers interested in developmental questions often undertook 'baby biographies', detailing the lives of their own children and treating them as participants in case studies (Anderson, 1956; Bradley, 1989). The sparsity of data captured within these biographies limited the kinds of questions researchers could ask, thereby limiting theories of child development.

One researcher who utilised the case study method was Charles Darwin. As part of his interest in the variability of expressed traits, in 1877 Darwin published what is considered to be the first child study, 'A biographical sketch of an infant' (Burman, 1994). Through this case study, Darwin sought to understand how certain abilities (such as language, creativity and intelligence) differ between humans and non-human animals, and how the emergence of these traits depends on environmental conditions versus genetic endowment.

Collectively, the theories proposed by Locke, Rousseau and Darwin offered a compelling reason to study children, in that the systematic study of children might reveal the origins of mind. The earlier in development an ability or trait (like intelligence) expresses itself, the more confident we might feel that it is innate (the result of genetics) versus the product of socialisation. In other words, the study of children might resolve once and for all whether it is the influence of 'nature' versus 'nurture' that determines human advancement (see Focus Box 3.1).

—Focus Box 3.1—

The Nature vs Nurture Debate

The phrase 'nature versus nurture' is shorthand to describe the competing influence of genetics and socialisation on behaviour. Developmentalists have long debated whether certain abilities and behaviours are innate, or whether they arise in response to external factors like physical surroundings and culture. Many people are surprised to learn, however, that developmental psychologists did not coin the saying. Instead, the origin story of the expression involves an academic feud, a few hundred famous scientists and lots of statistics.

In 1869, Francis Galton penned *Hereditary Genius: An Inquiry into Its Laws and Consequences*. In it he examined the lineage, traits and accomplishments of 'great men' (English judges, statesmen and premiers) to identify the factors likely responsible for their success and brilliance. The book presented a hereditarian case for intelligence, arguing that the sons of 'eminent' men were themselves more likely to achieve professional prominence compared to the children of ordinary citizens. Perhaps unsurprisingly, the Victorian scientific elite reacted favourably to the arguments presented by Galton, with one review claiming that the 'forcible and eloquent' book would 'take rank as an important and valuable addition to the science of human nature' (Wallace, 1870, p. 503).

But praise for the work was not universal, particularly outside British academia. French-Swiss botanist Alphonse de Candolle (1806–1893) criticised Galton's hereditarian hypothesis, arguing instead that culture exerted a much stronger influence on development. de Candolle detailed his critique of Galton in the nearly 500-page *Histoire des sciences et des savants depuis deux siècles* (1885). To make their work comparable, de Candolle adapted Galton's methodology by studying the biographies of over 300 eminent male scientists from across Europe. These scholars were notable because they had been inducted as foreign members into the elite learned societies of nations where they were not citizens (e.g. a Swiss scientist elected into a French society). Election of non-citizens into national societies was a rare distinction and thus qualified these men as internationally reputable scientists (Fancher, 1983).

According to de Candolle, hereditarian theories could not explain numerous patterns he uncovered in the data. First, a hereditarian account would predict the number of great scientists to be similar across nations after controlling for population size. The distribution of scientific geniuses within a nation should also be stable over time as those traits passed from one generation to another. de Candolle could not find support for either hypothesis. On the contrary, eminence varied tremendously over time and from place to place. For example, 5% of the men in his sample were from Poland and Russia (two nations together comprising a quarter of the European population at the time), but Switzerland (a country representing only 1% of the total European population) produced 10% of the scientists in his sample (Fancher, 1983).

On the surface, this finding could still be consistent with hereditary accounts—perhaps the genetic predisposition for scientific aptitude differed across nations. If so, the distribution of scientists would differ between countries as long as the number of great men within each nation remained stable. However, de Candolle ruled out this possibility as well by documenting strong historical trends in his data. The number of eminent men fluctuated dramatically within each nation over time in ways that de Candolle suspected had less to do with genetics and more to do with the intellectual atmosphere of each nation (Staum, 2011). He pointed to policies, such as the adoption of academic censorship, that seemed to suppress scientific achievement in places where it had previously flourished. Other patterns emerged from the data: scientific eminence seemed more common where climates were temperate and where scientists were well resourced with access to libraries, universities and laboratories. Eminence was also more common in places where vernacular language replaced Latin as the official mode of communication. Collectively, these factors made for more tolerant, open cultures that promoted independence and academic freedom as national values (Fancher, 1983). de Candolle concluded that environmental factors contributed to eminence, rather than it being driven solely by genetics.

Galton felt misrepresented by this critique and initiated correspondence with de Candolle. They debated statistical and theoretical assumptions, eventually arriving at common ground. Both Galton and de Candolle agreed that race exceeded all other potential explanations for eminence. Like Galton, de Candolle unequivocally associated eminence with whiteness and maleness. In a concession to Galton, de Candolle amended his views on how cultural values like independence might spread in a population. Transmission of values could be cultural, with values passing from institution to institution, but also genetic, with values passing from generation to generation. These forms of transmission might even interact; de Candolle suspected that migrant scientists were particularly prone to adopting the values of their new homes and thus more likely pass these ideas to their offspring (Fancher, 1983).

Over the course of their exchange, the origin of their disagreement became clearer. de Candolle admitted he had only undertaken his study because he disliked

(Continued)

how the title of Galton's book seemed to minimise and trivialise the importance of cultural factors (Fancher, 1983). This observation inspired Galton to run a follow-up study. He surveyed 200 scientists of the Royal Society with questions about their racial background, parental characteristics, physical health, education and social experiences. He also asked respondents to describe in detail what they could reconstruct about their childhood interest in science (Fancher, 1983). He believed a developmental approach might reveal signs of eminence inherent to the individual before any meaningful impact of socialisation. Most of his participants reported that their interest in science pre-dated any formal education. Another theme that emerged was the importance of travel–Galton's English respondents often mentioned education in Scotland as key to their professional development. In all, the data converged on a mixed picture (Fancher, 1983). The qualitative analyses of childhood interests pointed to hereditary influences, but Galton's survey data suggested that environment seemed important too. The resulting conclusion was a compromise. Galton titled his next major work *English Men of Science: Their Nature and Nurture* (1874) to highlight the dual role that genetics and environment play in behaviour.

Where do things stand with the nature-nurture debate today? Positions like probabilistic epigenesis (Gottlieb, 2007) and dynamic systems theory (Thelen, 2005) emphasise the flexible and reciprocal interaction of genetics and environment on behaviour. Although contemporary researchers debate the relative weight of 'nature' versus 'nurture', few would deny that both factors are critical to understanding how behaviour emerges and changes over time.

It became possible to empirically address the question of 'nature versus nurture' at the start of the 20th century when a wave of nurseries and kindergartens opened across the UK and USA. In the USA, President Woodrow Wilson declared 1919 the Children's Year and called for an increase in government and private funds to support research on education. Across North America and Europe, philanthropic investment in child studies skyrocketed, leading to the creation of childcare facilities as well as dedicated laboratory spaces for child studies (Bloch, 1991; Sears, 1975; Thompson, 2016). Many of these spaces were affiliated with university home economics departments, who touted developmental research as a selling point for their services. The influx of child labs and nurseries gave researchers access to large numbers of children who could participate in studies. Most of the research undertaken in these spaces was educational in nature, focused on individual differences in learning outcomes. In the USA, G. Stanley Hall (1846–1924) founded the Child Study movement by asking kindergarten teachers to systematically collect data on the intellectual aptitude of their pupils. He created training texts and published articles with the explicit purpose of making child studies as scientific as possible. In the UK, a similar movement started with the founding of the British Association of Child Study in 1895. Intelligence testing therefore emerged to objectively and systematically compare the intellectual abilities of children. The application of this knowledge was to improve educational materials so that each individual child might receive a standard level of instruction. Framed this way, proponents of intelligence testing argued that it had real potential to drive social mobility.

Implications for Education

The changing notion of childhood relates to intelligence testing—and to psychology more generally—in several ways. First, compulsory education laws in both the UK and USA led to a dramatic rise in the number of children in schools. This in turn meant that classrooms often comprised a mix of different abilities, backgrounds and needs (Smidt, 2006). Drawing on eugenic principles, intelligence came to be seen as a natural and scientific way to class children into groups based on ability. This paved the way for the invention of a psychometric tool that could reliably measure and grade the intellectual abilities of children. Many practitioners viewed such demographic management of students by mental ability as a way to save an educational system pushed to the limits of its resources, as evident in this passage from a handbook on child development:

> Since feeble-mindedness is not a disease that we can hope to cure, what methods are to be adopted to lessen the enormous burden that feeble-mindedness places on the community? The only procedures seem to be training, segregation, and sterilisation. (Pinter, 1933, p. 837)

Second, the idea of childhood as a sensitive learning period called for the development of standardised, evidence-based pedagogical practices that could be applied on a large scale. This was accomplished through the publication of textbooks and training manuals. These books drew heavily from the psychological literature of the time and thus put those canonical ideas into widespread circulation. For example, Tracy and Stimpfl's (1909) *Psychology of the Child* explicitly references evolutionary theory when contrasting the influence of genes and sociality on intelligence. Such texts advocated for evidence-based policies drawn from aggregated data and unbiased observation—assumptions we regard as canonical to psychology (see Chapter 1). The popularisation of intelligence testing therefore solved a problem for the growing field of developmental psychology. Intelligence testing became one of many forms of educational assessment undertaken by individual children in schools. This facilitated more complex analyses of child behaviour and opened to empirical testing questions that were previously limited to case study or ethnography.

In the USA, the massive amounts of data generated by intelligence and other educational testing necessitated a centralised hub to coordinate these efforts and systematically analyse the findings. This occurred in 1867 with the establishment of the US Department of Education (Sears, 1975).

Third, changing conceptions of childhood placed teachers in a place of tremendous influence and authority. This called for the professionalisation of the educational industry, from teachers to the psychometricians who administered intelligence tests. Roberts (2004) notes how educators seeking employment were expected to know about the most up-to-date findings in developmental psychology research. For example, teachers were routinely asked in job interviews to identify the psychological factors relevant to identifying and cultivating good character. Teachers' Colleges opened throughout the UK and USA to train educators in best practices. Staying informed of the latest scientific findings and 'being scientific' became a core part of how the profession cultivated credibility. Such legitimacy was especially important given popular impressions that teaching, like home economics, was a 'feminine' field and therefore subjective, unserious business (Bloch, 1991).

The need for intelligence testing arose in response to a seismic cultural shift that re-conceived the role of children in society. There was a perceived moral imperative to improve the collective welfare of children by mandating education. Identification of the feeble-minded was a pedagogical and political priority given limited educational resources. Proponents of intelligence testing claimed that it enabled more efficient and appropriate instruction tailored to the natural ability of the pupils (though see Chapter 7 for a counterpoint). In this way, schools served as a testing ground for eugenic theories about ability and heritability. Intelligence testing also enabled the state to control a growing urban population by segregating those persons society deemed unacceptable or abnormal.

THE BINET-SIMON INTELLIGENCE SCALE

At the end of the 19th century, La Société pour L'Etude Psychologique de l'Enfant (The Society for the Psychological Study of the Child) served as an academic think-tank enabling French practitioners and civil servants to collaborate on pedagogical research. In 1904, the French government tasked the group with establishing a 'Commission for the Retarded' to differentiate children with typical and atypical cognitive functioning (Wolf, 1973). Psychologists Alfred Binet (1857–1911) and his research assistant Théodore Simon (1873–1961) led the project. Their goal was to create an assessment that could capture variable intelligence. Most assessments at the time assumed that intelligence depended on sensory abilities. Binet's theoretical stance was unusual in that he posited that there were important mental processes like reasoning and judgement that were not being assessed by tests of perception and sensation (Curtis & Glaser, 1981). The Binet–Simon Intelligence Scale, first published in 1905, featured items of increasing difficulty that probed spatial reasoning (such as matching shapes, or doing basic mental rotation), hand–eye coordination, memory, listening comprehension and recall, and basic problem-solving. An extensive manual accompanied the test, providing guidance on the administration and interpretation of the assessment (Wallin, 1911).

The Binet–Simon Intelligence Scale featured thresholds for task difficulty against which mental ability could be compared. The test generated a single numerical indicator of performance that was then normed for chronological age (3–18 years), which enabled easy comparison of performance across individuals (Wolf, 1973). Ironically, it was this generation of a single output that inextricably linked the Binet–Simon test with theories describing intelligence as a singular, fixed ability. Binet himself conceived of intelligence as a dynamic suite of behaviours and abilities, and he advocated a range of approaches to understanding intelligence, including more qualitative measures (Wolf, 1973). Such theories of multiple intelligence did not gain traction until the 1930s when the rise of statistical techniques like factor analysis made it possible to see systematic patterns in correlations between test questions (Curtis & Glaser, 1981).

The Binet–Simon Intelligence Scale transformed the educational landscape. Originally published in French, the test was quickly translated into multiple languages: The noted eugenicist H.H. Goddard translated the measure into English in 1912, and by 1915 his lab had distributed more than 88,000 copies of the test (Curtis & Glaser, 1981). Within a decade of first publication, the Binet–Simon Intelligence Scales were revised several times. Each new iteration refined the existing corpus of questions and added new items testing new aspects of cognitive functioning. The original scale included 30 items; by 1911 that number had reached 54. The first Stanford–Binet iteration of the test, authored by Lewis Terman, included a whopping 129 questions (Mülberger, 2020). To a populace unused to standardised testing, administering or completing a test of this length represented a significant investment of time and energy.

The Binet–Simon Intelligence Scale enjoyed widespread use in both the USA and UK and was normed for multiple groups outside its original audience, including infants as young as 3 months (Kuhlmann, 1912; Mowrer, 1933). In 1916, Terman led a large-scale effort to make the test more relevant to the American populace (see Focus Box 3.2). He and his team of all-female researchers modified the questions to be more culturally meaningful to white, middle-class respondents and validated their new version on over 3000 individuals. It is this formulation of the measure that we now know as the Stanford–Binet Intelligence Test (Sears, 1975). Terman's team also popularised the idea of the intelligence quotient (IQ) as a way to intuitively compare and interpret test scores. An IQ score compares the mental age of the participant (as determined by the test) to their biological age and multiplies this fraction by 100. According to testing manuals for the 5th edition of the Stanford–Binet test, IQ scores tend to range from 40 to 160, with average scores falling between 90 and 100. Scores below 79 are often classed as borderline impaired, while scores above 120 are said to indicate superior intelligence (Kaufman, 2009).

─Focus Box 3.2─

Florence Goodenough

When faced with the daunting task of norming the Binet-Simon Intelligence Scale for the American populace, Lewis Terman determined that he needed a team of clever, dedicated scientists who could collect, analyse and synthesise data from thousands of participants. Terman did not believe that women belonged in academia; he advocated against opening higher education to female students and against the entry of women into learned societies. Despite these views, the team he built to complete his ambitious survey of intelligence was comprised entirely of women. Terman thought they would be naturally gifted at working with children and parents. To mitigate against their potential unsuitability for scientific work, Terman collected the IQs of the women he hired to the team, selecting only those with exceptionally high scores (Rogers, 1997).

Florence Goodenough (1886-1959) impressed Terman with her intelligence and was soon tasked as the chief data analyst for the study. She even completed her PhD under Terman's supervision. Goodenough's collaboration with Terman placed her at the centre of debates within educational circles about the genetic determinants of intellectual ability. Goodenough supported hereditary accounts of intelligence but recognised that the debate would not progress without a diversity of evidence. Consequently, she expanded the operationalisation of intelligence to include other abilities and skillsets not covered by the Binet-Simon or Stanford-Binet measures. Her Draw-a-Person-Test used minimal verbal instruction and allowed children to express their self-knowledge in more open-ended, free-form ways, making it more suitable to atypically developing and clinical populations (Goodenough, 1928). She also pioneered new measures of children's emotional intelligence by asking mothers to track the emotional outbursts they observed in their children. Her novel method of time-event sampling involved observing and recording everyday behaviour for defined, short periods (Harris, 1959). Although Goodenough's contemporaries expressed extreme scepticism at the idea of recruiting untrained and 'non-scientific' mothers, her work opened the door to more ecologically relevant methods of data collection. It also diversified the pool of topics that were considered appropriate to systematically assess in children.

Figure 3.1 Florence Goodenough

Goodenough's relationship to her gender was complicated. Despite her membership in the National Council of Women Psychologists, Goodenough insisted she was a psychologist first and foremost; she did not want the title to be qualified with her gender. At the same time, she recognised the importance of helping other women advance in science through female mentorship. Most of her doctoral students were women, including Ruth Howard, one of the first Black women in the USA to earn a PhD (Benjamin, 1980). In an interesting twist, in 1936 Goodenough received the honour of having her biography included in the 6th edition of 'American Men of Science' (Jolly, 2010).

Throughout her scholarship, Goodenough demonstrated that the experience of the researcher and the participant are both crucial to empirical work. She illustrated how drawing from non-traditional sources of information—such as a mother's observations of her children—could yield new insights that might refine existing measures. Goodenough modelled how objective, robust methods could systematically investigate topics like emotion recognition that were often perceived at the time as inherently subjective and therefore too difficult to measure. Her legacy of seeing the individual behind the research was best summed in this eulogy by a former student: '... children were not only objects of scientific study—they were also persons of intrinsic worth. To her, parents were not antagonistic to children and to trained professionals—they were fellow seekers after wisdom and after good things for children' (Harris, 1959, p. 306).

The success of the first generation of intelligence tests generated an interest in measuring other aspects of intellectual aptitude and resulted in the development of vocation-specific batteries, including assessments to classify soldiers into different branches of service (Curtis & Glaser, 1981). New techniques and nonverbal analogues of the original test were developed, including those for deaf and blind children (Goodenough, 1926, 1928; Pintner, 1927). Intelligence testing legitimised developmental research, and psychological science more broadly. It demonstrated how philosophical questions like 'nature versus nurture' could be studied objectively and in a way that had practical value to society. In the words of Terman, intelligence testing 'brought psychology down from the clouds and made it useful to men … [it] transformed the "science of trivialities" into the "science of human engineering"' (1928, pp. 105–106). In the next sections, we unpack this idea in more detail, exploring the ways in which intelligence testing made such 'human engineering' possible. Intelligence testing became a tool for promoting meritocratic advancement of some groups while controlling and limiting opportunities for others. It also contributed to the psychological canon ideas about personhood—and particularly about individuality personal responsibility—that continue to shape how we approach the discipline today.

THE SCIENTIFIC AND CULTURAL IMPACT OF INTELLIGENCE TESTING

Relatively soon after its introduction to the psychological community, scholars began using intelligence measures to test competing theories about mind and culture. The instrument was soon associated with evolutionary theory and eugenic policies. In this context, intelligence testing linked mental progress to cultural progress; just as individuals could be ranked in terms of their abilities and mental age, so too could cultural groups be ordered according to their degree of perceived primitiveness.

Development Is the Study of Age-Related Change

Binet and Simon normed their test by referencing the average abilities a child might be expected to demonstrate by a particular age. This yielded individual performance scores that classed children as mentally 'older' or 'younger' than this referent. Prior to Binet and Simon's test, chronological age did not feature prominently in most developmental theories (Curtis & Glaser, 1981). The popularity of the test ensured that consideration of chronological age would be part of most developmental theories moving forward. Piaget's constructivist account of development, for example, frames the acquisition of physical and cognitive skills in terms of benchmarks that children typically reach at particular ages.

Psychology Is About the Individual, Not the System

The intelligence testing movement conceived of intellectual ability as an individual trait. Subsequently, any atypicality of the individual was also an individual problem. If a child scored low on the Binet–Simon test, it reflected something impoverished about their internal qualities. The methodology of the intelligence test—the generation of a score that compares a single case to a larger distribution—highlights this emphasis on individuality. One consequence of individualising behaviour in this manner is that it also puts the burden of *fixing* perceived problems on the person. If an individual's test scores on an academic aptitude test are low, for example, it is their *personal* responsibility to improve performance by seeking out additional resources in the form of tutoring and study aids. This ignores the larger systemic context in which the behaviour is based. In Chapter 7 we present a case study about the consequences of streaming 'sub-normal' children of Caribbean descent in the London school system during the 1960s and 70s. We can also think about how the tendency to isolate and individuate personal outcomes from their societal context cements inequities into the research ecosystem (see Chapter 9).

Behavioural Abnormality Is Pathological ...

The methodology of intelligence testing reinforced the link between standardisation and normalisation (Burman, 1994). In creating an average profile of intelligence in the population, the test makers also created a sense of what 'typical' or 'normal' performance looks like. Creating a test standard that incorporated the child's chronological age also strongly implied that there was a 'normal' developmental trajectory. The result was a test that was believed to assess a set of traits that are universal, and that unfold in a consistent and invariant manner no matter the context in which they are measured (see discussion of WEIRD psychology in Chapter 8). As a result, children may be classed as 'atypical' or pathological if they do not reach these benchmarks by the anticipated age. However, there are many reasons why children might 'fail' or show delays on a given measure, some of which have nothing to do with their cognitive abilities. To counter this narrative of development as inherently normative, linear and unidirectional, Burman (2019) advocates that we replace the concept of 'growing up' with 'growing sideways'.

The fixation on universality is also apparent in the theoretical grounding of many intelligence tests. The evolutionary assumptions at the heart of the intelligence testing movement posit that intellect—like all heritable traits—is biological and therefore natural. Owing to a popular idea at the time—recapitulation theory (Haeckel, 2009)—development of this trait in the *individual* child was thought to mirror (hence *recapitulate*) the development of the trait over *evolutionary* time. For example, in early development, the human embryo has visible gills that eventually give rise to the structures of the head and neck. Recapitulation theory held that these gills reflect our link to a more primitive ancestor (fish); all the stages of human evolution are thus represented in the appearance of the developing foetus (Varga, 2022). In a similar fashion, the pre-linguistic phase of infancy echoes the existence of our pre-hominid ancestors who were without language. There was therefore a temptation to infer that 'lower' forms of intelligence reflected something bestial about children and suggested that their behaviour was 'primitive'.

We can extend this metaphor even further. Although Haeckel's recapitulation theory was eventually debunked, some of the assumptions have lived on indirectly, particularly in cross-cultural work where researchers often compare a particular trait (like intelligence) across groups of people. A popular contrast is to pit the behaviour of a person from a 'traditional' and small-scale subsistence-based culture against that of a person living in an urban, industrialised region. If differences emerge, they might reveal something about the likely constitution or psychological functioning of our human ancestors, particularly when the target sample performs better than the comparison group. According to this approach, the behaviour of a group living in 2023 acts as a stand-in for our early ancestors. 'Traditional' societies are thought to give us a window into a prehistoric world. The ethnocentric and racist implications of this position are difficult to ignore.

... and Therefore 'The Other' Is Pathological

The first intelligence tests were normed on white, largely middle-class populations but then tested extensively on other groups, largely without modification of the instrument to make it culturally appropriate. When these groups performed worse than their white, middle-class counterparts, the difference was attributed to demographic features and not shortcomings with the test. For example, using the Binet–Simon Intelligence Scale, Goddard compared performance of white participants born in the USA to that of recent Jewish, Hungarian, Italian and Russian migrants. According to the results he classed 80% of his immigrant sample as feeble-minded and 'mental defectives', a position that elsewhere has been described as a 'tame' interpretation for the time (Gelb, 1986; Goddard, 1917). Goddard was aware of the test shortcomings, including issues with standardisation practices, language and the cultural appropriateness of the test items, yet he chose to promote an interpretation of these findings that presented the immigrants as racially and ethnically inferior. Historical records paint a conflicting picture of the role Goddard's study played in informing the racist US Immigration Act of 1924, which placed quotas on the number of immigrants admitted to the USA from Eastern and Southern Europe. What is incontrovertible is that Goddard himself viewed intelligence testing as core to a healthy government: 'Democracy, then, means that the people rule by selecting the wisest, most intelligent and most *human* to tell them what to do to be happy' (Goddard, 1919, p. 237).

Uncritical acceptance of differences on intelligence measures forged a strong link between the seemingly 'atypical' abilities of minoritised individuals and notions of abnormality and pathology. Ascribing test labels such as 'moronic,' 'subnormal', or 'retarded' to the individuals themselves and not their performance provided a strong rationale for clinical intervention. On this basis, countless minoritised individuals were streamed into low-performing classrooms, denied employment, sanctioned to mental institutions and, in the most extreme cases, sterilised (Coard, 1971/2021; Mülberger, 2020). In many cases such practices were not merely conventional, but codified into law, as in the example of a 1927 ruling by the US Supreme Court to maintain forced sterilisation of 'feeble-minded people' on the basis of their intelligence scores (Kamin, 1974; Mülberger, 2020). We return to this point in Chapter 4.

Psychology and the Rise of 'Intellectual Labour'

A final, and perhaps unexpected, impact of intelligence testing concerns the rise of professions characterised by their intellectual labour. Goodey (2011) describes the exercise of intellect as the mental labour that goes into certain modes of production. Intelligence testing set a bar that test-takers were required to pass if they wanted to enter jobs defined by the production of knowledge, rather than material goods. Attaching a raw number to intellect provides a way for it to be commodified, marketised and exchanged. As we will see next, this intellectualisation of labour is central to the contemporary culture of marketised education.

The intellectualisation of labour represents another important historical turning point, a shift toward meritocratic models of societal advancement. In theory, linking one's achievements in life to *ability* rather than *nobility* had the potential to open doors of opportunity to individuals regardless of their class or position in life. In 1921, the Indian government undertook a massive social experiment using intelligence testing to determine fitness for higher education and government employment. The sprawling British Empire required local governance, and thus it was important to have reliable ways to determine who amongst the colonised population might be a good fit for the civil service. In decades prior, psychoanalysis and lengthy personal interviews were used to assess the suitability of candidates.

These methods suffered a number of drawbacks, including that they were time-consuming and yielded highly subjective, often ambiguous results. Consequently, intelligence testing flourished in the British colonies because it was a more objective and efficient way of finding appropriate candidates for schools and government positions (Linstrum, 2016). Thus, whereas in the UK and USA intelligence testing was often used to demonstrate the racial inferiority of non-white groups, within the colonies themselves intelligence tests became a tool for meritocratic advancement amongst racialised people (Regmi, 2023). Linstrum (2016) notes that by the end of the 19th century, standardised aptitude testing was widespread throughout the British Empire. The 'Cambridge Local Examinations' used starting 1858 screened applicants for higher education and government employment in Trinidad, South Africa, New Zealand, Jamaica, Ceylon and the Gold Coast. Today, the University of Cambridge Local Examinations Syndicate (UCLES) still oversees the administration of the updated Cambridge Assessment. One branch of the organisation—known as the Oxford, Cambridge and RSA Examinations (OCR) board—is one of the five main examination boards in England, Wales and Northern Ireland. Far from being a relic of the past, the test craze started by the Binet–Simon Intelligence Scale continues to influence society today.

WHAT NEXT?

In this final section, we demonstrate how the Binet–Simon Intelligence Scale inspired a multitude of educational assessments, all aimed at objectively quantifying elements of intellectual performance, academic aptitude and reasoning ability. Collectively and for the sake of conceptual clarity we refer to this phenomenon as 'educational testing'. Some of these assessments are what we call standardised measures because they require the test takers to answer identical questions in a similar format, as in the example of multiple-choice tests. This in turn enables the test to be scored in a consistent manner that makes results easy to compare across individuals. Other forms of educational testing—what are known as summative assessments—attempt to measure what an individual has learned after a period of study. Here there may be variability in how the test is administered or evaluated, as in the example of writing an essay in response to a given prompt. Regardless of whether the assessment is standardised or not, the assumption at the heart of all educational testing is that an individual can be reduced to a score that reveals something about their abilities, experiences, or qualifications. Educational testing has become a core feature of the higher education system. As such, it is a powerful tool for maintaining the institutional barriers faced by minoritised persons.

Educational Testing and Higher Education

Educational testing is big business. Millions of people take some form of standard-ised aptitude test or summative qualifying examination each year. This is often in an educational context, such as applying for university or determining if a pupil requires additional support at school. As a general rule, such standardised tests and qualifying examinations do not measure intelligence proper; test creators argue that they are a better indication of whether students have suitable skills or back-ground knowledge in the topics they will study at university.

In UK, for example, two different summative exams confer pupils with educa-tional qualifications. Both the General Certificate of Secondary Education (GCSE) and A-level examinations provide an assessment of students' knowledge and skills in core subjects at the end of compulsory education. These tests average close to £40 per exam for the GCSEs and cost approximately £100 per test for A-levels according to the most recent data (O'Reilly, 2022). A small number of companies dominate the educational assessment market in the USA, from administering and scoring standardised tests to publishing study resources for the same. These com-panies are corporate behemoths. Their products reach millions of students each year, and the companies are valued in the millions and billions of dollars.

The true cost of educational testing, however, is the opportunities that are lost if one does not gain entry into the elite circles of education. In the UK, along with other criteria, qualifying examinations determine placement in private schools. Advocates of private education point to the wealth of resources available to sup-port students and enhance learning outcomes. With the gap between state school spending per pupil and average private school fees rising each year—doubling from £3100 in 2010 to £6500 in 2020—it is no wonder that competition to enter these schools is stiff. For the approximately 7% of students who attend private school, the benefits of private education do not stop there (Sibieta, 2021).

According to recent estimates, the rate of top A* grades at A-level awarded to private schools (58%) is 50% greater than that of state institutions (38%). Given the importance placed on these qualifying examinations, private secondary educa-tion effectively functions as a way for families to buy access to the higher education system (Mason, 2022). University education has a profound effect on future employment and earning. Comparisons of tax records indicate that pri-vately educated women and men earn more than individuals attending state schools; this effect is true of non-university-attending people, but especially so for those who pursue higher education. This translates into higher lifetime returns for people who attended private schools (Britton et al., 2021). And the long-term benefits of private education are not limited to salary, either. Students attending university—but particularly elite institutions—gain access to social networks that open doors to numerous social, financial and intellectual opportunities. It raises the question of what purpose private education serves except to keep these doors closed to everyone else.

In conclusion, we argue that the ultimate legacy of intelligence testing—what was once seen as an optimistic engine of social mobility—is the entrenchment and reproduction of privilege. The educational reform movements that first pushed for intelligence testing did so out of a growing concern for the welfare of children, particularly those forced by poverty into the labour force. In the hands of the eugenic scientists of the 19th and early 20th century, however, intelligence testing provided a rationale for segregating society in ways that concentrated power and influence in the hands of a few elite. That dynamic exists today, with educational testing replacing intelligence tests as the mechanism by which entry into influential circles is determined. The cumulative impact of these interlinked stories has been the creation of an educational culture that inflicts great harm on minoritised persons. Curtis and Glaser make this point succinctly: 'In a society struggling to provide equal opportunities for all its members, classification and prediction are no longer the prevalent social needs. The fact that intelligence tests were not designed as diagnostic instruments to help diverse individuals succeed in available educational and occupational opportunities has contributed to resistance to their use' (1981, p. 133).

Qualifying examinations and standardised tests taken in adolescence have the potential to propel students on a path towards financial security. We now know that these tests do not measure intellectual ability as much as intellectual opportunity. But even if these tests could definitively quantify intelligence, how should we feel about a system that guarantees dignity, security and financial stability to only a small subset of the highest achieving in our midst?

FURTHER READING

Goodey, C. F. (2011). *A history of intelligence and 'intellectual disability': The shaping of psychology in early modern Europe*. Routledge. [book]

A fascinating history of how we think about intellectual ability.

Burman, E. (1994). *Deconstructing developmental psychology*. Routledge. [book]

A critical take on developmental psychology with a focus on how modern developmental theories have been abstracted from historical, cultural and political context.

Joffe-Walt, C. (2022). *Nice White Parents*. 30 July 2020. https://www.nytimes.com/2020/07/30/podcasts/nice-white-parents-serial.html [audio podcast]

A podcast series that illustrates some of the points in this chapter by documenting how educational programs oriented toward intellectually gifted children often privilege white students, even in schools that are racially and ethnically diverse.

4

MENTAL ILLNESS AND MARGINALISATION

PSYCHIATRIC DIAGNOSIS AS AN UNTRUSTWORTHY LEVER OF POWER

We have plenty of reason to reckon with the history of psychiatry—the branch of medicine concerned with the treatment of mental illness. There is a direct line from today's therapies to harms done to those suffering the same illnesses in the not-so-distant past. From insulin therapy to antidepressants, from lifetime institutionalisation to electroconvulsive therapy (ECT), popular media has not shied away from harrowing accounts of life-altering effects of psychiatric treatments.

Perhaps because of this reckoning, students of psychopathology are given greater training in the context of their studies than is given in other areas of psychology. Culture-bound syndromes[1] such as dhat (originating in South Asia) and koro (Malaysia) form part of the canon, albeit exoticised and localised in 'alien' cultures.[2] We also hear of the export of our own assumptions of mental illnesses, for example

---

[1]Culture-bound disorders have been reformulated as cultural concepts of distress in a text revision to the fifth edition of the Diagnostic and Statistical Manual of Mental Disorders (DSM-5TR; American Psychiatric Association, 2022).

[2]Note that the vast majority of the DSM's disorders, those that primarily affect English-speaking people of the Global North, are not referred to as culture-bound, as though they are situated not in a culture but in the norm.

via well-meaning attempts to make Sri Lankan tsunami survivors aware of the symptoms of post-traumatic stress disorder (PTSD), citing their continued resilience as denial and therefore unfalsifiable evidence of their anticipated response to trauma (Watters, 2010)! The fact too that Rosenhan's (1973) 'On being sane in insane places' study is part of the canon, is remarkable. That a study so often associated with the antipsychiatry movement—a movement whose proponents argue that psychiatric diagnosis is more harmful than helpful—is an integral component of the canon suggests a field that is open to challenge in the most intellectually mature of ways.

Before we take too much reassurance though, it is worth glancing back at psychiatry in the middle of the 20th century, to understand how practitioners viewed their field then. In 1949, Portuguese neurologist António Egas Moniz (1874–1955) won a Nobel Prize for the development of a revolutionary treatment for psychosis (Gross & Schäfer, 2011). This treatment was the pinnacle of the contemporary understanding of mental illness, based on the understanding that psychopathology was caused by localised brain dysfunction. Moniz's procedure would go on to be known as the lobotomy—the surgical severing of the frontal lobes from the rest of the brain—with typical consequences of dampening not only aggressive emotional behaviour, but *all* emotional response. It would have massive negative consequences for the popular opinion of psychiatry, but at the time, heralded a new era of psychiatric treatment. Psychiatry has had a string of false dawns. We may well be in the midst of another one.

In this chapter, we seek to understand why modern psychiatry takes the approach it does in treating psychiatric disorders. Whilst this is a critical examination of psychiatry, it is important to emphasise that we are not denigrating a profession that has had a positive impact on, and even saved the lives of, many vulnerable people. Nonetheless we must examine psychiatry as a medical specialty that strives to apply the ever-advancing pathological understanding of disease to disorders of the mind, even if the fit is often inappropriate. Whilst some chapters in this book have focused on the groups of people affected by the branches of psychology in question, here we will do this only briefly. Predictably, it is the same groups of people not sat at the top table of society in the Global North. We will then examine in more detail what is sometimes referred to as the 'bad barrel' of modern psychiatry—the dysfunctional system of scientific and capital incentives that has led the discipline to its current state of ideological, and financial, dominance.

DEVIANCE AND 'DEVIANTS'

The groups of people pathologised by psychiatry are the same groups minoritised throughout the history of Western civilisation. If we are to learn anything from the stories in the book, it is that the psychological canon may as well have been deliberately crafted to protect the most powerful by marginalising, disempowering and harming those without power. Whether it is on the judgement of mental health or cognitive ability alone, or in combination with sex, sexuality, gender identity, or race, the psychiatric canon has been expert at punching down.

Eugenics

Eugenics, of course, rears its head as a malign driving force behind the treatment of those whose psychological health or cognitive capacity made them a burden to society (see also Chapter 3). Under the Aktion T4 campaign, Hitler's Nazi regime killed tens of thousands of learning-disabled children and adults and those with mental illnesses (Klee, 1985). Children with conditions including Down syndrome, hydrocephaly and microcephaly were assessed at hospitals and institutions before being killed. Adults with schizophrenia, epilepsy, Huntington's chorea and dementia were similarly assessed before being killed. Aktion T4 continued until the denouncing of the campaign by the Catholic Bishop of Münster, Clemens von Galen, in 1941, and until the invasion of the Soviet Union, at which point many of those in line for extermination were transferred to the eastern front (Ericksen, 2012). It is easy to dismiss the atrocities as actions of a genocidal regime, but it is vital to understand that they did not emerge from a vacuum. The application of eugenic principles in early 20th century USA, particularly California, where disabled children were 'passively' killed, e.g. by the feeding of milk from tubercular cows, heavily influenced Hitler's ideology (Black, 2003).

Women

Women have been notoriously and disproportionately targeted by interventions for the mentally ill. In Chapter 6 we trace the history of how psychology has pathologized gender, with a particular focus on mental disorders such as hysteria. From the European witch trials of the 16th to 18th centuries, to the disproportionate incarceration of women in 18th century madhouses, the tradition of pathologizing then removing women from society has taken many varied forms (Scull, 2015). Much is made of the historic disparities in ECT and psychosurgery (surgery to the brain as a treatment for psychopathology), but even today, English National Health Service data reveal that women are twice as likely as men to be administered ECT (Read et al., 2018).

Homosexuality

From the inception of the Diagnostic and Statistical Manual of Mental Disorders (DSM), homosexuality was classified as a sexual deviation within the category of 'sociopathic personality disturbance' disorders (American Psychiatric Association, 1952). In the wake of the New York Stonewall riots, and growing social and academic disquiet, including from sexologist Alfred Kinsey (1894–1956) and psychologist Evelyn Hooker (1907–1996), the 1973 6th printing of the DSM-II saw homosexuality removed as a disorder (Hooker, 1957; Kinsey et al., 1949, 1953). Nonetheless, queer people could be diagnosed with sexual identity disturbance until 1987, and distress about one's sexuality, specifically homosexuality, remained in the DSM until the DSM-5's first publication in 2013 (Drescher, 2015). Including homosexuality in the DSM legitimised all manner of psychotherapeutic conversion therapies—pseudoscientific practices that aim to treat away the patient's sexuality—under the guise of treating a psychological disorder. Similarly, removing homosexuality from the DSM has gone hand-in-hand with shifting societal attitudes towards acceptance of queer people, and queer people being given legal rights to participate in social practices such as marriage, child-rearing and adoption.

Transgender People

The political debates over transgender people, identities and experiences are perhaps the most recent examples of the power of pathologisation. Scotland's 2022 Gender Recognition Reform Bill acknowledges, amongst other things, that trans people should not need to be pathologised, i.e. diagnosed with gender dysphoria, in order to obtain a gender recognition certificate—a document that legally recognises that their gender is not the gender they were assigned at birth (Scottish Parliament, 2022). By legislating for removal of the need for a diagnosis of gender dysphoria, the Scottish Parliament proposed to bypass the UK requirement of a psychopathological diagnosis according to the DSM, something that trans people have argued conflates trans experience with abnormality and distress (Schulz, 2017). That the UK's Westminster government then looked to exercise its power to overrule this Scottish legislation adds a layer of culture war complexity to the debate on the need for a contentious medical diagnosis for someone to have their gender acknowledged in law.

Race

It should come as no surprise that mental health has long been used to reinforce societal privilege and disadvantage along racial lines, an idea we explore in more depth in Chapter 7. Nineteenth-century, Black, enslaved people in the USA were diagnosed with psychological disorders in response to the various manifestations of their rational urge to escape slavery (Cartwright, 1851). This is an important starting point for this brief discussion, as it establishes what was then considered a psychological disorder as something we now consider a rational response to horrendous circumstances. This idea is extended into the 20th century in Jonathan Metzl's (2010) *The Protest Psychosis: How Schizophrenia Became a Black Disease*. Metzl looks at the history of schizophrenia diagnosis in the USA, noting that prior to the Black civil rights movement of the 1950s and 60s, white women were much more likely to be diagnosed with schizophrenia than any other group. This changed with the acceleration of the civil rights movement as well as publication of the DSM-II (American Psychiatric Association, 1968), which added diagnostic criteria of 'hostility' and 'aggression' to the disease. These were exactly the qualities being encouraged in the civil rights struggle. Whilst the DSM may have been altered without racist intent, Metzl argues that this contributed to a racially politicised shift to the over-diagnosis of Black men, and thus positions the DSM as a tool of structural racism. Once again, a set of behaviours that we consider rational, commendable and that ultimately agitated successfully for societal change, were pathologised and made the problem of the individual, not of society.

Social Control

This idea of pathologising the expression of one's sexuality or the rejection of subjugation is, of course, part of a broader pattern of correcting societally distasteful behaviours. In the 18th and 19th centuries, in reaction to the overcrowded and barbaric madhouses of the time, the desire for *humane* madhouses swept across the English-speaking world. The York Retreat, an English 'moral' asylum that employed a system of incentives on the understanding that 'whatever tends to promote the happiness of the patient, is found to increase his desire to restrain himself, by exciting the wish not to forfeit his enjoyments' (Tuke, 1813, p. 177). In some institutions, what we now class as occupational therapies were then called incentives and included language classes, theatre productions and lectures. This paints a picture of retreats that sound very much like modern facilities for those with the money to avoid state-provided care—pleasant places in which to convalesce as one overcomes the stressors of a hectic life. The idea of moral asylums, though, can be construed in two ways—as places that practised a moral treatment of their patients, or as places that coerced patients into moral behaviours. French philosopher Michel Foucault took the latter view, arguing that this system of coercion, however wilfully it was received, was a 'gigantic moral imprisonment' (Foucault, 1965, p. 233). Perhaps surprisingly, Foucault's view is not inconsistent with the views that those running the retreats had. W.A.F. Browne, a Scottish moral asylum founder, is said to have described his hope that the moral activities of the day would extend their reach into the night, so '[c]ontrol may thus penetrate into the very minds of the insane' (Scull, 2015, p. 208).

This brief overview shows how psychopathology has been used to disempower marginalised groups and justify inhumane actions, highlighting the skewed power dynamic that allows disempowerment to go unchecked. Members of marginalised groups who object can easily be dismissed as acting irrationally or even pathologically. Additionally, pathologising societal problems to the level of the individual allows them to be ignored. According to such a view, the problem lies not in the unequal social structure, but in the capacity of certain individuals to deal with their lot. Even today, the urge to pathologise structural problems seems irresistible. From interventions aimed at promoting resilience in children from disadvantaged backgrounds to mindfulness sessions for workers close to burnout, we begin to realise how much easier it is to blame the individual for their response to an unmanageable situation than it is to change the systems that put people in those situations in the first place. We address this point as it relates to higher education in Chapter 9.

Focus Box 4.1

Frantz Fanon and Decolonial Psychiatry

Frantz Fanon (1925-1961) was a Black psychiatrist and political philosopher born on the French Caribbean colony of Martinique. He is regarded as one of the most influential decolonial thinkers of the 20th century, and his work has influenced countless anticolonial liberation movements, including the American Black Panthers and the South African anti-apartheid movement (Jansen et al., 2017).

Figure 4.1 Frantz Fanon

When German collaborationist Vichy forces took over Martinique, the teenage Fanon fled his home to join the Free French Forces of Charles de Gaulle (Zeilig,

2021). After fighting in World War II, Fanon completed his psychiatry training in France, before embarking on a professional career practising and writing. In 1953, he moved to Algeria, then also a French colony, where he worked as head of the Blida-Joinville Psychiatric Hospital until 1957. During this time he grew so disillusioned with colonial rule that he joined the National Liberation Front–the force that ultimately secured independence for Algeria in 1962. Fanon died of leukaemia a year before Algeria gained independence.

Fanon's written work blended his psychodynamic training with observations on sexual and racial politics, relationships between colonisers and the colonised, and his observations on anticolonial uprising and liberation. Many of his most influential decolonial ideas arose from his psychiatric work in Algeria. Crucially, he situated mental ill-health in colonial contexts as a response to multi-generational oppression and cultural denigration. He rejected institutional care in which patients were coerced into adapting to their oppressive environments as yet another way in which the coloniser enacts violence on the colonised (Gibson & Beneduce, 2017). His alternative was care that acknowledges cultural traditions and the need for social liberation, through group activities including patients' union meetings, handcrafts, gardening and sports (Robcis, 2020). While this might sound very much like the occupational approach of the moral asylums, it came from a vastly different position–rejecting authoritative control and empowering the patient from a position of cultural authenticity.

Fanon was clear that decolonisation could never be a solely intellectual exercise. In *The Wretched of the Earth* (1961) he wrote that decolonisation always requires violence. He dismissed the argument that there are peaceful means by which to ensure greater satisfaction for the colonised as a double standard, given the means by which the colonisers obtained their power. In presenting the argument for peaceful, incremental change, Fanon argued that colonisers would use *colonised intellectuals*, members of the colonised people who had been indoctrinated into supporting the colonial regime, to water down and ultimately ensure the failure of revolutionary change.

Fanon's words carry weight, and force those of us who might ourselves be considered colonised intellectuals to introspect. As if we needed any more reminding, the title of Tuck and Yang's (2012) seminal paper on contemporary efforts within higher education puts it succinctly: 'Decolonization is not a metaphor' (p. 1).

THE BAD BARREL

In the decades since its inception, the Diagnostic and Statistical Manual of Mental Disorders (DSM) has had a growing influence on psychiatry. It has ballooned from 132 pages in 1952, to 947 now. This growth has been necessary to accommodate the number of disorders that the manual can be used to diagnose, from 128 to 541 (Blashfield et al., 2014). This increased diagnostic specificity might be expected given the increasing biotechnological diagnostic capabilities of modern medicine. But this assumption falls flat when we consider that most psychiatric conditions cannot be tested for like, for example, COVID-19 can. There is no laboratory test for depression; instead, it is diagnosed on conversation with a doctor or psychiatrist. The same model of diagnosis is true of all mood disorders, all anxiety disorders, schizophrenia and all personality disorders, to name but a few. Advancing biomedical technology has nothing to do with the increasing number of mental health conditions we can be diagnosed with. So what is causing the DSM expansion? To understand this, it is helpful to understand the recent history of psychiatric diagnosis.

The Pathogenic Revolution

In the 19th century, medical researchers made great leaps in their understanding of disease. Germ theory, aseptic surgery and the identification of bacteria responsible for cholera, anthrax and tuberculosis heralded the pathogenic model of disease. According to this model, disease can be caused by the effect on the body of pathogens—agents such as bacteria and viruses that disrupt the body's healthy functioning. Armed with this knowledge, those looking to reduce disease could take a preventative approach. By reducing contact with pathogens, for example by cleaning drinking water, or conducting surgery in aseptic conditions, it was possible to greatly reduce the likelihood that those pathogens would cause infection and therefore disease (Ackerknecht & Rosenberg, 2016).

If prevention failed, it follows from the pathogenic model that a diseased body could be cured by eliminating the pathogens causing disease. By the early 20th century, agents that could eliminate bacteria from the body—antibiotics—had been discovered, and were being used not just to treat, but to eliminate certain diseases. The idea of pathogenic cause and effect, of physiological balance and imbalance, was not new to Western medicine, but the identification of biological agents that physicians could be sure caused and cured disease was.

This biomedical revolution largely left psychological disease untouched. One exception was syphilis, for which a bacterial pathogen was identified (Tampa et al., 2014). This sexually transmitted infection causes sores and growths before progressing through a long-lasting asymptomatic latent stage, to a final stage which can involve brain damage manifesting as mania, depression, dementia and psychosis. Patients with psychological symptoms resulting from syphilis comprised up to 20% of those in 19th century British asylums, and were typically given a diagnosis of 'general paralysis of the insane' (Davis, 2012). As the pathogenic model was embraced, treatments were developed to much acclaim. Malarial therapy—the infection of syphilitic patients with malaria on the assumption that malarial fevers destroy the syphilis pathogen—even won the Nobel Prize in 1927 (Scull, 2015). This therapeutic approach was swiftly ousted by antibiotic therapy, which effectively cured syphilitic patients, including those with psychiatric symptoms, and allowed them to leave asylums. This understanding of how general paralysis could be treated was key to cementing the idea that mental disorders are governed by the pathogenic model of disease and can be treated with a biomedical approach.

Keeping Up with Medicine

Spurred on by the successes of the pathogenic model and the biomedical approach, doctors treating mental disorder sought to apply the same principles to revolutionise psychiatry. American psychiatrist Henry Cotton (1876–1933) attributed all psychological ill-health to untreated infection, and set about removing the organs harbouring pathogens. According to Cotton, teeth, tonsils, testicles, ovaries and colons were all likely suspects, and their removal was key to his patients' recoveries (Cotton, 1921). There is little evidence to suggest that Cotton's cures could have been effective. Indeed, evidence from Cotton himself suggests that his surgeries often led to death rather than cure (Cotton, 1923).

An alternative to removing a host organ for pathogens was to make the host body inhospitable to them by other means. Shock therapies were devised for this purpose. We are used to thinking of electroconvulsive therapy (ECT) as *the* shock therapy, but in the early 20th century, a great many physiological shocks were experimented with. Scull (2015) collected accounts of many of these now-abandoned therapies, including the previously mentioned deliberate infection with malaria, the cooling of the body, the deliberate infection with meningitis on the assumption that the immune system would be mobilised, and the injection of poisons. In some cases, neurological disorders were themselves understood to generate shocks that could drive off other psychopathologies. The shock therapy that survives into the 21st century, ECT, was initially devised on the false premise of an antagonism between epilepsy and schizophrenia (Shorter, 2009). The idea was that if one could induce seizures, the hallmark of epilepsy, then one might be able to alleviate the symptoms of schizophrenia. Whilst ECT survives as an effective treatment for otherwise-untreatable depression, its hypothesised mechanism of action has long since moved away from the idea of an epilepsy–schizophrenia antagonism (Kellner et al., 2012).

When considered alongside the development and rise of the lobotomy, the first half of the 20th century ushered in a range of biomedical therapies founded on the pathogenic model of disease. They were heralded within the scientific community and the media at large, commanding Nobel Prizes (for lobotomy and the malarial treatment of syphilis) and glowing write-ups in *Time* magazine and the *New York*

Times (for insulin shock therapy; Scull, 2015). But that didn't last. Most 20th century biomedical therapies have faded into obscurity, and a few have risen to infamy. Nevertheless, the appeal they had illustrates quite how voracious the appetite was for the application of the pathogenic model to psychological disorders.

Paradigm Shift

The culmination of the pathogenic model of psychological disorder came in 1980. It arrived not as a discovery or a treatment, but as a 494-page book—the third revision of the DSM (American Psychiatric Association, 1980). Prior to the DSM-III, the manual had taken a psychodynamic, Freudian approach. Given the shift that had occurred in medicine, and the extent to which these ideas had taken hold of psychiatry in the first half of the 20th century, a shift away from Freud seemed long overdue. When it came, the revised DSM took a *neo-Kraeplinian* approach, and set into action a seemingly inevitable chain of events that has led us to modern-day psychiatry (Mayes & Horwitz, 2005).

Focus Box 4.2

Emil Kraeplin's Taxonomy of Psychological Disease

Emil Kraeplin (1856–1926) was a German psychiatrist and colleague of neuropathologist Alois Alzheimer. In 1907, Alzheimer published the case-study of a 51-year-old woman presenting with memory impairment and delusions (Berrios, 1990). On post-mortem examination, she was found to have brain atrophy accompanied by clusters and twisted strands of protein known as neurofibrillary plaques and tangles. Kraeplin assisted with Alzheimer's work to describe the disease and its neurobiological basis, and in the eighth edition of his textbook for students and doctors, published in 1910, named the disease after Alzheimer.

In integrating Alzheimer's disease into his classification of mental disorders, Kraeplin was drawn to a taxonomy of psychological diseases that was organised according to patterns of disease symptoms (Berrios & Hauser, 1988). This taxonomy deviated from previous classifications that had focused on major symptoms, and instead provided a more comprehensive approach to characterising diseases according to their constellation of symptoms and how they progressed. Kraeplin proposed that, as with Alzheimer's disease, there was a unique biological pathology underpinning each psychological disorder. Kraeplinians of the time argued that his descriptive taxonomy would, with continuing advances in medical research, be proven with the discovery of these pathologies (Moncrieff & Steingard, 2019).

The neo-Kraeplininan approach of the DSM-III reflected Kraeplin's original taxonomy. It described psychological disorder according to constellations of symptoms and behaviours exhibited by patients, and categorised them according to presumed underlying biomarkers. This was a massive shift from the psychodynamic approach of previous editions. According to the previous approach, unconscious conflict stemming from past events, notably childhood experience, was key to the formation of mental illness. These psychological factors required psychotherapeutic skill to tease of out of participants, often with a great deal of inference from the therapist in the process. The neo-Kraeplinian approach, on the other hand, was behaviouristic. Observable symptoms were defined by consensus, and compiled into check-list style, diagnostic criteria (Karter & Kamens, 2019).

To illustrate this difference, we can examine the example of depression from each version of the DSM. Whilst many defined disorders included depressive symptoms, the characteristic psychodynamic approach was clearly evident in the DSM-II's definition of 'depressive neurosis' as 'manifested by an excessive reaction of depression due to an internal conflict or to an identifiable event such as the loss of a love object or cherished possession' (American Psychiatric Association, 1968, p. 40). The criteria for 'major depressive episode' in the DSM-III were much more procedurally operationalised, as: (a) dysphoric mood or anhedonia, in combination with; (b) four of eight separately listed symptoms and; (c) the ruling out of three other potential causes (American Psychiatric Association, 1980). For better or worse, the DSM had been re-shaped into a manual that could be used to diagnose mental disorder without a great deal of psychotherapeutic training.

But why, half a century after Kraeplin outlined his approach to the classification of psychological disease, did the American Psychiatric Association align themselves with this approach? One reason came from the fringe movement of *antipsychiatry*. Antipsychiatry gained traction in the 1960s and 70s, as a challenge to the dominance of the psychodynamic psychiatric model. Many of the ideas explored so far in this chapter contributed to the movement: the control that therapists and asylums had over patients; the pathologisation of individual responses to societal forces; and reactions against the harmful ineffective therapies of the early 20th century (Dain, 1989). Another reason, the highlighting of major problems with the dominant psychiatric model, came not from the fringes, but from squarely within the establishment, in the pages of *Science* magazine.

'On being sane in insane places' was the *Science* report documenting two studies conceived by psychologist David Rosenhan. In the first study, healthy 'pseudopatients' were admitted to psychiatric institutions, mostly with a diagnosis of schizophrenia, because they presented to the admission team with auditory hallucinations. In the second study, a psychiatric institution volunteered to detect pseudopatients, and did so at a high rate, only to discover that *no* pseudopatients had been sent there by Rosenhan. Beyond these findings, the article described the demeaning nature of the psychiatric care received by pseudopatients, and the potential impact of diagnoses of 'schizophrenia in remission' when they were eventually discharged. Rosenhan's paper contributed to a growing scientific discontent with the reliability of psychiatric diagnoses (e.g. Spitzer & Fleiss, 1974), with its publication in *Science* doing so in one of the most prestigious scientific journals.

After the attention Rosenhan's paper received, something needed to be done to shore up the reliability of psychiatric diagnoses. Though the seeds had been sown decades previously, the time was right for the old approach to give way to the new. Robert Spitzer, one of the key critics of DSM-II reliability was tasked with leading the revision of the DSM by the American Psychiatric Association. By adopting a neo-Kraeplinian approach, Spitzer's team succeeded in making the DSM-III far more reliable than its predecessor (Andreasen et al., 1981; Scull, 2015). But in doing so, they also imbued psychiatry with another Kraeplinian assumption, that psychological disorders stemmed from biological pathologies—pathologies that would soon be treatable.

The Pharmacotherapeutic Treatment of Mental Illness

The descriptive diagnostic approach taken by the DSM-III played into another mental health revolution that was taking hold of society. In the 1950s, an anti-psychotic drug marketed under the name Thorazine (chlorpromazine) began to be prescribed to treat schizophrenia (Adams et al., 2014). Whilst it had side-effects, Thorazine reliably relieved symptoms and improved functioning. Without definitive biomarkers for schizophrenia, the introduction of a diagnostic system that focused on symptoms and functioning, and a drug whose efficacy was assessed by its action in these domains, closed the loop. From 1980 onwards, the medical treatment of schizophrenia *appeared* as though it was acting on a biological understanding of the causes of schizophrenia. In reality, no such understanding existed.

There were also other forces at play. The costs of institutional care were increasingly being scrutinised by governments, who were looking for cheaper ways of dealing with the mentally ill (Scull, 2015). In 1961, Health Minister Enoch Powell (who would go on to speak of 'rivers of blood', see Chapter 7) gave a speech to the National Association of Mental Health in which he outlined the British government's plans to replace dedicated institutions with care in the community (Nuffield Trust, 2023). Patients were to be discharged, with their institutional care replaced by contact with social workers and community services. Whilst the merits of this approach are increasingly being called into question, it would have been unthinkable without the pharmaceutical treatment options that were increasingly being viewed as viable ways in which the mentally ill could manage their symptoms.

Without institutional care, the need for pharmaceutical treatments grew. Fortunately for drug companies, from the third edition onwards, the DSM has provided a symptom-focused manual that could be used to target drug development, and a much more reliably diagnosed pool of patients: (a) in whom to evaluate drug efficacy during development and (b) to whom the drugs could be administered once approved. It matters little to drug companies if biomarkers for disease are not developed as long as their drugs relieve symptoms. Indeed, drugs that relieve symptoms of intractable disease present drug manufacturers with greater financial opportunity than those that provide a one-off cure (Scull, 2015). In this context, antidepressants, anti-anxiety drugs, antipsychotics and mood stabilisers have all become part of the symptomatic treatment of psychological disorders, whose biological causes we still know very little about.

If we now consider drug manufacturers' priorities as financial entities, and their place within this ecosystem alongside the DSM, a curiosity already alluded to in this chapter makes sense. The reason for the DSM's growth, in disorders identified and therefore number of pages, is down to its success as a diagnostic manual. Reliable diagnoses led to its widespread professional adoption, and subsequent consideration by regulatory entities (Harper, 2013). This consideration is important as, for example, if a drug is to be approved by the US Food and Drug Administration (FDA) that drug must be effective in treating a disease. Without a disease to treat, there is no justification for approving a drug. One of the ways in which drug manufacturers can continue to grow financially, then, is to ensure that they have an ever-increasing pool of diseases. And without disease biomarkers, the arbiters of what constitutes a disease are the authors of the DSM.

This sounds conspiratorial, but has support from formal analyses. Whitaker and Cosgrove's (2015) book *Psychiatry Under the Influence* explored the growth of successive versions of the DSM, culminating in an analysis of the DSM-5. They found that the lack of biomedical diagnostic tests for psychiatric disorders, coupled with the financial conflicts of interest faced by psychiatrists who both assist with pharmacological clinical trials and revise the DSM, makes the treatment of psychiatric disorders particularly susceptible to institutional corruption. Psychiatrists tasked with developing the DSM-5 invariably had ties to drug companies. Not only did the drug companies stand to gain from the growth of the DSM, an outcome that the psychiatrists were capable of influencing, but in healthcare models such as those of the USA, the same psychiatrists stood to gain from the day-to-day prescription of drugs (Karter & Kamens, 2019). The biases at play, however small or well regulated, all push in one direction—the identification of a greater number of psychiatric diseases.

The swing towards drug prescription over other forms of treatment prompted the president of the APA to acknowledge that '[f]inancial incentives and managed care have contributed to the notion of a "quick fix" by taking a pill and reducing the emphasis on psychotherapy and psychosocial treatments' (Sharfstein, 2005,

p. 3). Meanwhile, the noticeable increase in disorders identified by the DSM prompted Allen Frances, the chair of the taskforce developing the DSM-IV, to declare '[i]t's very easy to set off a false epidemic in psychiatry … [t]he drug companies have tremendous influence' (Ronson, 2011, p. 46). And whilst there is a temptation to point the finger at corrupt psychiatrists, it is difficult to identify any individual bad actors. In fact, we can all point to the good that psychiatrists, members of successive DSM task-forces and drug treatments have done in helping patients with their conditions. Nonetheless, this good is being increasingly incorporated into a system of institutional corruption driven by the financial interests of the drug companies. This paradox has been referred to not as a problem of 'bad apples' but of a 'bad barrel' (Cosgrove & Vaswani, 2019). The seemingly inevitable progression of psychiatry as concerning the biomedical treatment of pathogenic diseases has set the modern discipline on a trajectory that few would otherwise have plotted for it.

WHAT NEXT?

The dominance of the pharmacotherapeutic model of psychiatric treatment carries with it a huge influence on popular and even professional perceptions of the scientific understanding of mental illness. Whilst psychiatrists using the DSM adopt a descriptive diagnostic framework, the pharmacological treatments they prescribe suggest the use of a pathogenic, biologically causal framework (Moncrieff & Steingard, 2019). Of course, there are some diseases for which the latter framework applies, which complicates the big picture—no single model is universally appropriate. From a medical ethics perspective, though, it is surely important that patients presented with pharmacotherapeutic treatments be free to make informed decisions about the treatments available to them.

The Drug-Centred Approach

Communication of the drug-centred approach to psychiatry is one way by which patients could be more fully informed about their treatment. This approach stands in contrast to the traditional disease-centred approach and aims to re-orient our understanding of the efficacy of pharmacological treatment as being driven by the psychoactive effects of the drugs themselves (Moncrieff, 2018). Whereas the disease-centred approach leads us to believe that drug treatments correct an abnormal brain state, the drug-centred approach provides an understanding in line with how psychopharmacological drugs are, in many cases, developed—that drugs themselves alter physiology and psychology in ways that may be useful in balancing out the symptoms of the disease (Moncrieff, 2019). Wider communication of the drug-centred approach would go some way towards breaking the chain of inference that leads people to assume a pathogenic understanding of psychological disease.

The Biopsychosocial Model

The biopsychosocial model, proposed in 1977, calls for psychiatrists to move beyond a simple biomedical model, and consider *all* the factors contributing to the expression of psychiatric disease (Engel, 1977). It re-introduces the need for understanding of psychological and social processes, in addition to biomedical processes, to better understand why a person's condition manifests the way it does, and why they have chosen (or not chosen) to seek treatment. Considering psychological disease in this way emphasises the importance of talking and occupational therapies, and even societal power dynamics, introduced to us by writers such as Fanon (see Focus Box 4.1). It is easy to see why a return to such a holistic model would be resisted. Spitzer's rationale for the DSM-III was to remove human judgement, and therefore human error, from psychiatry (Ronson, 2011).

One approach that uses the biopsychosocial model is community psychology. Community psychology extends beyond psychiatry, and seeks to understand the complex interplay between people and their socio-political environments in understanding behaviour (Kloos et al., 2012). Practitioners place the values of appreciating human diversity, empowerment and participation, and social justice, as central to their approach. Relevant to the topics covered in this chapter, community psychology shifts the focus from disease to wellness, seeking to foster environments that promote good health and prevent the conditions that lead to poor health. Moving away from the current status quo—wryly termed the bio-bio-bio model (Sharfstein, 2005)—will require re-engagement with the complexities of psychological disease beyond the individual, but approaches like community psychology provide the frameworks within which this can begin.

Psychiatric Reform

Even before the publication of the DSM-III, it was hard to imagine psychiatric reform, specifically a move away from the biomedical model (Engel, 1977). With the established intertwinement of the APA, Big Pharma and worldwide health-care industries, it is now almost impossible to conceive of. Nonetheless, suggestions continue to be made for how to move back towards a psychiatry that moves away from the influence of Big Pharma, and best represents current understanding of psychiatric disease and its treatment (Sharfstein, 2005;

Steingard, 2019). The challenge of such reform cannot be underestimated, especially if we take at face value the claim that the current model is 'a colonisation of the psychological and social by the biological' (Read, 2005, p. 597). Fortunately, the psychiatric profession is no stranger to the idea of decolonisation. With this in mind, it is crucial to acknowledge the societal context that psychiatry finds itself in. There will be no hope of psychiatric reform if it does not go hand-in-hand with governmental healthcare policy reform.

Integrating alternative perspectives into the practice of clinical psychology has the potential to create a more comprehensive and nuanced approach to mental health. Fixing the bad barrel will require honest examination of the corruption that currently drives the system, and collaboration between professionals, policymakers and communities, especially those marginalised within the current systems, in a way that puts people before profits. In looking for alternatives, we should not be afraid to shift the culture of mental health care towards embracing models that better reflect the complex interplay between biological, psychological and social factors. As with all culture change, this will require those who benefit from their current positions of power to acknowledge this, and cede their privilege. If we can enact this sort of change, we will have played a vital role in fostering a more inclusive, empowering and socially just mental healthcare system.

FURTHER READING

Scull, A. (2015). *Madness in civilization: A cultural history of insanity, from the Bible to Freud, from the madhouse to modern medicine.* Princeton University Press. https://doi.org/10.2307/j.ctvc77hvc [book]

A fascinating examination of the history of perceptions of mental health and psychiatric treatment.

Ronson, J. (2011). The kids are not alright. *New Scientist, 210*(2815), 44–47. https://doi.org/10.1016/S0262-4079(11)61329-8 [magazine article]

A distillation of how revisions to the DSM changed mental health diagnosis, with a focus on childhood diagnoses of bipolar disorder.

Fanon, F. (1961). *The wretched of the earth* (C. Farrington, Trans.). Penguin. [book]

Seminal work by Fanon exploring the psychological impact of colonialism on colonised peoples.

5

PHRENOLOGY, NEUROIMAGING AND THE TECHNOLOGIES THAT SHAPE OUR UNDERSTANDING OF THE MIND

'Are you left-brain or right-brain dominant? Do you gravitate to facts and logic, or feelings and creativity?' This false dichotomy proposing two supposedly discrete halves of the brain is found everywhere—from online quizzes to assessments carried out at school or work— and illustrates a myth that pervades in the public understanding of the mind. Even though a cursory internet search reveals that there is no basis for this division of brain function, we are still drawn to this idea, and plenty of others like it. In this chapter, we will explore a vulnerability in our understanding of how the mind works, to show how unscrupulous technologists have presented, and marketed, neuroimaging as a tool for reading the mind. Viewing modern neuroscience through the historical lens of phrenology—the debunked notion that cognitive faculties and personality traits could be inferred from the shape of the skull—demonstrates our susceptibility to pseudoscientific misrepresentation when faced with the potent combination of science and technology.

THE RISE AND FALL OF PHRENOLOGY

Phrenology was devised by the German physician Franz Josef Gall and rose to its peak in English-speaking nations in the 19th century. As interest in phrenology grew, it was refined and extended by Scottish lawyer George Combe, with the consequence that, within the British Empire, Edinburgh rose to be the seat of phrenological study. According to the phrenological framework, the outer layer of the brain, the cortex, is divided into a number of 'organs' (27 according to Gall, 35 according to Combe), in which a particular faculty or trait is *localised*. Whilst many phrenological faculties would not appear out of place in a modern psychometric battery—e.g. capacity for language, conscientiousness—others have fallen out of favour—e.g. secretiveness and acquisitiveness (Combe, 1828). The location of the phrenological organs meant it was assumed that their size would be evidenced in the contours of people's skulls. It followed that the organs could be indirectly measured by examination of the head, either by hand or with measuring calipers. These examinations yielded an understanding of the individual that could both support observations of their character and presuppose it.

Explanations of the mechanism by which phrenological organs influenced thought and behaviour drew on state-of-the-art mechanical and physiological analogies (Zarkadakis, 2017). The larger the organ, the more it was thought to drive its faculty. It was understood that individuals could exercise and grow their phrenological organs like muscles, but also that different peoples had different starting points, according to the head shape that typified their races. The latter understanding was employed extensively across the British Empire to characterise Indigenous peoples, and justify the theft, disenfranchisement and slavery they were subjected to (Poskett, 2019). To add insult to injury, skulls supporting racialised phrenological claims were disinterred and treated as scientific collectables. They were sent to museums and private collectors, and used to perpetuate the oppressive systems of thought regarding colonised peoples that would last far beyond phrenology itself.

In evaluating phrenology for the purpose of deriving insights from its history, it is crucial to determine the factors that contributed to its downfall. What ultimately brought an end to phrenology, and how could a more rigorous brain science avoid similar pitfalls? In 1824, an article published in the *Encyclopaedia Britannica* provided a scathing review of phrenology and proposed a series of tests to challenge its assumptions (Roget, 1824). The author then proceeded to explain how phrenologists had failed to produce convincing evidence to support their claims. He stated that there was no evidence for the critical assumptions that a larger phrenological organ was linked to a greater capacity for that faculty, or that the phrenological organ could indeed shape the skull. These failings were reinforced by the work of two French physicians, Jean Pierre Flourens and Paul Broca, with Flourens using crude animal lesion studies to argue against the idea of localisation at all (Pearce, 2009), and Broca finding neuropsychological evidence for the localisation of language, but not where any of the phrenologists had placed it (Broca's area, as it would go on to be called, is situated in a lower lateral region of the left frontal cortex, not between or immediately behind the eyes as Gall and Combe had placed it; Greenblatt, 1995). Perhaps most pertinently, the *Encyclopaedia Britannica* article finished with the criticism that the arguments phrenologists used were entirely circular—'he assumes as true the thing to be proved, namely, that faculties of a certain class reside in a certain department of the head, and then applies it to establish the very proof on which the proposition itself ought to have rested' (Roget, 1824, p. 436).

With the absence of evidence seemingly necessary to establish phrenology as a science, how then did it take hold to such an extent that phrenological busts are *still* being mass-produced, well over a century after it fell out of favour? This appeal likely derives from a number of forces that worked together to elevate phrenology far beyond that warranted by its scientific basis.

1   Its **intuitive appeal** is inescapable. Gall made no secret of the origins of phrenology in his own attempts to find links between the personalities of his friends and their observable physical characteristics (Roget, 1824). We see evidence of our own desires to find patterns all around us, from the rules we learn implicitly as we pick up a new language, to the superstitions we hold and the stereotypes we maintain.

2   Phrenology presented a **technologically advanced** science to aid the new-found understanding of the mind. Craniometric tools, plaster busts and printed photographs were all technologies that allowed phrenology to spread across the English-speaking world in a way that emphasised its universality (Poskett, 2019). These were truths of nature that modern technology was unmasking!

3   These technologies evolved into **industries**, which had a vested interest in promoting the success of phrenology. Collectors traded in skulls and casts, whilst travelling educators gave classes and sold their materials. A perfect embodiment of these interconnected industries was the Fowler Brothers, who printed guides, manufactured busts and founded the *American Journal of Phrenology* (Greenblatt, 1995). They promoted phrenology through readings (adapting to changing technologies by offering to read people's skulls from early photographs; Poskett, 2019), and training new phrenologists. The brand is so synonymous with phrenology that it persists on new busts sold on Etsy and eBay.

4   It was a **tool that consolidated power**. Its perceived scientific legitimacy, coupled with the absence of any real scientific grounding, allowed those in

positions of power to use phrenology to show whatever they wanted to show. Just as it was used to dispossess peoples of the British Empire, so it was used in North America to defend slavery. American physician Charles Caldwell used phrenology to argue that differences in the sizes of 'animal organs' in Black enslaved people and their white 'owners' was evidence that they belonged to different species (Erickson, 1981).

Taken together, these forces allowed advocates of phrenology to ignore the lack of evidence for their ideas, and point to the intuitive appeal, modern technology and popularity of their ideas, especially amongst the respectable elite, as evidence for their credibility.

In the next section, we move on to discuss contemporary neuroimaging. Whilst based on significant advancements in technology and scientific understanding compared to the pseudoscience discussed so far, neuroimaging and phrenology share some key characteristics. As with phrenology, neuroimaging allows us to think of faculties and thoughts as localised within the brain, and it does so with the weight of medical technology behind it (in a manner not dissimilar to the 'hardening' of psychology with statistics; see Chapter 2). Moreover, certain uses of neuroimaging are lent credibility by industrial backers, to an extent that should lead us to ask *'why?'*. As we make the comparison between neuroimaging and phrenology, we hope to prompt consideration of how scientific technologies can be used to misrepresent scientific understanding for the purposes of perpetuating existing power structures.

THIS IS YOUR BRAIN ON POLITICS

In November 2007, more than 200 years after phrenology was developed, and almost exactly one year before the 56th Presidential election in the USA, the *New York Times* published an op-ed titled 'This is your brain on politics' (Iacoboni et al., 2007). The authors of the piece, four university academics and three commercial researchers, gave their insights into what swing voters *really* thought of the candidates vying for party nomination. They based these insights on a state-of-the-art procedure that would eliminate the biases and inaccuracies that arise during focus groups and conversations, where people hide, misrepresent and lie about their political beliefs (Hammer, 2007). Instead of asking voters about the candidates, the research team examined their thoughts directly, laying their participants in a multi-million dollar brain scanner and reading their brain activity in response to pictures and videos of the candidates. Following a sophisticated analytic process, they distilled their findings into eight points, which included the following: '1. Voters sense both peril and promise in party brands', based on amygdala activation;

'2. Emotions about Hillary Clinton are mixed', based on anterior cingulate activation; and, '8. Barack Obama and John McCain have work to do', based on the absence of any marked increase in activation. According to the levels of brain activity measured, Obama looked to be in particular trouble.

Obama and McCain, the candidates creeping into the final point of the op-ed, were the candidates who would go on to receive the strongest support in the regional caucuses and primaries. They were selected as their parties' nominees for president, with Barack Obama arousing fervent support during his rallies, and going on to a decisive election victory. A cautionary tale then. Social science, particularly psephology, the science of polling, tries to reduce uncertainty, but it can't eliminate it altogether. As we saw in the 2016 Trump election and the Brexit referendum, we can't expect pollsters to get it right every time. Except that the op-ed authors chose the methods they chose to eliminate precisely this sort of uncertainty. They looked directly into people's brains didn't they?

APPEALS TO INTUITION

Functional magnetic resonance imaging (fMRI), the neuroimaging method used in the op-ed, is a brain-scanning technology that infers brain activity from minute changes in the flow of oxygenated blood. The more blood is present in any of the tiny subdivisions of brain measured by the scanner (cubes with sides of length ~3mm), the more the brain tissue occupying that area can be assumed to have been active. Scans are carried out by research teams in scanners that costs millions to buy and install, and hundreds of thousands per year to maintain. Each participant's stimulus-driven brain response, though, forms only a very small part of the analytical puzzle. Because the elevated signal from oxygenated blood is so small, minuscule sources of error—a brief distraction, even the tiniest head movement from a blink or intake of breath—can drown it out. A single participant's scan therefore requires hundreds of observations, generating the average response for that individual. Each participant's brain is different too, so each participant's averaged brain map is itself averaged into the entire study sample. The compelling figures that reveal brightly coloured blobs on greyscale brains show activations in configurations that likely haven't been observed once in any single person, but emerge from the statistical milieu.

The personal experience of having worked on and published studies using neuroimaging provides a good basis to explore the assumptions that neuroimagers make when we present and explain the results of brain imaging studies. The first concerns *causality*. When we show participants our experimental stimuli, we hope to elicit a brain response that is specific to those stimuli. We attempt to isolate this response by also presenting control stimuli, and looking only for brain responses that differ when we compare experimental stimuli to these. Even when we do this, and go on to identify a specific response, we have only ever examined one direction of causality. Stimulus (e.g. psychological state) → Response (e.g. brain activation). Assuming that this causality also works in reverse, i.e. observing a brain response and assuming a psychological state must be present, is known as making a *reverse inference*, and falls under the logical fallacy of *affirming the consequent* (Poldrack, 2011). A straightforward example of this error of reasoning comes when we consider the following statements:

(A) When I think about my dog, I smile;

(B) I am smiling, so I must be thinking about my dog.

We know that any number of things can make us smile, so even though (A) is true, that does not mean that (B) is. Just because we reliably observe a reaction in response to a thought, that does not mean that the reaction is exclusive to that thought. In the same vein, just because we observe localised brain activations in the amygdala during studies of anxiety, that does not mean that whenever we see elevated amygdala activation, we are anxious.

It could be that we are particularly prone to reverse inference because of another assumption we tend to make about the brain, 'modularity'. We tend to think of it being made up of modular units that switch on and off. Just like the labelled bumps on a phrenologist's bust, we intuitively understand the brain as divided into regions that deal exclusively with specific functions, activating to carry out the function, and deactivating when they are done. The illustrations that accompany fMRI papers, and indeed the way in which brain activity is communicated, actively promote this way of thinking. The brightly coloured blobs give the impression of brain regions as lightbulbs, stripping away the skull so you can see the flickering brain beneath. This impression is totally inconsistent with what we know about the minute changes in blood-flow and the statistical averaging needed to detect any difference at all. In reality, what we are doing when we show activated brain regions is using a process known as statistical thresholding to highlight reliable changes in image intensity as low as 0.1%. Looking at arbitrary units of image intensity that might underpin a brightly-coloured blob—56.25 off-task, and 56.30 on-task—gives a very different impression of what is happening than we might otherwise get from the visualisation. Simply put, this is because brain regions *do not* turn on and off. Individual neurons do, but each tiny cube of brain activation measured using fMRI contains approximately one million neurons (Huettel et al., 2009). Based on the summed activations of all the neurons contained within a brain region, all brain regions are always on. Yet, the visual shorthand we use, and the misleading metaphor this evokes, is powerful.

What this means is that when we see a brain activation in response to a thought, we are lured into thinking that the discrete activation in the brain region in question is necessary for this thought to take place.

Another problem with the assumption of brain modularity is one we ought to recognise from the fall of phrenology—findings from functional neuroimaging don't always point to the same function-region correspondences as the findings from other methods of investigation. Take remembering as an example. fMRI studies consistently find that parietal and frontal cortices become active during memory tasks (Wagner et al., 2005). Neuropsychological studies (studies that investigate altered cognitive performance in people with known brain injuries) find that patients with damaged or missing parietal and frontal cortices do indeed have a number of impairments (e.g. hemispatial neglect, famously presented by Oliver Sacks, 1985), but these don't include obvious memory dysfunction. In fact, the only brain region whose removal decimates memory, the hippocampus, is tucked away in the folds of the temporal cortex, and is difficult to observe fMRI activations in at all.[1] All this points to a messy understanding of the brain and how it supports memory. This isn't to say that fMRI-evident memory regions aren't involved in some aspect of memory function, but that what we assume to be a neat metaphor of regions being computer parts is not so neat after all.

TECHNOLOGY, INDUSTRY AND POWER

The issues outlined above are problematic because they tap into a faulty but dominant discourse on brain function. *All* imaging studies that use statistical thresholding to illustrate activations, or describe brain regions simply as active or inactive, rely on, and perpetuate, a modular understanding of brain organisation. There are different ways of thinking about brain function, and we will look at one of these later in this chapter. First though, we will deal with some of the other problems with the work described in the *New York Times* op-ed—problems that evoke and extend the issues we have already discussed when critiquing phrenology.

In this example, our discussions of technology, industry and power all point to the influence of money. Here, we step through each one in turn, to build an

---

[1]To complicate things further, the hippocampus *is* one of the few brain regions that magnetic resonance imaging has shown us to have modularity in the way in which we typically think of it—London taxi drivers, who specialise in navigational memory use, show increases in the size of the hippocampus corresponding to their experience (Maguire et al., 2000).

understanding of how these seemingly independent components of neuroimaging compound, to generate a seemingly inevitable pseudoscientific spiral.

Technology

Whether in the form of equipment or ideas, technology represents a practical advancement for humanity. The typical neuroimaging participant—a person lying serenely in a snug tube, whilst around them, a humming machine monitors their internal state—is a staple of space exploration stories. It is hard not to be in thrall to this vision, especially when it looks so much like the science-fiction utopia we have been asked to imagine for hundreds of years.

Of course, those who know how this technology is implemented in HAL, the computerised intelligence from *2001: A Space Odyssey* (Kubrick, 1968), understand that this can also be the stuff of dystopia. Regardless, *we* aren't the arbiters of how these technologies get used. Just as we could not individually afford to fund a private flight to space, or build a social media network with billions of users, none of us can afford to install a multi-million pound MRI machine, fill it with super-cooled helium and use it to tell us what we *really* want for dinner. We have these technologies proffered onto us, either as aspirational spectacles to showcase wealth and advancement, or as low-cost or free services offered by billion dollar corporations.

We are still far from walk-in MRI centres being used in psychotherapy or conflict mediation, but should this be pitched, the cost could be overcome. On a large scale, eye-wateringly expensive technology is paid for by the prospect of what can be done with our data. This is a business model that excites investors, as is evident in the trading prices of tech companies that offer free services such as social media, internet search, cloud storage and health tracking. The prohibitive cost of cutting-edge technology then, becomes a rallying call to investment. It takes the hardware out of consumers' hands, and places it and the user data it generates into the hands of the corporations providing the service.

Industry

For any researcher, whether in academia or industry, the goal of developing a technology is to use that development to further their organisation's goals. In academia, the organisational goal is to consolidate the university's reputation as a seat of learning at the forefront of research. To this end, the path that universities encourage their researchers to take, one that has its origins in the power that learned societies had in shaping academic discourse (see Chapter 9), is to publish in peer-reviewed journals (Moxham & Fyfe, 2018). The key aspect of this process is the involvement of other academic experts as a form of quality assurance—an iterative, lengthy process that aims to ensure that the work satisfies a collective standard of scientific rigour. In industry, the organisational goal is to use the technology to gain a competitive advantage in developing or selling a product or service (Stephan, 1996). Instead of publishing findings for the scientific community, a corporation typically protects its intellectual property with patents, and gets it to market as efficiently as possible. If the technology offers the organisation an obvious competitive advantage, it also makes sense to promote this to potential clients and investors (Wood et al., 2021). Importantly though, without the expectation of peer-reviewed publication, there is no need for transparency in how the technology works, or the scrutiny of the broader scientific community.

Bringing this back to the op-ed, the commercial researchers were part of a now-defunct organisation called FKF Applied Research, a neuromarketing firm whose website claimed to 'provide Fortune 500 marketers with previously unattainable understanding of consumer choice and decision making' (FKF Applied Research, 2007). The *New York Times* article appears to have been part of a drive to drum up interest in the capability that this technology offers them—an effort that included conversations with venture capitalists (Hammer, 2007). Importantly, although much of the op-ed read like the summary of a peer-reviewed paper, no such source material exists. This is it. If it had been peer-reviewed, the findings presented would likely have been toned down so much that it would not have been reported in the *New York Times*. The op-ed served its purpose—to increase awareness of the organisation, to raise investment and to sell their services.

That's not to say that the academic approach is good, and the industrial approach is bad. They each serve their own purpose, and when those purposes align, can work very well together. For example, in the past few years, medical research organisations have mobilised in historic ways, both as solely industrial bodies and academic-industrial partnerships, to develop and deploy COVID vaccines (Kalinke et al., 2022). There is no *right* model for the development of technology. What we ought to be wary about, though, is a way of doing things that pretends to be one thing when it is another. Just as we might view a phrenologist starting a journal to sell more busts as a charlatan, we should also be cautious of neuromarketers presenting dubious observations as peer-reviewed science in order to attract investments from those eager to capitalise on the next big opportunity.

Power

Power, particularly modern political power, is inextricably linked with technology and science (Morgenthau, 1964). In the examples that have formed focus points within the book so far, we have seen the statistics develop hand-in-hand with the political lobby for eugenics, and phrenology justify the dominant practices of colonialism and slavery. It goes without saying, then, that the proposed technological breakthrough in polling offered by the *New York Times* op-ed garnered political interest.

Of course, the subject of the op-ed's research was political. But the political connections ran deeper, to the origins of FKF Research itself. Two of the organisation's founders, Tom Freedman and Bill Knapp, were political strategists who worked on Bill Clinton's successful presidential campaigns. Indeed, they are fixtures in the political establishment—following the op-ed's publication they continued their political strategy work under more recent Democratic candidates and presidents. Going back to their backgrounds working with Bill Clinton, though, it should now come as even less of a surprise that the op-ed focused so extensively on the candidate they knew best, Hillary Clinton. And given *all* of this, it should be absolutely obvious why FKF's methods were presented as a technology that would give political strategists the edge in understanding how candidates were being received by the populace. Power does not emerge from a vacuum, and nor it seems does an article in the *New York Times* touting a dodgy technological breakthrough in polling.

Once again, it is important to state that none of these links *needs* to be a problem. The combination of technology, industry and power is integral to modern life and has been responsible for huge advances in how long and how well we live. But problems arise in any situation that leverages misinformation: either through misrepresenting a science's capabilities and obfuscating its limitations, or through misrepresenting the work as academic, and obfuscating its industrial and political backing. fMRI itself is not the villain of the piece. What is problematic is how we fMRI researchers have bootstrapped onto a widely held, simple, but flawed, phrenological understanding of modular brain function, whilst simultaneously avoiding discussion of the many, often complex, assumptions that are necessary to fit complex brain responses to simple cognitive events. Whilst phrenologists got a lot wrong, their core assumption, that the root of cognition is in the brain, is the basis for modern cognitive neuroscience. fMRI researchers get a great deal right too, undoubtedly far more than their phrenological counterparts. But we have a responsibility to communicate openly about what neuroimaging can and cannot do. This is even more important to do if we are to close the door on those who would otherwise use it to line their pockets or further their political ambitions.

AN ALTERNATIVE APPROACH TO LOCALISED BRAIN FUNCTION

In this book, we propose alternatives to the dominant, canonical approach for the reader to consider. They are not presented as replacements or as without fault themselves, but to provide a window into other ways of understanding the topic in question. The alternative approach we focus on here is of cognition as emerging from immeasurable complexity. Whilst this idea forms a part of mainstream neuroimaging in a number of guises, e.g. dynamic functional connectivity (Menon & Krishnamurthy, 2019), and is implied in others, e.g. electroencephalogram (EEG) spectral analysis (Glomb et al., 2020), in the form in which we describe it below, there is no plausible technique for its measurement or analysis. We present it simply as a thought-provoking alternative to the intuitive understandings of brain function outlined so far.

Even when considering the brain as comprising a mere 40 phrenological organs, Roget, the contributor to the 1824 *Encyclopaedia Britannica* article on phrenology, understood that it would be strange to consider each organ as only being capable of acting independently.

> If the brain be a single instrument it cannot be at once both weak and strong; it cannot exhibit one faculty in its perfection and another in a very limited extent. But all difficulty vanishes if we admit it to be an assemblage of many organs; for the combination of these organs may be as infinitely diversified as the actions and powers of man. (p. 425)

As soon as we consider that brain units interact, we introduce both spatial and temporal complexity to brain function. Which brain regions signal to which others? In what order do these interactions take place? Even by considering these questions within a basic, phrenological framework, we can see the limitations of static representations of brain function. A single module for a single cognition requires that the brain scientist localise to one of 40 brain regions. When you introduce the possibility that two regions interact, this becomes 1560 possible combinations (3120 considering order), and with three regions, this jumps to 59,280 combinations (177,840 considering order). The problem quickly becomes intractable, and that is entirely the point. The impossibility of conceptualising the *infinitely diversified* combinations of billions of neurons requires us to think about brain function in a radically different, and exciting, way.

Within this infinitely complex system, there must be a starting point from which insight can be gained. Here, we draw on a method that has long existed in psychology: the comparative approach, with which we aim to understand the human complexity by examining a simpler organism. In this case though, the simpler organism is an abstract one—a thought experiment aimed at understanding what the simplest artificial life-form might be.

John von Neumann (1903–1957) was a Hungarian-American mathematician and physicist known for his work in a range of disciplines including game theory and digital computing. Shortly after working on the Manhattan Project during

World War II (in which he coined the term 'kiloton' as a unit of nuclear explosive measurement; Brown & Borovina, 2021) von Neumann turned his hand to creating artificial life, specifically a rule-governed collection of cells that could reproduce itself. He imagined a two-dimensional graph paper-like grid, in which each cell behaves according to the state of each of the four cells it borders (Bhattacharya, 2022). His *cellular automaton,* laid out in a posthumously published book (von Neumann & Burks, 1966), was capable of reproducing itself, but required each of its 200,000 cells to have the possibility of being in 29 different states. It was so computationally intensive that it was not until 1994 that a computer powerful enough to simulate it was developed (see Figure 5.1).

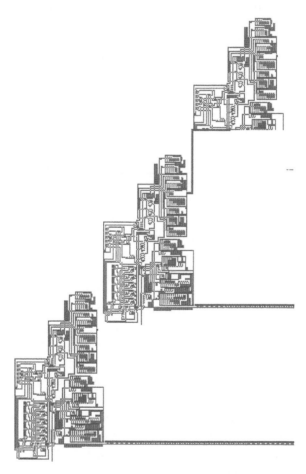

Figure 5.1 Three generations of von Neumann's self-replicating cellular automaton. The automaton in the bottom left created the middle automaton, which is in the process of creating the incomplete automaton at the top. Automata simulated using Golly software (Golly – SourceForge, 2021).

A huge problem with von Neumann's automaton was how large and complex it needed to be to work. Whilst it could replicate itself, it was not something that could have emerged from a simpler automaton. It required von Neumann as its highly intelligent designer. Nonetheless, this work kickstarted an interest in simple, artificial life amongst mathematicians.

John Horton Conway (1937–2020), an English mathematician, shifted the focus from the specifics of designing automata to designing their environments (Bhattacharya, 2022). In 1970, he used von Neumann's two-dimensional environment but simplified it so that its cells could hold only two states: alive or dead (Gardner, 1970). Within Conway's 'Game of Life', each cell was influenced by the state of all eight contiguous cells (including corner cells) according to the following rules:

1   live cells stay alive if they are contiguous to 2 or 3 live cells;
2   dead cells come to life only if they are contiguous to 3 live cells;
3   all other live cells die.

In *this* environment, no designer was needed for an immense variety of lifeforms to take shape and persist over time. When seeded by noise (each cell assigned as alive or dead at random), cell configurations that reproduce, move, interact and eject missiles materialised. It was also possible to design complex lifeforms that mimic von Neumann's huge automaton (dvgrn, 2013). With the right environmental conditions, sustained complexity simply emerges.

But how does this relate to our understanding of brain function? The answer lies in how Conway demonstrated that complexity can, under the right conditions, emerge without a plan. Switching our frame of reference to the brain, the granularity and simplicity of the 'Game of Life' is such that each neuron can be represented as being in two states: firing or not firing. With the right hard-wired connections in the form of the brain's white matter, and constant perturbations being input to the system from the senses, it is plausible that clusters of neurons order themselves to behave in concert as brain regions. In fact, this idea isn't new at all. In the 1950s, an American psychologist named Frank Rosenblatt developed a model for artificial intelligence, the 'Perceptron', that conceptualised decision-making as the product of many neurons, coded as either firing or not firing. Decision-making was adjusted on the basis of reinforcement by changing the weights assigned to each neuron (with each weight representing the statistical importance of its corresponding neuron to the decision being made; Rosenblatt, 1958). Within this framework, neural activity is plastic—afforded the capacity for change—not only as it emerges from a small number of undifferentiated cells, but also in response to experiences throughout all stages of development and ageing.

A critical difference between the phrenological, modular approach and this idea of *emergent complexity* is the difference in how information and information processors are considered. Modular approaches consider brain structure to be static, and the information the brain processes to be temporary and ephemeral—a set of silicon processors through which electricity flows. But this analogy is inconsistent with the extent to which we understand experience shapes not just *what* we think about, but *how* we think about it (e.g. Green & Bavelier, 2008). Processors are changed by what they process, with layers of meaning built upon each other, and connections that change according to their relevance over time. It is also inconsistent with the extent to which we know that much cognitive function can recover, even after severe brain injury (Robertson & Murre, 1999). Specialised processes can get re-instantiated, even when the cellular hardware in which those processes were thought to be situated no longer exists. This is all possible as emergent complexity, where information and information processors are one and the same: tens of billions of interlinked neurons sparking chain reactions that reverberate through an infinitely diversified system (Epstein, 2016).

Focus Box 5.1

Technological Solutions and Technological Problems

Were we able to collect detailed, reliable physiological data targeted at understanding emergent complexity, a traditional statistical approach would be ill-suited to their analysis. In such circumstances, a more data-driven approach could be considered. These approaches to big data have been enabled by the explosion of modern-day computational power, and are now widely used across a range of fields (O'Neil, 2016). Data classification algorithms are systems that will *learn* how to classify complex data based on training datasets for which this has already been done. For example, if we wanted to train an algorithm to identify Attention Deficit Hyperactivity Disorder (ADHD) from brain scans, we could image people with and without ADHD diagnoses, and ask the algorithm to determine what differentiates these two sets of scans. We could then use the fully trained algorithm to make future diagnoses without a lengthy and costly clinical assessment. Whilst this algorithmic solution is appealing, it comes with its own problems that, if we are not careful, reproduce many of the problems already outlined in this chapter.

A major problem with algorithms is their opacity. Algorithmic tools are often difficult to intuitively understand, and as such, we entrust their development and operation to mathematicians and computer engineers. These developers do not always have experience of or training in human-facing work, resulting in decisions that pay little regard to ethical consequences of algorithm use (Gelfand, 2016; though this is certainly not to say that ethics training ensures that all psychologists act ethically). In tension with other priorities, for example commercial or national intelligence priorities, these algorithms can be used to justify unethical decision-making, or incentivise antisocial behaviour, in ways that only become clear when they are spelled out by those who develop them (as detailed by Frances Haugen in the *Wall Street Journal*'s Facebook Files, Horwitz, 2021).

The lack of insight into and control over how the algorithms enact themselves is another function of their opacity. The example given above, of using neuroimaging scans to classify people with and without ADHD, is a real one that formed the basis of a 2011 scientific competition, The ADHD-200 Sample (ADHD-200, 2011). Whilst the aim was to use imaging data to most correctly identify those with ADHD (and not misidentify those without it), the team that scored the highest in the competition actually used no imaging data at all (Yarkoni, 2011). The University of Alberta team used demographic data alone and outperformed their competitors despite the seeming richness of the imaging data available to them. They were, of course, fully aware of this, and were transparent in stating this to the competition organisers (Sidhu et al., 2012), but it is not hard to envision a situation in which a neuromarketing firm would be less honest, hiding behind the investor-friendly smoke and mirrors of algorithms and neuroimaging (especially if the data were entered into the algorithm but ultimately proved useless). As we know from phrenology, the appeal of cutting-edge technology does not always align with its utility. We should be mindful of this, even when technologies are otherwise well regarded and scientifically validated.

The final issue for consideration here is the pernicious bias introduced by training an algorithm using human judgement. Again, this is not so much a problem with the technology, as a problem introduced by the difference between what we *think* a technology is doing, and what it *actually* does. For most of us, when we think of machine learning, we assume that a computer is employing a digital rationality to make objectively accurate classifications–seeing through the fog of human error to find the ground truth. What it is actually doing is examining how *we* have previously made classifications in the training dataset, and finding ways of reliably reproducing these classifications. If we trained an algorithm to make classifications using data from a human expert with 80% accuracy, the algorithm would likely reproduce an accuracy around 80%. If we trained it using data from an amateur with 60% accuracy, this lower value would likely be reproduced in the algorithm's results. The problem gets more complicated if we think about classifications for which a ground truth does not exist (e.g. culturally variable mental health conditions), and it gets downright sinister if we know that this is how algorithms work, yet we present them as ways of eliminating racism and sexism when they are in fact perpetuating it (as happened when St George's Hospital introduced a computerised admissions

(Continued)

process for medical student applications; Commission for Racial Equality, 1988). By portraying algorithms as the saviours of decision-making, we run the very real risk of both hiding and legitimising the very bias we are trying to eliminate.

How then to do we mitigate these problems? Cathy O'Neil's brilliant book *Weapons of Math Destruction* (2016) suggests a number of solutions which, if embedded into the development cycle, would help: amongst them, engaging in cross-disciplinary work and providing opportunities for negative reinforcement of technologically aided decision-making. Genuine, good-faith, cross-disciplinary, cross-sector work, carried out across disciplines with a range of ethics and priorities, would minimise the potential for many of the problems outlined above. Under a truly collaborative framework, the engineering, ethical and financial choices that have been made in development would become more transparent and accountable, allowing a greater variety of stake-holders to input their priorities into what the technology is aiming to achieve. In the case of technologies like decision-making algorithms, that have the potential to have positive and negative social impacts, negative reinforcement would see technologies evaluated not just against decisions that have been made before (either by humans, or more insidiously, by the technologies themselves), but against the pattern of decisions we wish to see in future. Under such a system, a technology yielding outcomes that exacerbate existing social biases would be revealed as doing so, and re-tuned with this in mind. If computational power can perpetuate inequity on a terrifying scale, then it can also do the same to promote equity.

WHAT NEXT?

In this chapter we have explored the limitations and consequences of the dominant, canonical approach to understanding brain function. We have seen that technology can burnish psychological narratives in ways that mask bad science, and that our desire to reduce brain function to a series of digital modules often obscures the complexity and beauty of brain function. Even as we attempt to better understand this complexity, we will inevitably recruit even more powerful, even more complex technologies to help us, and we must be wary of being in thrall to these tools to the extent that we lose sight of the assumptions they make and once again risk accepting bad science. With the advent of large language models (LLMs) like ChatGPT, the potential utility of algorithmic approaches to understanding brain function has expanded further, giving us new ways of analysing complex data, simulating brain processes and generating hypotheses. However, the growing opacity of LLMs—they are trained on such enormous amounts of data that it is unlikely the organisations releasing them can be aware of the contents of the corpus on which they have been trained (Heikkilä, 2023)—also has the potential to further entrench the biases mentioned in Focus Box 5.1. We must be careful not to assume that each new tool wipes the slate clean of known technological problems, and instead understand that these issues pervade, and should themselves be considered part of psychology's technological canon.

FURTHER READING

Epstein, R. (2016). The empty brain. *Aeon*. https://aeon.co/essays/your-brain-does-not-process-information-and-it-is-not-a-computer [magazine article]

A call to abandon the information processing metaphor of brain function.

Gardner, M. (1970). The fantastic combinations of John Conway's new solitaire game 'life'. *Scientific American*, 223(4), 120–123. http://www.jstor.org/stable/24927642 [magazine article] and
Martin's (n.d.) online implementation of Conway's 'Game of Life' at https://playgameoflife.com/ [web game]

Introduction of Conway's 'Game of Life' and an online version of the game.

O'Neil, C. (2016). *Weapons of math destruction: How big data increases inequality and threatens democracy*. Crown Books. [book]

Exposé of the dark side of big data, exploring how biased algorithms and opaque mathematical models perpetuate inequality.

6

HYSTERIA, HAPPY PILLS AND HORMONES

PSYCHOLOGY'S WOMAN PROBLEM

The Western cis straight white male worldview masquerades as the invisible background that is taken as the 'normal,' 'standard,' or 'universal' position ... those outside it are racialised, gendered, and defined according to their proximity and relation to colonial whiteness ... people who are coded as anything other than white have limited to no access to the field, as reflected in the demographics from undergraduate courses to professorships ... This is especially apparent when we consider that many positions of social and political power reflect the broader demographics of the societies in which scientific institutions are embedded, while these same scientific institutions lag behind in terms of representation. (Lugones, 2016, p. 62)

'Why do [women] not feel well? And what can we do about it?' The problem is as much patriarchy and corporate greed as viruses ... In medicine as in politics, the abuse of power leads to the loss of authority. The medical industry, from doctors to hospitals to pharmaceutical industries to insurance companies, has long gotten fat from denigrating, ignoring, and prolonging the suffering of vulnerable patients in its care. If people are so worried about women taking mystery pills and chugging bone broth to rid themselves of mysterious pains, they could better spend their time fighting to socialise the whole system. Only then, with the female body given the same monetary and medical concern as the generic body, can we all finally be well. (Crispin, 2018, p. 49)

From the (mal)treatment of female hysteria to the persistent use of gendered language in scientific writing, psychology has played a substantial role in legitimising the stigmatisation of women and suppressing their participation in civic life. In this chapter we identify some of the central figures and beliefs that have contributed to psychology's troubled treatment of gender.

This chapter is divided into three sections. In **Women as Research** we addresses how colonial conceptualisations of gender have influenced psychological research about women. A key theme of this chapter is the way in which gender essentialism—the belief that differences in female and male psychology are natural and fixed—has systematically erased or minimised women's contributions to the canon. We present the history of hysteria as a case study to illustrate this point. We follow this with a discussion about how essentialist beliefs impact the way psychologists operationalise and measure gender. In **Women as Researchers** we trace the history of female scholars in the discipline, and we document the ways in which gender disparities continue to manifest in higher education. Finally, in **Breaking Down the Gender Binary** we explore alternative models of scholarship that move away from the colonial and patriarchal roots of psychological science.

WOMEN AS RESEARCH

Gender essentialism lies at the centre of psychology's troubled treatment of women. In this section we explore the interplay between gender essentialist beliefs and research practice. Gender essentialist views have had far-reaching consequences for how women are portrayed and studied. Throughout the history of the discipline, women have often been reduced to simplistic stereotypes. Research practices in psychology have at times perpetuated these harmful beliefs, resulting in biased investigations and a limited understanding of gender and sex as properties that are static and invariant. As we will see here, a critical examination of these foundational assumptions paves the way to a more dynamic and equitable understanding of human behaviour.

Gender Essentialism

Gender essentialism maintains that inherent temperamental traits and intellectual abilities differentiate women from men. These traits are natural, fixed and invariant qualities; strong versions of gender essentialism claim that gender differences are biologically determined. Many proponents of gender essentialism argue that gender is binary and assign gender identity (the social and cultural categories of 'woman' and 'man') on the basis of biological sex ('female' and 'male,' defined here with reference to genital, gonadal and genetic attributes; Morgenroth & Ryan, 2020; Rippon et al., 2014).[1]

Biological differences between men and women—particularly in musculature, height and weight—are often used to naturalise differential social treatment of individuals based on perceived sex. These subjective interpretations of biological fact have been used to legitimise the view of women as inferior, weaker than men in mind and body. In modern Western history, the larger physical size associated with masculinity has been associated with physically active gender roles, such as hunting and farming. In contrast, the female capacity to bear children has been associated with domestic gender roles. From here we can see how psychological traits and abilities also become essentialised. Men must be more aggressive, competitive, risk-taking and sexually promiscuous. Women are innately nurturing and therefore must be natural caregivers and homemakers (Roberts, 1993).

Appealing to biological differences provides a seemingly objective way to categorise and discriminate between individuals. Over historical time, certain facts of biology—such as menstruation, pregnancy and menopause—have been used to construct an understanding of women as physically and psychologically unstable and therefore inherently inferior to men (Boyd et al., 2020; Stone & Sanders, 2021). On this basis, women have often been denied opportunities for self-determinism. In Victorian culture, for example, the ideological rewards of motherhood were considered the appropriate compensation for household labour rather than monetary pay and economic freedom (Hedges, 1973; Roberts, 1993).

A particularly potent example of gender essentialism—and one that has a long history in Western psychology—is evident in the diagnosis and treatment of hysteria. In what follows we provide a brief overview of the history of hysteria to better contextualise how the behaviour was understood at various points in the development of our discipline. We can see from this story the ways in which psychology adopted, reinforced and promoted gender essentialist views that disadvantaged women.

---

[1]Throughout most of this chapter we frame our analysis through the lens of gender to underscore the fact that binary identities are culturally constructed. However, in some places we refer to gender/sex as a composite term to reflect the understanding that both can be conceptualised as a binary.

A Case Study in Gender Essentialism: Hysteria

Colloquially, hysteria is a catch-all term to describe emotional excess, but at various points in Western history it has also been a physical and psychiatric diagnosis characterised by paralysis, fainting, amnesia, seizure, anxiety, insomnia, sensory impairments, shortness of breath and pain. Although it is no longer a formal diagnosis in most of the world, hysteria is considered the first mental disorder attributed to women (Tasca et al., 2012). As we show here, the diagnosis and treatment of hysteria was justified using gender essentialist beliefs, many of which were developed and endorsed by prominent psychologists and neurologists.

Western historical explanations for hysteria start from the assumption that women are more emotionally fragile and labile than men and therefore less rational and objective. This perceived emotional volatility has long been linked to women's reproductive capabilities. Hippocrates suggested that women are constitutionally 'cold and wet', which in turn made them 'prone to putrefaction of the humors' that could lead to uterine infections, chills, disorientation and convulsions (Tasca et al., 2012, p. 111). Plato described the womb as an autonomous animal living independently within the female body. Physical illness, emotional disturbance and psychic instability arose when the uterus roamed too far from the genitalia. Curiously, the uterus only seemed to migrate when women neglected their biological imperative to bear and raise children (Cleghorn, 2021). In a nod to this belief, the root of the word 'hysteria' stems from the Greek *hyster* (for womb), inextricably linking female biology to notions of mental illness (Morris, 1991).

Advances in anatomical knowledge during the 1800s suggested that hysteria resulted from injuries to the nervous system, at least in men (Malane, 2005; Morris, 1991). Women, however, did not usually present with an observable, acute physical cause that could be clearly identified as the source of their hysteria. The lack of a clear physiological origin suggested to doctors that women were either malingering and faking their symptoms, or else that the cause was psychic. As a result, some theorists started characterising hysteria as a female personality disorder, the outward expression of distress caused by the need to repress unnatural thoughts or desires (Chodoff, 1974). French neurologist Jean Martin Charcot (1825–1893) suggested that hereditary degeneration of the nervous system predisposed individuals to hysteria. An acute psychological trauma could exacerbate this degeneration, and the subconscious suppression of such trauma might therefore result in hysterical outbursts. Charcot speculated that hypnotism might cure hysteria by allowing patients a chance to vocalise these subconscious thoughts. For Charcot, hysteria could befall people of any gender, but he tended to focus on women when discussing the disorder. He demonstrated his hypnosis treatment almost exclusively on hysterical female patients during live lectures. One of the men who attended these lectures left convinced—Sigmund Freud departed

Charcot's lecture auditorium with the conviction that subconscious drives played a key role in female hysteria (Cleghorn, 2021).

Like Charcot, Freud attributed hysteria to the repression of traumatic memories, particularly those that were libidinous in nature (Micale, 1989). But because he presumed the cause of hysteria was psychological, not neurological, Freud advocated for psychotherapeutic treatment. It was through the process of psychoanalysis that hysterical women might recognise and unpack the psychosexual nature of their trauma. Freud's philosophy of the mind was distinctly patriarchal and reinforced numerous gender essentialist positions. In an explicit reference to colonial conquest and exploitation, Freud described women's sexuality as a 'dark continent', something primitive and enigmatic that must be dominated and tamed to be properly understood (Khanna, 2003; Swartz, 2022). The psychotherapeutic relationship between patient and clinician also carried distinctly gendered overtones. In exploring her traumatic memories, a hysterical patient would subordinate her own self-knowledge to the authority of the (typically male) clinician whose expertise would illuminate the source of any suppressed psychic conflict (Linstrum, 2016).

Whether psychological or neurological in origin, one commonality across the various conceptualisations described here is that they all framed hysteria as a disease caused by the perversion or disruption of natural impulses. In Victorian Britain, a diagnosis of hysteria was a convenient way to stigmatise and pathologise the behaviour of women who did not conform to gender norms. This included sexually promiscuous women as well as women who opted not to bear children in favour of pursuing careers or education. Gender essentialism provided both a rationale and a method for controlling women's behaviour. Women who abandoned their traditional and naturally defined domestic roles were abnormal and required treatment. These medical interventions were often invasive, dangerous and debasing. For example, hysterical women often suffered forced ovariectomies and clitorectomies at the recommendation of neurologists who believed this would suppress sexual appetites and nervous fits (Morris, 1991). Another barbaric practice known as the 'rest cure' forcibly restrained the hysterical woman to her bed where she was kept in complete isolation for weeks or months. To encourage lethargy, compliance and total emptiness of mind, women subjected to the rest cure were force-fed a high-fat diet at all hours of the day and prohibited from any form of mental or physical stimulation (Cleghorn, 2021; Morris, 1991). Author Charlotte Perkins Gilman fictionalised her experiences of the rest cure and published them as a short story entitled 'The Yellow Wallpaper' (Stetson, 1892). In the story, Gilman suggests that hysteria is not a legitimate medical disorder, but rather a rational response to oppressive societal expectations that thwart women's personal ambitions (Hedges, 1973). In later writings, Gilman argued that economic freedom outside marriage was the only cure for hysteria. She called for the development of childcare centres and community kitchens to enable career-oriented women to pursue alternative employment. These centres would relieve such women of their caregiving responsibilities while valuing and compensating the time of women who chose to remain in domestic labour (Hedges, 1973).

Practices like the rest cure were common, not because they were efficacious, but because they were consistent with prevailing theories that essentialised women as physiologically and psychologically erratic. One popular eugenic theory of the time was that during development, the nervous system and reproductive system compete for the same nutrients. Education threatened the health of middle- and upper-class women by placing too much strain on their reproductive systems, leading to painful periods and potential infertility. The ultimate consequence to society was disastrous: low birth rates amongst the class of people most vital to the nation's economic and political success (Albee, 1996). One of the first female physicians in the USA, Mary Putnam Jacobi, countered this narrative by collecting anonymous data about menstruation from hundreds of patients of varying backgrounds (Cleghorn, 2021). With this data Jacobi demonstrated that education did not adversely impact menstruation and that extreme menstrual pain was the consequence of undiagnosed gynaecological conditions, not learning (Cleghorn, 2021).

Efforts by women in psychology also undermined gender essentialist claims that women were incapable of educational pursuits (Hollingworth, 1914, 1916). To cite one specific example, Helen Woolley (1910) demonstrated that gender differences in brain size did not translate to gender differences in behaviour or ability. She noted that gender essentialist claims seemed motivated by political concerns rather than empirical evidence:

> The cry is no longer that woman will injure herself by the mental and physical over-strain involved in higher intellectual training, but that she will injure society by reducing her own reproductive activity (later marriages, fewer marriages, fewer children, opposition between intellectual and sexual functions), and thus lessen the chances of the best element to perpetuate itself. (Woolley, 1910, p. 342)

Hysteria and its treatment were thus part of a larger ecosystem that sought to suppress women's participation in civic activities that could threaten the established order.

We can see from our case study that the conceptualisation of hysteria changed over time to match societal preoccupations about gender roles and gender relations. Perhaps unsurprisingly then, no single, canonical explanation for hysteria ever crystalised (Micale, 1989). In most Western contexts, after the 1940s hysteria ceased to be a formal diagnosis. Eventually the symptoms associated with hysteria were subsumed into other mental disorders like anxiety and depression (see Focus Box 6.1), and hysterical neurosis was removed from the DSM-III (Tasca et al., 2012). However, in many nations of the Global South, and particularly those in Asia and

Africa that were once British colonies, hysteria remained a popular diagnosis until well into the 1970s. In this context hysteria was arguably a reaction to the forcible adoption of colonial practices and values that alienated women by destroying local customs and conceptions of health (Tasca et al., 2012).

The diagnosis and treatment of hysteria were strongly influenced by gender essentialist perspectives that themselves reflected colonial, patriarchal and capitalist value systems. In some cases, this reductionist approach ignored the true underlying causes of hysterical symptoms, contributing to misdiagnosis and inadequate treatment for women who were genuinely unwell. In other cases, the diagnosis of hysteria functioned to control and subjugate women under the guise of medical care. In the next section we will examine the legacy of gender essentialism in psychological research beyond the treatment of hysteria. Although changing social norms eventually led to the decline of hysterical diagnoses, gender essentialist beliefs are still apparent in many contemporary aspects of psychological research and practice.

Focus Box 6.1

Happy Pills and Hysteria

Anxiety is one the most common symptoms associated with hysteria, and its treatment reveals a great deal about gender essentialism. Early pharmaceutical remedies for anxiety (such as Lydia Pinkham's Vegetable Compound or Wright's Indian Vegetable Pills) were little more than home-brewed elixirs with high alcohol content and often dangerously high levels of toxins like mercury, arsenic and lead (Crispin, 2018). Prior to the 1940s, barbiturates were the only sedatives widely available to treat anxiety, and doctors prescribing them had to balance their clinical benefits against serious risks like long-term dependency, depressed respiration and accidental overdose (López-Muñoz et al., 2005). That changed with the invention of safer, less habit-forming drugs like mephenesin. Frank Berger, a Czechoslovakian scientist working in Yorkshire, England accidentally discovered the tranquilizing properties of mephenesin while trying to synthesise new antibiotics to aid with the war effort. Doctors used the drug as a sedative in surgical wards and a muscle relaxant for patients with multiple sclerosis and Parkinson's disease (Radke, 2018).

In the 1950s, pharmaceutical companies realised the commercial potential of safe anti-anxiety drugs that could be targeted to hysterical women. They started promoting mild tranquilisers as a treatment for anxiety, depression, insomnia, headaches and muscle tension. These medications included meprobamate (a long-lasting oral derivative of mephenesin that sold under the name Miltown) as well as a class of drugs known as benzodiazepines (sold under the names of Librium and Valium; Radke, 2018; Speaker, 1997). Advertisements for the drugs branded them as 'peace pills' and 'emotional

(Continued)

aspirin', claiming that although they might not be able to cure mental illness, they could prevent it (Speaker, 1997, p. 343). Doctors often prescribed these 'happy pills' in conjunction with diet pills (amphetamines) as a cure-all cocktail marketed toward the modern woman (Radke, 2018). By 1955, the American Psychiatric Association estimated that approximately 30% of the American populace had been prescribed anti-anxiety drugs, and their usage was so ubiquitous that the Rolling Stones referenced the pills in their 1966 song 'Mother's Little Helper' (Speaker, 1997).

The medical establishment may have embraced happy pills, but public reactions grew increasingly sceptical. A 1979 US Senate hearing concluded that the country had become a 'nation of pill-poppers and potion-pushers', and that the total erasure of anxiety from daily life might erode personal responsibility, economic drive and motivation (Speaker, 1997, p. 340). Gendered pharmaceutical advertisements drew condemnation for their harmful, stereotyped depictions of women as neurotic, hapless victims of emotional instability (Radke, 2018). Other critics, including feminist activists, raised concerns about the public health implications of widespread tranquiliser use. They noted the hypocrisy in policy-makers' tolerance of prescription drug abuse amongst the middle class compared to their punitive approach towards harder drugs and alcohol in the working class. They also highlighted problematic behaviour on the part of pharmaceutical companies. Librium, for example, had been safety tested on inmates in a Texas prison. (Advocates for Librium saw this as a selling point rather than an ethical lapse; prison testing proved the drug's efficacy because the incarcerated men reported feeling placid despite their stressful surroundings; Speaker, 1997.) Feminists claimed that the popularity of anti-anxiety pills was a form of social control (Zola, 1972). They argued that general practitioners were ill-equipped to treat mental health problems; as a result, they prescribed psychiatric medication indiscriminately, without any consideration for the contextual factors underlying poor mental health in their patients (Speaker, 1997). Individualising stressful or traumatic experiences and treating them solely with medication ignored the possibility that anxiety might be a social disorder requiring social support as a cure (Zola, 1972).

In many ways the rise and fall of happy pills reflects a market response to a psychological problem. The pills arguably declined in popularity over time not because of advances in psychiatric care, but because they garnered bad press (Radke, 2018). And at least in the United States, prescriptions for happy pills became too cumbersome to manage in a healthcare system dominated by the endless bureaucracy of insurance companies (Speaker, 1997). Meanwhile, the underlying problems that drove women to seek pharmaceutical care have largely remained unaddressed. Gender disparities in the treatment of anxiety remain a feature of contemporary psychological and psychiatric practice. Women seeking medical care for physical symptoms (particularly pain) are more likely than men to have their experiences dismissed as psychiatric problems, leading to increased risk of misdiagnosis and medical complications (Ballweg et al., 2010). Perhaps as a consequence, women are more likely to report abusing prescription psychiatric medications to alleviate psychological distress, whereas male patients report higher rates of illicit drug abuse (Jamison et al., 2010). In brief, the story of happy pills is a cautionary one. The medicalisation and marketisation of psychological problems often overlooks the structural issues that underlie poor health. It kicks the can of mental health down the road until the next wonder drug comes along.

Operationalising and Measuring Gender

As our historical analysis of hysteria demonstrates, there is a longstanding tradition in Western psychology of treating women's experiences as aberrant. In contrast, male perspectives have often been normalised and used to define what 'typical' or 'average' behaviour should look like. In this section we explore how this bias influences research design and methodology.

Mainstream psychological science often treats gender as a 'nuisance variable', a demographic factor that introduces undesirable variability into data (Chrisler & McHugh, 2011, p. 39). There are two primary methods for addressing the variability associated with gender. The first is to omit gender from the study design or to exclude any mention of gender in an experimental write-up. Indeed, the gender or sex composition of research samples in psychological and neuroscientific studies often goes uncommented (Mamlouk et al., 2020). The assumption underlying this approach is that if gender is not relevant to the research question, then it need not factor into sampling decisions or analyses. An alternative approach is to focus sampling efforts on just one gender, the rationale being that it is useful to establish a phenomenon in one group before extending it to others. As a result, major findings, methods and tools in psychological science have been based on participant samples that are disproportionately male (see Focus Box 6.2 for examples of how biased sampling has impacted neuroimaging). As a result, we often have an incomplete picture of how gender does or does not impact on key aspects of psychological functioning. We can think of this as a problem about representativeness—biased samples make it difficult to generalise a finding to a broader population. But there is a larger point to make here about power relationships. One method by which individuals are indoctrinated into endorsing patriarchal systems is by suppressing knowledge about gender diversity (Hollingworth, 1916). Our understanding of biological and psychological functioning historically centres around men and male experiences, which then become normalised and considered 'default'. As we will see here, this narrow focus results from a complex interplay of pragmatic considerations, theoretical assumptions, socio-cultural biases and policy choices.

Some of the barriers limiting gender diversity in research studies have their origins in policies originally intended to protect vulnerable groups, such as pregnant individuals and children. For example, in the 1950s and 60s, the use of a sedative called thalidomide resulted in increased rates of miscarriage and serious birth defects throughout the UK, USA and Europe (Newbronner et al., 2019). Although the drug was originally marketed as a safe treatment to alleviate anxiety and morning sickness, it was not tested on a sample of pregnant people. As a result, pregnant patients took the medication without any knowledge of the potential risks involved. Public outcry following the controversy led to stricter pharmaceutical regulation and reforms to clinical research practices. One particularly influential response came in 1977 from the US Food and Drug Administration (FDA), which banned women of childbearing potential from certain kinds of clinical studies (National Institutes of Health Office of Research on Women's Health, 2018). Ironically, the widespread use of a drug not tested on women then became the basis for systematically excluding women from research.

The unintended consequence of this reform and others like it was a decades-long shortage of data about gender in the biomedical and psychological sciences. These policies inadvertently established a research culture in which gender came to be seen as largely irrelevant. Even when they did not necessarily have to exclude women from their studies, researchers often did so out of convenience. Over time, the research landscape reverted into one that was strikingly similar to the one that precipitated the thalidomide controversy. Policy shifted once again in the UK and USA; this time, policy-makers seemed to acknowledge the importance of acquiring representative samples but only with more thorough informed consent procedures (Bartlett et al., 2005; Brown et al., 2001). In the USA, for example, the National Institutes of Health (NIH) mandated that researchers include women and racialised groups in clinical research, regardless of cost or geographic constraints. Other governmental and professional organisations have similarly authored policies on inclusive sampling and reporting practices. For example, in 2020 the American Psychological Association (APA) *Publication Manual* (7th Edition) updated its guidance to recommend that researchers address the gender composition of their samples in published reports. Where sampling is skewed or limited, researchers are encouraged to address the potential impact of underrepresentation on their findings.

Despite these shifts in policy and cultural attitudes, gender bias remains a significant problem, one that is so pervasive that it even influences sampling decisions in non-human animal work. For example, Mamlouk and colleagues (2020) examined the frequency with which authors publishing in six flagship neuroscience journals reported the gender or sex of their model organisms, from fruit flies to chimpanzees. Studies comprising only male samples were much more common than those comprising only females, though this depended on species. Some authors provided a clear rationale for the bias of their samples. For example, in many bird species only the male sings, so studies examining the neural basis of song flexibility routinely exclude females. More often, however, researchers provided pre-emptive rationales for excluding females from their samples, such as speculating that female hormones and reproductive cycles might introduce too much variability to justify their inclusion in the sample (Mamlouk et al., 2020). Although this might be a defensible position, we caution readers to consider how data are then framed in such papers. In their discussion have the researchers explained how hormonal variability may have impacted their results? Are the findings presented as relevant to a particular subgroup, or more broadly applicable across the spectrum of sex/gender? Addressing such questions is critical if researchers seek to avoid normalising male experiences to the exclusion of any other perspective (see Focus Box 6.2).

Focus Box 6.2

Representing the Canonical Brain

Localising brain imaging activity to known neuroanatomical brain regions works according to a relatively straightforward principle. Researchers take a scan of a participant's brain—obtained using technology like magnetic resonance imaging (MRI)—and compare it to a canonical, average, reference brain. That canonical brain, as it turns out, is mostly male.

To understand the significance of this statement, it is helpful to know a little more about the history of neuroanatomical atlases. Neuroatlases provide a standard or template for what the brain looks like. They define regions of the brain and identify anatomical locations using 3D spatial coordinates, resulting in a standardised reference system (Davatzikos, 2009). As a reference tool, a successful atlas provides a good correspondence or match between its representation of brain anatomy and the anatomies of individual brains that are compared to it. Neuroanatomical atlases seem objective and neutral because they are based on spatial coordinates. However, the information that informs the atlas is itself selective, and numerous subjective (ethical, moral, theoretical, aesthetic) judgements go into the visualisation of a reference brain (Beaulieu, 2001; Daston & Galison, 2007).

Prior to the 1990s the most popular neuroatlases were either based on drawings or on photographs of post-mortem brains. The Talairach and Tornoux atlas, for example, was based on just one brain—that of a 60-year-old French woman (Beaulieu, 2001; Brett et al., 2002). Although this representation was highly idiosyncratic, the

(Continued)

atlas was enormously influential because it introduced the idea of a 3D coordinate system that could define the location of a brain region relative to other anatomical landmarks. Talairach and colleagues also devised a method for directly comparing individual brains by spatially transforming them; this system scaled brains using a proportional grid system that could roughly match brains on overall size and shape, laying the foundation for later efforts that would automate this process using statistical algorithms (Brett et al., 2002).

During the 1990s, a massive influx of funding in the USA and Europe enabled large-scale, multi-national collaborations like the International Consortium for Brain Mapping (ICBM) which dedicated itself to the creation of a new neuroatlas representing an 'average' human brain (Beaulieu, 2001). To create their average brain, the ICBM scanned 305 'normal' participants who were young (average age 23 years old), mostly male (78% of sample) and right-handed. Researchers also screened for other determinants of good health, collecting data on prescription and illicit drug use, blood pressure, surgical history and basic cognitive functioning (Mazziotta et al., 2009). The new atlas was created by comparing these individual brains to the original Talairach brain using manually defined landmarks. Once the shape and scale of the individual brains were transformed into this uniform coordinate system, they were averaged together using statistical algorithms to create the MNI305 atlas (Brett et al., 2002).

Since development of the MNI305, numerous other atlases have been created using similar techniques, and included as referents in popular brain imaging analysis packages (Brett et al., 2002). The atlas known as 'colin27' created an average brain from multiple images of a single male participant. As of 2017, it had been referenced in over 800 scientific papers (DelViscio, 2017; Holmes et al., 1998). Another popular referent known as the Human Brain Atlas comprised scans from 27 Scandinavian men (Roland et al., 1994). The ICBM152 was built from scans of 86 male and 66 female brains.

A major benefit of contemporary atlases is that they have democratised the study of brain anatomy and function. The process of comparing an individual brain to a referent is algorithmic, and thus it can be standardised, computerised, streamlined and automated. Researchers who want to use imaging techniques do not need to be experts in neuroanatomy to make relevant comparisons. However, the approach is not without criticism. Though brain imaging may seem like a fairly objective procedure, at each step of this process researchers make subjective judgements about how data should be refined, what data should be included and what variability should be excluded. In the example of neuroatlases, the resultant reference brains can be described as 'supernormal' because they are based on a highly selective subsample of participants. In addition to being young, mostly male and right-handed, the participants who had their brains scanned for the original MNI305 atlas were unmedicated, not pregnant, without psychiatric diagnoses or neurological disorders and self-identified as 'untraumatised' (Beaulieu, 2001). Other demographic information, such as socio-economic status and race, was not collected. The extensive exclusion criteria underpinning the creation of many modern neuroatlases removes or omits most of the variability that would otherwise be found in a typical, representative pool of adults. That variability may be important and relevant—a point we return to in our discussion of WEIRD psychology in Chapter 8.

Psychological instruments and tools make assumptions about what health and typicality look like. These assumptions may be defensible methodological decisions, provided they are made transparently. A failure to acknowledge the roots and potential limitations of these tools, however, only serves to reinforce the view that male, white and able-bodied experiences are the neutral, default perspective from which we should base our science.

The skewed treatment of gender/sex in neuroscience and psychology points to a larger issue than sample representativeness. In their attempt to control variability, researchers often reduce gender and sex to a binary of male and female. This provides conceptual clarity, but potentially at the expense of oversimplification. Many studies assume that hormones and brain structures are dimorphic, meaning they take one of two forms. For gonadal hormones, oestrogen and progesterone are considered 'female' whereas testosterone is considered 'male.' Dimorphism assumes that the levels of these hormones is static, so that women are characterised by having reliably more oestrogen and men more testosterone. This dichotomisation seems sensible and intuitive, until you realise that hormone systems are remarkably fluid and dynamic.

Oestrogen and testosterone are both produced by women, men, and non-binary persons, and classifying adults based on the concentration of these hormones is not straightforward; the average level of these hormones overlaps considerably across genders (de Ronde et al., 2003; DuBois & Shattuck-Heidorn, 2020; Fausto-Sterling, 2005; Liening et al., 2010; Oettel & Mukhopadhyay, 2004). Some historical analyses even suggest that the concept of 'sex hormones' is itself a legacy of gender essentialist thinking: because scientists first thought to measure them in testes and ovaries, the earliest data on oestrogens and androgens seemed to reinforce a view of sex as binary (Oudshoorn, 1994). Decades of subsequent studies, however, demonstrate that the so-called sex hormones are linked to many organs and organ systems, not just those involved in reproductive or sexual functions (Sanz, 2017).

In fact, if we were to base a gender binary on average hormone levels, a very different classification system might emerge: pregnant versus non-pregnant people (Hyde et al., 2019). Pregnancy is associated with remarkable brain plasticity and hormonal flux, and levels of gonadal hormones in non-pregnant women are, on average, more comparable to those in men than to those of women who are pregnant (Dahan, 2021; Hoekzema et al., 2017; Hyde et al., 2019; Martinez-Garcia et al., 2021; Orchard et al., 2023). A sex binary based on hormone levels does not adequately describe developing populations, either. Foetuses and prepubertal children cannot be reliably differentiated into female/male identities according to gonadal hormones, and even in adolescence there is still considerable fluidity and overlap in the levels of androgens and oestrogens across genders (Granger et al., 2004; Matchock et al., 2007; Nguyen et al., 2013).

Like hormones, brain structure and function are often characterised as dimorphic. Here too evidence suggests this may be an oversimplification. There are more commonalities in brain size, shape, volume and connectivity between sexes than there are differences (Hines, 2020; Joel & Yankelevitch-Yahav, 2014; Persson & Pownall, 2021; White & Gonsalves, 2021; though see also Cosgrove et al., 2007 and Becker et al., 2005 on why brain-based sexual dimorphism may still be a tractable position). Meta-analyses also evidence greater similarity than difference regarding female and male behaviour, from performance on maths tasks to depression scores (Hyde et al., 2019). Taken together, the collective evidence suggests it may be more accurate to describe gender/sex as a spectrum or mosaic rather than a binary with clear-cut biological distinctions (Joel, 2021).

How we conceptualise gender and sex has profound consequences for scientific and cultural practice. Far from being naturalised and objective, these conceptualisations are culturally specific. In many parts of the world gender is not conceptualised as binary and psychological traits are not essentialised according to female/male categories. Samoan culture, for example, recognises male, female and *fa'afafine* genders. Individuals who describe themselves as fa'afafine identify with aspects of both masculinity and femininity (Farran, 2010). Binaries based on sexual orientation (such as being either straight or queer) do not capture fa'afafine identity either. Though fa'afafine individuals are often gay, homosexuality does not define what it means to be fa'afafine. Being fa'afafine does not cohere neatly onto Western understandings of identity based on binary distinctions. Similarly, Singh (2016) documents how transgender and gender non-conforming groups such as *hijras* were widely accepted within India before Empire. After colonialism, however, these communities suffered legal discrimination, societal prejudice and sharp declines in mental and physical health. Whereas hijras often held prestigious community positions before colonisation, British laws based on gender essentialist views of sex and sexual orientation criminalised their lifestyle and isolated hijras from their support networks (Hunter, 2019; Singh, 2016). Western binary concepts of gender and sexual orientation simply do not capture the experience and meaning of personhood in places like Samoa and India, and the imposition of Western values into cultures that have traditionally upheld more dynamic conceptualisations of gender has been extremely harmful.

Rather than treating the gender/sex binary as natural, normal and inevitable, Western psychology must reflect on the historical and contemporary reasons we maintain such distinctions. For whom do these distinctions matter? How do gender binaries and gender essentialism maintain power structures that privilege some over others? What cultural, social and scientific issues are at stake if we challenge these canonical positions? It is only by addressing such questions that psychology can truly begin to move beyond its colonial, patriarchal, heteronormative roots.

WOMEN AS RESEARCHERS

So far we have explored how psychology has treated women when they are the topic of research. In this section, we discuss what happens when women are the researchers themselves. In brief, women have faced numerous systemic barriers to their participation in research. From a historical perspective such barriers include gatekeeping from male colleagues who justified the exclusion of women from the discipline by appealing to essentialist beliefs and stereotypes. Although these exclusionary practices were successfully challenged by widening educational access and women's organisations and campaigns, other barriers remain. As we shall see toward the end of this section, implicit biases in academic practice have a huge impact on whether women stay in the discipline.

Gatekeeping, Educational Reform and Social Organising

Many of the eminent male psychologists we have met in the book thus far mentored female students, supporting their research ambitions and in some cases even supervising their doctoral degrees. Boring, Hall, Titchener, Terman—all provided support to a limited number of seemingly exceptional women on an individual basis while maintaining parochial and discriminatory attitudes towards women in general (Proctor & Evans, 2014). Consider a group known as The Experimentalists: Titchener founded the influential club in 1904 to connect like-minded male scientists who were sceptical of applied and other 'soft' research topics. Women were almost universally excluded from the group; a few, exceptional women were granted membership on the basis that the total exclusion of women would be perceived as unscientific (Rutherford, 2015). There was no sustained objection to this policy, even amongst members who themselves trained female students. Even after the ban was lifted in 1929 following Titchener's death, few women were elected to the society. As a result of this gatekeeping, female representation in North American experimental psychology remained low for decades (Unger, 2001).

For much of the late 19th and early part of the 20th centuries, many prominent male psychologists advocated against policies to expand educational opportunities for women (Rutherford, 2015). Although these men framed their prejudices as rational and empirically grounded, we can identify the cultural concerns that likely fuelled their beliefs. Expanded access to education and employment threatened established (white, male) power structures in several ways. First, it opened routes to economic liberation for women. Subordination of women was an essential requirement for colonial and capitalist powers to maintain dominance (Chrisler & McHugh, 2011). Second, participation in the labour force might expose women to new forms of social organising which could also be used to further consolidate political power. Third, education and employment might distract or even deter women from their God-ordained duty to raise children (Hollingworth, 1916). The resulting depopulation would shrink quality genetic stock and enable those of lower class and inferior race to gain more political influence and control. It should be noted here that even as they advocated for their own emancipation, as a collective white women reinforced this racist narrative and were highly complicit in crafting a feminism that deliberately excluded racialised women, both within the UK and USA, and further afield in their colonies (Kumar, 2011; Roberts, 1993).

Women's entry into the scientific workforce during the 1940s created new economic tensions as researchers competed for post-war funding. Appeals to gender essentialism provided a way to justify the exclusion of women from the academy in this competitive economic climate. During this time psychology witnessed a resurgence of masculinisation in rhetoric and cultural conventions that were first promoted by early eminent men in the field. Researchers like Titchener and Boring valorised objectivity as the bedrock of scientific progress and civic society, and they lamented the intrusion of feminine subjectivity into otherwise rigorous, apparatus-based experimentation. These gendered attitudes penalised women, but they also hurt men: male researchers were devalued if they seemed too sensitive to frank criticism, or if they were unskilled at using tools and technology as part of their lab work (Rutherford, 2015). Influential male mentors tried to address psychology's 'woman problem' by encouraging women towards more reflective forms of scholarship, such as book writing on generic psychology topics. Ambitious women could neither identify as feminists nor pursue traditional activities like marriage or childrearing; anything other than total focus on scholarship indicated a problematic 'divided allegiance' between personal commitments and intellectual responsibilities (Unger, 2001).

These formal and informal barriers to progress did not spontaneously disappear during the feminist movement of the 1970s. Change required concerted activism and the creation of professional networks for women.[2] Even with such organisational

---

[2]Advocates for a women's section in the British Psychological Society (BPS) organised conferences, and attendees were encouraged to submit conference papers on the topic of gender equality. One submission featured the heart-breaking title 'What can the behavioural sciences do to modify the world so that women who want to participate meaningfully are not regarded as and are not in fact deviant' (Unger, 2001, p. 8).

support, policy changes represented hard-fought, protracted battles for equal rights. For example, the leadership council of the British Psychological Society (BPS) rejected an initial proposal in 1975 to create a 'Women in Psychology' section of the organisation. For BPS leadership, this label represented an intrusion of politics into science; the organisation did not want to be perceived as pushing a feminist agenda. The group was officially added to the BPS 12 years later in 1987, and only then after organisers amended the name of the section to 'Psychology of Women' (Unger, 2001).

Where Are We Now? The Leaky Pipeline

One long-term consequence of the political activism described above is that women are now well represented in psychology, at least when we consider entry-level employment and undergraduate education. In 1946, women comprised 30% of those registered with the APA as psychologists. That figure has since risen to 53% by recent estimates (Cramblet Alvarez et al., 2019). In the USA, the majority of undergraduate degrees in psychology (approximately 70%) are awarded to women, and the numbers are even more dramatic in the UK, where approximately 80% of psychology undergraduates are women (Ceci et al., 2014; Johnson et al., 2020). We don't know why women are now so much likelier to pursue psychological studies relative to men. The reasons could be cultural, perhaps pointing to implicit gendered stereotypes about the field; in particular, clinical, developmental and applied areas of scholarship have long been stereotyped as more female-oriented (Rutherford, 2015). Economic motives are also likely: women tend to earn less for the same work, a phenomenon known as the gender pay gap (Office for National Statistics, 2022). Fields with an over-representation of women may therefore trend towards lower salaries.

What *is* clear is that beyond undergraduate education, equality of opportunity remains beyond the reach of many women in academia. The life sciences and social sciences suffer from a problem known as 'the leaky pipeline': female graduates with PhDs in these fields are less likely than those from other disciplines to progress further in their academic careers (Blickenstaff, 2005). At all stages of career progression, from temporary contracts to first hires to professorships, women in scientific disciplines are more likely than men to leave academia or to have their careers stall prematurely. Psychology is a particularly leaky field in this regard (Ceci et al., 2014).

The causes of the leaky pipeline are complex and multiple. Table 6.1 identifies several areas of academic activity (funding, publishing and professional networking) where gender disparities likely contribute to the exodus of women from the discipline. The metrics summarised below are drawn from across the range of science, technology, engineering and mathematics (STEM) disciplines, including psychology. Across these various indices, men routinely experience advantages relative to women: they are more likely to obtain funding, to have their written work receive better evaluations, to have their publications widely disseminated and to occupy prestigious leadership positions in influential professional organisations. With regard to psychology in particular, female academics publish significantly fewer papers than male colleagues, even after controlling for age and career stage (Ceci et al., 2014). As a result, metrics that quantify academic impact using citation frequency (e.g. h index) are lower for women in psychology than they are for men (Geraci et al., 2015).

Table 6.1 Gender disparities across core academic activities

Academic Activity	Metric	Outcome
Funding	Likelihood of obtaining grant Value of obtained grant	Women are funded at lower rates and receive less material support when obtaining grants (Murphy et al., 2014; Titone et al., 2018; van der Lee & Ellemers, 2015)
Publication	Paper rejections	Authors with assumed male gender less likely to receive rejections (Smith et al., 2023)
	Authorship credits	Men more likely to publish single-author papers and to occupy prestigious authorship positions that signify leadership roles (Odic & Wojcik, 2020; West et al., 2013); globally women comprise only 30% of scientific authorships (Larivière et al., 2013)
	Publication frequency	Men in psychology publish 2.8 papers for every 1 published by a female colleague (Ceci et al., 2014)
	Citation rates	Papers with female lead authors receive fewer citations (Murphy et al., 2014); only nine countries have achieved gender parity in citation rates (Larivière et al., 2013)
	Paper evaluations	Articles perceived to be written by men receive better evaluations (Paludi & Strayer, 1985) compared to female or gender-neutral authors
	h-index (quantification of a researcher's influence based on citation metrics)	Female faculty in psychology have lower h-index relative to male colleagues of similar age (Geraci et al., 2015)
Professional networking	Leadership roles in professional organisations	Men more likely than women to occupy leadership roles or receive nominations into prestigious societies (Vaid & Geraci, 2016)
	Efficacy of social network	Women characterise their social networks as less helpful than men (Rose, 1985)

Taken independently these inequities would be problematic enough, but consider their compounding nature. Less funding means female researchers have fewer resources to accomplish their work. They are thus less likely to produce a high volume of internationally recognised published papers. As a result, their work is less likely to be referenced by other researchers. Lower citation rates lead to lower quantifications of scholarly impact, which in turn reduces the probability of being inducted into professional societies. The overall impact of these gender disparities is an academic ecosystem in which women are more likely to be employed on part-time contracts, less likely to be promoted to positions of seniority and less likely to earn the same pay as their male colleagues (2021/2022 data from HESA, 2023a; Jack, 2022; Science and Technology Committee, 2014).

Differences in productivity metrics might be one reason that women are more likely to be employed on part-time contracts compared to men (2021/2022 data from HESA, 2023a). Part-time employment may also differ in caregiving dynamics, and it is important that universities allow flexible contracts to accommodate such responsibilities. However, part-time employment and leave of absence from the university may result in lower academic productivity and thus negatively impact career progression. We know that proportionately more women than men take a leave of absence for caregiving purposes (36.7% versus 25.5%; Equality Challenge Unit, 2017), and some estimates suggest that women experience career interruptions at twice the rate of men (Science and Technology Committee, 2014).[3]

Perhaps unsurprisingly, then, women in universities are promoted at lower rates than men. Women are more likely to hold junior positions, or to be employed on non-academic contracts (i.e. department administration, technical staff, librarian, IT services; 2021/2022 data from HESA, 2023a). Recent data indicate that although they represent 46% of the workforce, women comprise 30% of the professoriate and 41% of other senior positions (2021/2022 data from HESA, 2023a). While this is certainly higher than in decades past, it is still well below the rates at which men obtain the most senior employment posts in academia. These data also speak to a persistent racial bias that has not been addressed by policies promoting gender equality; the number of Black women and other racialised

[3]The gender gap regarding career interruptions may have widened as a result of lockdowns during the COVID-19 pandemic. Preliminary evidence suggests that female academics were disproportionately likely to take over the majority of childcare and home management responsibilities during lockdown compared to their male colleagues, potentially resulting in suppressed manuscript submission and publication rates for women compared to men (Cardel et al., 2020; Krukowski et al., 2021; Manzo & Minello, 2020).

academics occupying professorial positions is vanishingly small (2021/2022 data from HESA, 2023a).

Promotion is one means by which universities communicate that they value employees. So is pay, and here again we see evidence of disparity that likely contributes to women leaving the field. The gender pay gap is a quantification of the difference in remuneration paid to men versus women. This is calculated by comparing average hourly earnings (excluding overtime pay) for women and men. Across the UK higher education sector, some estimates place the gender pay gap as high as 14.8%, and men earn more than women at all but one UK university (Jack, 2022). Pay discrepancy is a pattern that starts early, usually with an employee's first contract, which then sets the base-rate for all future compensation. At UK universities, starting salaries for women tend to be lower compared to men (Science and Technology Committee, 2014). The gender pay gap is apparent even at the highest career ranks, with male professors earning 6.2% more than their female colleagues (who, as we read earlier, are already fewer in number; Jack, 2022).

If you read through these paragraphs and found the data overwhelming—yes! That is precisely the point. Inequalities—of access, of opportunity, of outcome—do not arise because of one bad policy, or even a handful of bad policies. The data we summarise here exist even *with* policies in place to safeguard against explicit gatekeeping and other employment inequalities! The issues are cultural and systemic, and in many cases they have historical antecedents steeped in white male supremacy. A single institution may have excellent policies that should, in principle, ensure gender equality in the workplace. The way in which those policies are enacted, and the degree to which an individual feels included in their community, however, are very much cultural issues. Deeper systemic change may therefore require a radical rethink of how we view universities and the purpose of higher education (see Chapter 9).

Diversity leads to better work (Campbell et al., 2013; Clark et al., 2021; Murphy et al., 2014). When women—or indeed members of any minoritised group—leave the university, their voices and perspectives leave too, and our community is poorer for the loss.

BREAKING DOWN THE GENDER BINARY

We have suggested here that gender essentialism lies at the heart of many cultural assumptions and policies that disadvantage women. Our discipline has contributed to this problem by legitimising gender essentialist claims. In some cases, this has been accomplished by erasing gender altogether, ignoring it as a factor in experimentation. In other cases, psychologists have supported androcentric worldviews that limit what counts as acceptable, credible evidence. The same power structures that render women invisible as the subjects of scientific discourse also minimise their voices in the process of creating and sharing scientific knowledge, and the gradual loss of women from the discipline compounds these problems. We close by considering the implications of these findings, and by making concrete suggestions about how to move the field forward.

Gender essentialism exacts an additional cost that we have so far not considered. It reduces complexity and homogenises a diversity of experiences into a single, generic concept of 'woman'. Consider the story we have told here, about how gender norms in the Global North shifted as women entered the workforce, first in response to the Industrial Revolution and then again in the post-World War II era. That story makes sense—but mostly for white, middle-class women. However, white accounts of women's liberation only tell the story of white women entering professional, elite, white-majority workforces (Roberts, 1993). This ignores the reality of racialised women who were already in the workforce in low-prestige and low-paying positions. For example, by some estimates, in 1880 (after the American Civil War), 50% of Black women in the USA (but only 1.6% of white women) held paid employment (Roberts, 1993). So to generalise and say that social norms changed when *women* entered the workforce is to ignore an important set of racial and class dynamics that are undoubtedly relevant. We can see a similar friction in recent debates about how legal recognition, health care and antidiscriminatory policies apply to trans individuals. Gender essentialism is apparent in the way language and policy often differentiate between being born a 'natural' woman or man and self-identifying as one. We hope the evidence reviewed here about the stability of gender/sex categories proves food for thought in this regard. Gender essentialism homogenises women, when the point is that there is no single, fixed way of experiencing gender or the problems caused by gender discrimination.

As it manifests in psychology, feminism is often inadequate in its efforts to make scholarship less colonial. This is because white feminism is largely grounded in neoliberal thought that reproduces the same hierarchies of dominance and power that have historically disenfranchised women (Kurtiş & Adams, 2015). This form of white feminism takes its insights from the narrow subset of women living in the Global North and treats this knowledge as universal (see Chapter 8). White women suppress and weaponise equalities discourse when they reduce it to a single dimension, such as critiques focused exclusively on patriarchy (Birhane & Guest, 2021; Lugones, 2016). Gender equality movements that centre their advocacy around the concerns of white, able-bodied and heterosexual women are simply not equipped to single-handedly discuss let alone dismantle the complex and intersecting legacies of coloniality.

WHAT NEXT?

So far we have written at length about the many ways in which gender essentialism creates problems in psychology. We close by offering concrete suggestions about how the field can move beyond these limitations to create a science that is inclusive in theory and practice.

1   **Adopt diverse methodology:** As a scientific community we often avoid any interrogation of our disciplinary roots as political and therefore unobjective. But failure to interrogate our underlying assumptions— especially for those concepts that we see as fundamental to the field— is itself a political choice that only serves to maintain the status quo (Birhane & Guest, 2021; Chrisler & McHugh, 2011). Moving beyond the problems inherent to gender essentialism requires a shift in perspective. One possible way to do this is by expanding the scope of how we practise science. Feminist epistemologies rethink the importance of experimentation in understanding natural phenomena (Harding, 1995; Keller, 1985, 2003). According to such views, the scientific method is one tool amongst many for observing, evaluating and documenting the world. Other tools—such as oral histories and personal testimony—may avoid overly reductive interpretations about group differences. Mixed methods in research designs provide a way to complement quantitative approaches with qualitative ones. There are valuable insights to be gained by considering the knowledge and practices of individuals outside the framework of empirical investigation.

2   **Investigate theoretically motivated questions:** Our discussion about the treatment of women in psychological science points to a tension. Problems occur when gender is excluded from research designs, generating an incomplete picture of a phenomenon. At the same time, the inclusion of gender into study designs has often been used to cherry-pick evidence that supports gender essentialist claims. One way to resolve this tension is to engage in research practices that seek to elucidate mechanisms rather than effects (van Rooij & Baggio, 2021). Lindqvist and colleagues (2021) suggest that gender should be included in study designs and analyses *when that construct is relevant*. In other words, researchers should attempt to test specific, theoretically driven questions about the meaning or cause of gender differences, rather than provide a mere descriptor of how outcomes vary across different groups.

3   **Reconceive operational definitions of gender:** Open-ended questions about gender identity and sexual identity do not impose categories onto

participants and allow participants the dignity of providing information that is meaningful and relevant to them. Continuous measures of gender may also be useful to measure the relative fluidity or stability of gender identities. Some examples of continuous measures include asking participants the extent to which they identify with different aspects of gender, or asking about the frequency with which they engage in various activities that are assumed to be gendered (Hyde et al., 2019; Massa et al., 2023).

4   **Avoid androcentric language:** Language can be a powerful force for cementing—or challenging—gender/sex binaries and gender essentialist stereotypes. Androcentric language describes communication styles that are focused on men, often to the neglect or exclusion of other groups (Eagly & Riger, 2014). Some examples of androcentric language include using male pronouns as the default to describe an otherwise generic individual or group (i.e., 'mankind' or 'manpower'); referring to male professionals with gender-neutral titles ('psychologist') while using gendered terms for female professionals ('female psychologist'); and using biased descriptors (e.g. describing identical behaviour as 'confident' for men but 'aggressive' for women). Conscientious adoption of gender-neutral language fosters inclusivity, demonstrates cultural sensitivity, improves accessibility and challenges harmful stereotypes.

5   **Consider participant recruitment:** Researchers should carefully consider any ethical issues that arise when working with minoritised groups and act to ensure the well-being of all participants (see Edmiston & Juster, 2022 for a useful guide). For example, transgender people, queer people, and those who have experienced gender-based violence may have concerns that their participation risks identifying or 'outing' them in ways that are harmful and dangerous, or that participation may affect their access to healthcare and social support. Efforts to diversify research samples cannot compromise the safety and dignity of participants.

What we hope we have achieved with this chapter is to make readers curious about the cultural and scientific assumptions that ground much of our psychological approach to gender. Essentialist beliefs—whether they are about gender, sexuality, race, class, or any other characteristic—impact everyone. The pressure to conform to rigid behavioural expectations is not limited to women, nor are the harms that can occur when individuals internalise damaging stereotypical views of their gender. A critical approach to gender essentialism allows us to better understand the potential impact these views have on women, men and individuals outside the binary who find themselves marginalised within this restrictive framework.

FURTHER READING

Hollingworth, L. S. (1916). Social devices for impelling women to bear and rear children. *American Journal of Sociology, 22*(1), 19–29. https://doi. org/10.1086/212572 [journal article]

A bold essay about gender equality written by a woman who was working as an experimental psychologist in the early 1900s.

Hyde, J. S., Bigler, R. S., Joel, D., Tate, C. C., & Van Anders, S. M. (2019). The future of sex and gender in psychology: Five challenges to the gender binary. *American Psychologist, 74*(2), 171–193. https://doi.org/10.1037/amp0000307 [journal article]

Great tips for how researchers can rethink their treatment of gender.

Rutherford, A. (2015). Maintaining masculinity in mid-twentieth-century American psychology: Edwin Boring, scientific eminence, and the 'woman problem'. *Osiris, 30*(1), 250-271. https://doi.org/10.1086/683022 [journal article]

A nuanced take on influential male psychologists who mentored female students while gatekeeping their research efforts.

7

I DON'T SEE COLOUR

PSYCHOLOGY'S RACE PROBLEM

Most chapters in this book focus on specific domains within psychology, exploring the origins of the narratives that shape these disciplines. Here we shift our approach, examining how Black people in the UK and USA have been affected by their encounters with psychology and related disciplines. This restructuring introduces overlap with a range of issues covered in other domain-specific chapters in this book, and in doing so illustrates the extent to which Black people have been relentlessly aggressed on by psychology as a whole.

The factors contributing to this aggression have been established over time—carried out both directly by scientists and indirectly by societal systems that scientists have influenced. Each factor might individually be dismissed as minor, defensible given the circumstances, or an outcome that scientists regret but could not have anticipated. Viewed together, they form a pattern of systemic hostility, akin to death by a thousand cuts, perpetrated by scientists and the systems they legitimise.

In the final section of this chapter, we suggest that psychology must go beyond merely acknowledging the harm it has done to Black people, and embrace an active, reparative approach. This entails using our influence to address the long-lasting effects of injustices that our field has committed and perpetuated. Just as proponents of Public Sociology urge sociologists to be active in considering the needs of the peoples and societies they influence, and the responsibilities they have to them, so too can we.

SCIENTIFIC RACISM IN AMERICA

Polygenism

The term 'race' was defined in the 1700s as a way of categorising humans into groups with underlying biological characteristics (Bancel et al., 2014). Unlike the much more recent term 'ethnicity', which incorporates socio-cultural characteristics into a set of dynamic and imprecise categories, race was defined as a biological truth. It has though, with advances in genetic science, been found to have no clear scientific basis (Witzig, 1996). As such, the reminder that race is a social construct is necessary as a reminder that 'race science' has no rational legitimacy beyond folk taxonomy (Sternberg et al., 2005).

The scientific categorisation of humans was formalised by the Swedish taxonomist Linnaeus, who is credited with popularising binomial nomenclature (e.g. *Homo sapiens*) in *Systema Naturae* (1735). For many editions of this text, Linnaeus referred to humans as having four varieties: 'Europaeus albus' (white); 'Americanus rubescens' (reddish); 'Asiaticus fuscus' (tawny); and 'Africanus niger' (black). Linnaeus did not used the term 'species' to subdivide humans, and in a later text wrote with subtlety about the extent to which environmental factors influence characteristics that are typically described as racialised (1737). This detail, however, was lost on those who co-opted Linnaeus' taxonomy to propose that humans comprise separate species with distinct ancestral origins. This idea, known as 'polygenism', had depressingly predictable consequences.

Slavery in the Americas provides a harrowing illustration of atrocities polygenism was used to justify. During the 19th and 20th centuries, white supremacists applied Darwinian arguments to contrast the evolutionary fitness of Black people with their own, thereby justifying enslavement, rape, abuse and forced labour. The baseless evolutionary argument used to excuse these atrocities was that the stock of enslaved people in the Americas had already been made inferior by environmental pressures in Africa (Washington, 2006). Enslaved people were therefore being afforded a better life and greater chance of species survival than they would otherwise have as free people. So strong was belief in the idea, known as the Black extinction hypothesis, that many of Du Bois' World's Fair exhibition panels were intended to demonstrate that Black people could thrive socially, economically and physiologically, free of the shackles of slavery (see Focus Box 2.1). Refuting the idea that Black people would not survive without 'assistance' was an integral component of Du Bois' data-driven celebration of Black American lives (Battle-Baptiste & Rusert, 2018).

Bolstered by their conviction that Black people were members of a different species, defenders of slavery made an array of baseless claims about Black physiology and psychology. They asserted that Black women experienced increased sexual appetite, which excused their rape (Washington, 2006), and that Black people experienced the mental disorders of 'drapetomania' and 'dysthesia aethiopica'. These diseases were concocted by Confederate physician Samuel Cartwright (1793–1863), and represented the psychological disorders of impulsively seeking freedom, and laziness (Cartwright, 1851). Drapetomania, Cartright proposed, was exacerbated by the 'owners' of enslaved people who treated Black people as anything other than 'submissive knee bender[s]' (p. 332) and could be prevented by whipping. Dysthesia aethiopica was evidenced by skin lesions and could, predictably, also be cured by whipping.

The circularity of these *treatments* generating more symptoms left the 'owners' of enslaved people with absolute peace of mind that their brutality was justified. Crucially, it also reframed universally human responses to subjugation as disease, medicalising the societal ill of slavery as a malady unique to Black people. The echoes of racialised medicalisation are evident even in modern psychiatric diagnoses. For example, Black people in the USA and England are many times more likely to be diagnosed with schizophrenia than their white counterparts (Halvorsrud et al., 2019; Olbert et al., 2018). The pathologisation of rational responses to systemic structural inequality is further explored in the opening to Chapter 4 and in Focus Box 4.1, but it is important that we emphasise here that the pathologisation of Black people for objecting to inhumane treatment is not a modern phenomenon, and has been occurring for centuries. When considering the diagnostic rates of psychological disorders, we would do well to consider whether over-representations of disease in minoritised peoples are manifestations of societal expectations that people should just accept systemic racism, with medicalised consequences should they fail to do so (Metzl, 2010).

Eugenics and Birth Control

Despite the eventual emancipation of Black people from chattel slavery, scientific racism had taken hold of popular discourse in the USA, providing fertile ground for its manifestation in eugenics. Given our relative comfort with the selective breeding of species different to our own, it is straightforward to understand the importance of polygenism in realising eugenics on Black people.

It may come as a surprise that an organisation held up as a poster-child of modern liberal values rose to prominence in early 20th century America thanks to its promotion by eugenicists. Planned Parenthood, a charity that today provides reproductive health care, including abortions, has its origins in another organisation, the American Birth Control League (the name was changed in 1942), set up in 1921 by nurse and activist Margaret Sanger (1879–1966). In 1939, the American Birth Control League instigated the Negro Project, a scheme to bring widespread birth control to Black communities. As the face of the effort, Sanger gained personal support, and support for the American Birth Control League from racist organisations such as the Ku Klux Klan (Douglas, 1969).

A key component of Sanger's approach was the delivery of her message and promotion of her organisation's services by trusted Black pastors and Black physicians. In a letter to a supporter, Sanger wrote: 'We do not want word to go out that we want to exterminate the negro population and the minister is the man who can straighten out that idea if it ever occurs to any of their more rebellious members' (Sanger, 1939, p. 2). Whether or not Sanger intended to communicate that the word going out was the real intent of the project, or an unfounded worry within Black communities, is unclear from the letter. Arguments can be made for both interpretations on the basis of the varied sources of support that Sanger received. In favour of the first, malign interpretation is that the letter itself was written to Clarence Gamble—grandson of Proctor and Gamble company founder James Gamble—a eugenicist physician whose Human Betterment League of North Carolina supported involuntary sterilisation schemes. These schemes were targeted at those whose reproduction was judged to be a drain on the public coffers, who comprised a majority of Black people (see Chapter 6 for similar arguments made about the urban poor). In favour of the second, benign interpretation is that the project was supported by civil rights activists like Martin Luther King and W.E.B. Du Bois. Du Bois even published in an issue of Sanger's *Birth Control Review* journal titled 'A Negro Number' (Du Bois, 1932), decrying the ills of unfettered reproduction on Black communities using entirely eugenic language:

> the mass of ignorant Negroes still breed carelessly and disastrously, so
> that the increase among Negroes, even more than the increase among
> whites, is from that part of the population least intelligent and fit, and
> least able to rear their children properly. (p. 166)

Whether racist or not in her intentions, Sanger took advantage of how willingly received eugenic ideas were in the first half of the 20th century, especially by racist groups who wished to impose any restriction they could on Black people. She garnered support for her ideas from those with track records of racialised hate, whilst selling the same ideas to Black communities as methods of personal control and empowerment.

Whilst some Black women embraced the reproductive freedom that the success of the American Birth Control League and Planned Parenthood offered, others argued that it was part of a hidden, coordinated approach to use eugenics to enact Black genocide (Caron, 1998). The hidden and coordinated aspects of the eugenic approach in the USA were noticed by the Eugenic Society of Britain who sought to emulate what they called crypto-eugenics (MacKenzie, 1981). When viewed alongside other programmes of sterilisation and coercive contraception described in Harriet Washington's *Medical Apartheid* (2006), like the 1930s North Carolina Eugenic Commission's sterilisation of 8000 'feeble-minded' people, 5000 of whom were Black, the 1970s involuntary sterilisation of 100,000 to 150,000 women in Alabama, half of whom were Black, and the 1990s coercion into contraception in exchange for lenient criminal sentences or money offered to drug addicts from Black communities, it becomes clear that there was a pattern of attempts to control Black women and Black births by those who subscribed to eugenic ideals. The fact that this was still happening at the turn of the 21st century illustrates the influence that eugenic ways of thinking still have on society, evident in well-meaning medical programmes and law enforcement, long after the eugenics movement has fallen out of fashion.

Regardless of the intent of any individual actor, it is totally understandable that there should be a distrust of a social care and medical system that has harmed so many Black people, especially in the South of the USA. Black women have been particularly disadvantaged by their intersectional identities—put in a position to mistrust the birth control movement that empowered so many other women. Uvelia Bowen, a Black social worker, perfectly summed up this impossibility in an account given to the 1966 *Population Crisis* hearings before US Senate committees: 'Negroes don't want children they can't take care of, but we are afraid to trust you when your offered help has so often turned out to be exploitation' (US Senate Subcommittee on Foreign Aid Expenditures of the Committee on Government Operations, 1970, p. 274). As for Planned Parenthood, the organisation has gone some way to recognising the harm Margaret Sanger did for the cause of birth control with minoritised peoples (Planned Parenthood, 2021):

> Margaret Sanger was so intent on her mission to advocate for birth control that she chose to align herself with ideologies and organizations that were explicitly ableist and white supremacist. In doing so, she undermined reproductive freedom and caused irreparable damage to the health and lives of generations of Black people, Latino people, Indigenous people, immigrants, people with disabilities, people with low incomes, and many others. (p. 1)

Margaret Sanger certainly limited reproductive freedom for individuals who did not fit her narrow perspective of those deserving the right to make their own choices. But, she was only able to do so by taking advantage of the toxic narratives and pseudoscience that scientific racism had established in the decades preceding her time.

THE SOCIAL CONSTRUCTION OF INTELLIGENCE, AND EDUCATION IN THE UK

Central to the evaluation of an individual's civic worth by eugenicists was intelligence. The realisation of potential civic worth was argued to come when natural intelligence was built on by societal education. Education then, was viewed as a crucial lever with which society could be engineered. Although we have moved on from explicitly eugenic ways of thinking, or perhaps because of this, the emphasis we place on education to maximise individual potential remains. Moreover, narratives concerning personal development, especially in schools, have focused on the concepts of 'grit' or 'resilience'—the idea that a student who has passion and perseveres in the face of difficulty is a student who will eventually reap the rewards of their hard work in realising their potential (see Chapter 9 for discussion of how these concepts raise their heads again at university; Duckworth et al., 2007). This narrative seems readily accepted because it is so consistent with the more contemporary, meritocratic ideals that we hope exist in our education systems and in society more generally—that those who show merit will be rewarded for this demonstration. Working backwards from these assumptions, though, we might be tempted to infer that any individual who has not achieved their meritocratic potential did not *try hard enough* (a faulty argument discussed in great depth by Sandel, 2020). Through a different route to the one taken by eugenicists, meritocrats achieve the same result of attributing the individual's failure to achieve their potential to their own deficiencies.

The attribution of failure to the individual ignores structural barriers that make it far harder for some individuals, or groups, to succeed. Children facing structural barriers must not only excel to perform as though the playing field is level in the first place, but then excel even further to be perceived as worthy of meritocratic reward. The systemic disadvantage that Black students, specifically those of Caribbean origin, experience within the British school system was laid bare by Bernard Coard (1945–) in his 1971 booklet 'How the West Indian Child is made educationally sub-normal in the British School System'. Coard is a Black, Grenadian politician who, in the 1960s, studied and taught in the UK. During his time as a teacher, he observed that Black Caribbean students in London were removed from mainstream schools and sent to schools for 'educationally sub-normal' (ESN) students at far higher rates than their white peers. Outcomes for students in ESN classes were generally worse than students in mainstream classes— they were taught with lower expectations of their academic achievement, in classes that lacked educational resources, and faced problems integrating with others at school and, later, in work. Coard's experiences of working with Black students identified as ESN led to the publication of a 50-page booklet that outlined systemic, active suppression of Black students. Coard argued that British society and the education system set up expectations of failure in those who encountered Black students, and funnelled resources away from them when they met these expectations. He later referred to these barriers as 'weapons of mass suppression' (Coard, 1971/2021, p. xvii).

Figure 7.1 Bernard Coard

Amongst the weapons identified were cultural expectations held by white British teachers. Coard observed that, in contrast to British classrooms in which discussion and questioning of the teacher was encouraged, Caribbean classrooms discouraged talk-back. When white teachers unaware of this difference were faced with white students who participated actively and Black students who did not, Coard argued that this inevitably led to a tendency to evaluate Black students as 'dull'. Once this evaluation was 'confirmed' by IQ testing, and they were funnelled into the ESN path, the structure of the schooling system allowed no escape for the Black student, with too few resources to allow the curriculum to be effectively taught. If Black students did learn the curriculum, they learned that all the great men of history were white, with no expectation that they could ever achieve anything approaching greatness themselves. This educational system intellectually ghettoised Black students, and gave them no hope of success. Given the importance of educational success on further prospects, the school system set Black students on the path to societal marginalisation. Considering the range of barriers that Black students faced, Coard marvelled that the performance gap wasn't greater than it was.

What is crucial to Coard's approach is that he situated the 1960s British education system in the context of societal and scientific racism. As societal context, British political discourse had grown more openly hostile to immigrants. In the 1964 General Election campaign, the eventual Conservative Party winner was reported to have used the slogan 'If you want a n*gger for a neighbour, vote

Labour'. Meanwhile the Labour government's Race Relations Act of 1968, which outlawed racist discrimination in housing and employment, had prompted Conservative MP Enoch Powell to give his now infamous 'Rivers of Blood' speech, in which he described British immigration policy as akin to the nation building its own funeral pyre. In scientific discourse, the new field of genetics had ushered in another method by which scientific racism could be justified. Psychologists Arthur Jensen (1969) and Hans Eysenck (1971) had proposed hereditarian views on intelligence, arguing that the consistently lower IQ scores obtained by Black people, compared to white people, were 80% down to reduced inherited capacities for learning. These statements were not from fringe figures within the discipline, but in Eysenck's case, from one of the most respected and cited psychologists of his time—an expert in the fields of intelligence and personality. Although these claims have since been dismissed for want of evidence, at the time they did a great deal to shape the scientific discourse on race and intelligence (Colman, 2016). Coard recognised that Black schoolchildren in Britain were growing up in a society where it was acceptable for politicians to be campaigning for their repatriation, often to countries they had never even visited, and against the backdrop of a scientific community that was justifying, not questioning, their intellectual inferiority.

In spite of the bleak picture that Coard exposed, he made a series of recommendations to Black parents to minimise the chances of their children becoming identified as educationally subnormal, amongst them visiting schools often, reading and finding Black dolls for children to play with. He also proposed a range of education reforms that he believed would break the cycle of systemic disadvantage facing Black students. These included:

- recruiting Black teachers, under whose instruction Black students do better;
- providing an opportunity to have students' educational needs reassessed by a Black educational psychologist, moving away from a student's educational trajectory being set by single culturally loaded evaluation; and
- recognising that the IQ test is partly a test of culture, with children unfamiliar with the culture in which the test has been constructed bound to perform more poorly than those who are fully acculturated.

Coard's recommendations now have a wealth of evidence supporting them, and many are seen as good practice. What is perhaps most remarkable about Coard's message, though, is that he delivered it with humanity in a publication whose primary audience was the communities it affected. His community-centred, active approach empowered parents to build a steadfast movement working towards a better future for their children and their communities.

Focus Box 7.1

Robert Williams and the BITCH-100

In the 1960s, whilst many psychometricians had moved beyond explicitly *trying* to demonstrate that racial differences in intelligence existed, they still consistently found average IQ test scores obtained by Black Americans to be lower than those obtained by white Americans (a mean difference of 1 standard deviation, still observed to this day, e.g. Roth et al., 2001). If well-trained, liberally inclined civil rights-supporting psychologists at some of the most prestigious North American universities were still finding IQ differences between their Black and white study participants, was there actually something to the suspicion that white Americans had held for so long? The argument went that if the only difference between these two groups of Americans was their genes, then the lower intelligence scores obtained by Black people must be the result of a lower heritable capacity for learning.

Here we return to the difference between race and ethnicity. Whilst ethnicity explicitly acknowledges socio-cultural factors in a necessarily imprecise taxonomy, race does no such thing. When scientists engage in race science, they lead their colleagues and students, their readers and the public, towards the conclusion that racial differences are genetic differences. Using the social construct of race, without explicitly acknowledging the cultural differences inherent in the collective histories, dialects and practices in the communities from which people of differing racial backgrounds tend to be drawn, wilfully obscures a host of alternative explanations for one's findings.

Figure 7.2 Robert Williams

(Continued)

Robert Williams (1930-2020) was a Black professor of psychology and African and African-American studies at Washington University in St. Louis. In 1972, Williams published the 'Black Intelligence Test of Cultural Homogeneity', a 100-item vocabulary test (BITCH-100; Williams, 1972). Noting that standardised intelligence tests such as Wechsler Adult Intelligence Scale were normed for white Americans, to the exclusion of all other groups, Williams developed the BITCH-100 as a culture-specific test for Black Americans. Each test item required the respondent to identify how to correctly use a Black American English word (a language Williams would later name Ebonics; Williams, 1975).

The complete BITCH-100 is not publicly available, though small numbers of items can be found online. An encyclopaedia entry for the scale (West, 2010), lists two multiple choice questions asking respondents to define the following:

Boot: (a) cotton farmer, (b) Black, (c) Indian, (d) Vietnamese citizen; and

Clean: (a) just out of the bathtub, (b) very well dressed, (c) very religious, (d) has a great deal.

The correct answers, both (b), are illustrative of the extent to which test takers unfamiliar with Ebonics would have struggled to score well. Indeed, according to Williams (1972):

White [subjects] seemed to be quite challenged by the test and appeared tense. Many sighed and showed other signs of discomfort. A few questioned the validity of the instrument; others stated that if the test is valid, then they have little knowledge of the Black experience. (p. 9)

It was no wonder then, that white participants achieved far lower scores than Black participants, with mean proportions correct of .51 (standard deviation [SD] = .16) and .87 (SD = .07) respectively.

Williams' point was not that the Black people taking the BITCH-100 were more intelligent than the white people taking it, but that all intelligence tests make cultural and linguistic assumptions of those they are testing. In the case of the BITCH-100, Black Americans did better than white Americans because the test assumed and tested knowledge of Ebonics. Tests such as the Wechsler Adult Intelligence Scale, and the Stanford-Binet test on the other hand, had been developed in almost entirely white academic environments. It was no wonder to Williams that they advantaged white respondents. The injustice lay in the fact that white respondents and academics alike were quick to point out the problems of draw-ing conclusions about people on the basis of culturally specific tests when they were disadvantaged, but willing to argue the culture-free credentials of tests that disadvantaged others. Their willingness to attribute differences in test scores to heritable capacities for learning was clearly not something that cut both ways.

WHAT NEXT?

Across current measures of education, employment, health and wellbeing, there are outcome differences in favour of white people, relative not just to Black people, but a range of ethnically minoritised peoples. To tackle these outcome differences, educational institutions, employers and healthcare providers will often take an organisational approach, implementing well-intentioned, evidence-based programmes targeted at reducing them. These programmes deal with specific measures and how differences in these measures manifest within the organisation's sphere of influence. But, what we know from this brief review of a few topics, drawn from a near endless array of historic racism, is that the building blocks of inequality are woven into the fabric of society. This is not to say that organisational interventions are unnecessary—quite the opposite—but that they need to be implemented alongside broader, societal efforts that honestly examine inequalities, with a view to eliminating them.

Considered from this perspective, the possibility of change seems remote. How can we honestly engage with racial inequality as a society when government agencies such as the UK government's Commission on Race and Ethnic Disparities produce documents that identify inequalities but refuse to acknowledge that racist outcomes result from processes that enact racism (the Sewell Report; Commission on Race and Ethnic Disparities, 2021)? How can we dismantle structural racism in the face of structures that refuse to acknowledge its existence? We propose that the answer lies in the template that Bernard Coard laid out in his booklet for parents: we must take active responsibility for concrete actions that dismantle processes with racist outcomes, and do this in our own lives and workplaces and in broader society. Crucially, this is not solely the responsibility those directly affected by specific inequalities, but *everyone's* responsibility.

Such activism requires us to abandon ideas of race-neutrality, adopting an identity-conscious approach instead (Salter & Adams, 2013). We must ask people from minoritised groups about their experiences, and listen, even if what we hear is distressing to us and our own sense of allyship. For those navigating higher education as students or workers, we must examine how racist outcomes are enacted in our universities and in the towns and cities in which they are situated. It is not acceptable for our universities to take pride in the *impact* our research has on scholarly engagement if they are unwilling to also engage in antiracist impact efforts within our communities. In our teaching and learning, we must broaden the canon. Just as Coard wrote: 'if we do not want them to hate themselves, we must get them **Black** [Coard's emphasis] dolls' (Coard, 1971/2021, p. 44), and we must teach from the growing array of resources highlighting the contributions of minoritised scholars (e.g. Carmichael-Murphy & Danquah, 2022).

We can also look to allied disciplines in which the contributions of minoritised scholars have informed what we do. As psychologists, we can look to sociology, and the contribution made by Black cultural theorist Stuart Hall (1932–2014). Hall expanded cultural studies to include gender and race, and was described as viewing culture as 'a critical site of social action and intervention, where power relations are both established and potentially unsettled' (Procter, 2004, p. 1), a message that resonates with what is being outlined here. Also pertinent is the style of public sociology, which encourages sociologists to 'carry [sociology] forward as a social movement beyond the academy' (Burawoy, 2005, p. 25). This approach emphasises the responsibility of sociologists to actively communicate with the public, shifting the discipline away from the increasingly professionalised, insular approach of modern scholarship, and back towards an activism aimed at bettering the institutions of civil society.

The public style exists within psychology too, but has yet to be broadly adopted (Eaton et al., 2021). Nonetheless, those interested in how this has been enacted within our own discipline should consider African American psychology, liberation psychology and abolitionist psychology. African American psychology examines the Black diasporic experience in the USA, situating it within a unique culture that encompasses African influences and the need to navigate American systems where this culture is not readily accepted (Belgrave & Allison, 2018). Liberation psychology has its origins in South America and is intended to help the liberation of the oppressed from the structures and systems of thought that perpetuate oppression (Comas-Díaz & Rivera, 2020). Another approach that focuses on a specific struggle is abolitionist psychology, which places at its centre the responsibility to take an active role in in abolishing the USA's prison industrial complex (Klukoff et al., 2021). These approaches all foster personal and collective agency by encouraging psychologists to take active roles in shaping the cultures in which they do their work.

As we know too well from the various illustrations of scientific racism presented in this chapter, a publicly active organisation or individual has the potential to cause societal harm and human suffering. It is paramount, then, that we all engage reflexively with the public, hearing those who are disadvantaged by the activities of our disciplines, our institutions and our communities. This is vital to do even if, *especially* if, we have not intended to cause this harm. More challengingly, we must also recognise that a great deal of the privilege we have been afforded through our participation in higher education has been enabled by historic, and current, inequality. It is only by recognising this structural inequality that we ourselves benefit from that we can credibly work to reduce it in all the domains in which we hold power.

FURTHER READING

Coard, B. (1971/2021). *How the West Indian child is made educationally sub-normal in the British school system* (5th ed.). McDermott Publishing. [book] and McQueen, S., & Siddons, A. (2020) *Small axe*. Film 5, *Education*. Turbine Studios/ EMU Films/BBC/Amazon Studios. [film]

The booklet is a powerful call to arms for Caribbean parents of children in 1960s and 1970s Britain, explaining the system and how to navigate it. The film presents a fictional account of a Black child's experience of ESN school, and the power of Coard's booklet in bringing the Black Caribbean community together.

Williams, R. L. (1972). The BITCH-100: A culture-specific test. Paper presented at the American Psychological Association Annual Convention, Honolulu, Hawaii, September 1972. https://files.eric.ed.gov/fulltext/ED070799.pdf [conference proceedings]

A lesson in psychometrics accompanying the paper in which Williams set out the BITCH-100.

Carmichael-Murphy, P., & Danquah, A. (2022). *Hidden histories: Black in psychology*. University of Manchester. https://gmhigher.ac.uk/resources/hidden-histories-black-in-psychology/ [booklet]

Resource aimed at older schoolchildren, but worth reading by all. A beautiful introduction to a range of important Black figures in psychology, and discussion of issues facing Black psychologists today.

Akala. (2018). *Natives: Race and class in the ruins of empire*. Two Roads. [book]

Not cited in this chapter, but highly relevant to a range of topics discussed. A powerful observation of the British Black experience.

8

DE-WEIRDING RESEARCH

A STEPPING STONE TO A BETTER PSYCHOLOGY?

Around 1865, renowned anthropologist and anatomist Pierre Paul Broca (1824–1880) faced a serious problem. Unlike other French anthropologists of the time, Broca advocated for a distinctly quantitative approach to understanding the human mind. He valued numbers and placed importance on the measurement of physiological and behavioural characteristics over linguistic analysis or ethnography. Broca theorised that many cognitive processes could be localised in the brain, and through post-mortem investigations of patients with brain lesions, he demonstrated that the left, third circumvolution of the left frontal lobe was implicated in speech production. This would become known as 'Broca's area'.

Despite this discovery, a decade later, Broca felt stymied in his efforts to understand the mind. Broca interpreted his numerous craniometric and anthropometric measurements as evidence for polygenism—the theory that human racial groups derive from different origins (see Chapter 7 for discussion of consequences of the belief in polygenism). In line with this interest, he subsequently sought to quantify the relative influence of heredity on brain development and cognition. However, Broca was beginning to realise that his expansive collection of measurements was only as extensive as the sample from which they had been drawn. He and his fellows at the newly founded Société Mutuelle d'Autopsie (which translates to English as the Mutual Autopsy Society) depended on charity hospitals for cadavers, performing their autopsies on the mostly nameless and penniless people who died there (Wright, 2022). Relying on the 'poor and unattached' of society presented major scientific obstacles (Hecht, 2003). First, the life course of these anonymous people was often a mystery, making it difficult to test hypotheses about the relative role of life experience on brain morphology. Second, Broca recognised that whole theories of human behaviour were being developed by testing and generalising from a very narrow subset of the broader population. To address these problems, Broca sought to study the brains of people from different social strata. To do this, he launched a campaign targeting the Parisian elite, soliciting socialites and scholars to donate their bodies to science. In a move reminiscent of Galton's use of expositions to collect data (see Chapter 2), the Société Mutuelle d'Autopsie recruited at the Paris World's Fair of 1889, providing applicants with a template will specifying how their brains should be donated for anatomical study (Hecht, 2003). Completed personality questionnaires accompanied these wills, allowing researchers to correlate brain metrics with self-reported psychological characteristics, and allowing donors to find meaning in death by advancing science (Wright, 2022).

Broca's call to broaden the participant base for scientific studies would find accord with contemporary researchers, even if his solution for this problem might not. Over 130 years later, Arnett (2008) documented how the vast majority (96%) of data published in top-tier psychology journals were drawn from participants in the UK, Europe, North America, Australia and Israel, with 68% of those studies focusing specifically on North American undergraduates alone. Building on this work, Henrich and colleagues (2010) popularised the acronym WEIRD—Western,[1] educated, industrialised, rich and democratic—to characterise these *atypical* samples. Scholars addressing the WEIRD phenomenon converge on two claims: first, that many of the theories of human behaviour have been developed and validated on a very narrow and non-representative sample of human beings; and second, that even where broader sampling exists, researchers do not escape the WEIRD problem because they typically employ tools and concepts that were developed for and by this same narrow subset of individuals. More representative scholarship in the form of cross-cultural comparisons is often suggested as a remedy for these philosophical and methodological problems. As we will see in the next section, there is a long history of considering the importance of culture and context in human behaviour. Why then has the nature of our scholarship been so slow to change? To address this question, it is useful to understand how cross-cultural approaches came to dominate psychology and what implications this has had for decolonising and diversifying our practice.

---

[1]Throughout this chapter, we use the term 'Western' as it typically appears in cross-cultural psychological literature as a way to refer to institutions and research based in the English-speaking Global North.

This chapter is a reflection on the role that culture and context play in psychological science. In it, we seek to understand how certain approaches to studying variability in human behaviour have become canonised, and what consequences this has had for our discipline as well as the larger ecosystem of knowledge exchange in which academic activity is embedded. We also seek to provide an alternative account of the WEIRD problem—one that situates psychological research in a larger framework of scientific values that stem directly from histories of colonialism and imperialism. In doing so, we argue that the limitations of WEIRD science cannot be solved by broader sampling alone.

WHERE DID WEIRDNESS COME FROM?

Broca was prescient though not unique in his observations about the importance of culture and context to addressing representativeness and generalisability. In many ways, the story of culture in psychology is one about whether variability is the signal or the noise—the phenomenon to study and understand, or the source of error and unpredictability in an otherwise universal and stable system.

Measuring and Defining Culture

One goal of cultural studies is to understand the degree to which observable variability in behavioural repertoires stems from true differences in physiological and cognitive processes, or whether these differences are more superficial in nature. As a theoretical starting point, *universalism* assumes unity of human experience. Ultimate, evolutionary level causes of behaviour should be constant across groups, with variability reflecting differences in how those superordinate processes, motivations and functions are realised. Universalism therefore assumes coherence, that diverse behaviours and phenotypes can stem from common roots. In contrast, *relativism* maintains that culture and mind are not dissociable, and that differences in behaviour can only be understood in local terms (Poortinga, 2016). According to this view, psychology is embedded in cultural context, not separate from it.

Cross-cultural approaches are necessarily comparative, contrasting a behaviour across multiple groups. The underlying assumption is that there is some common core to each behaviour that facilitates a meaningful comparison between groups. Rather than treating culture as the signal—the phenomenon of interest—comparative approaches treat culture as a quasi-independent variable that explains noise (or error) in a dependent measure. For this reason, cross-cultural approaches are more aligned with 'hard' or 'experimental' science and are arguably viewed as more mainstream than cultural studies.

In the comparative approach, and when viewed as an independent factor, culture could conceivably have multiple 'levels'. While many studies do indeed contrast multiple socio-cultural groups, a more common approach has been to reduce cultural differences to highly contrasted dichotomies. These dichotomies function to simplify study designs and make interpretation of results more straightforward. However, if a variable (e.g. culture) is designed with only two levels (e.g. collectivism versus individualism), then any group differences can only support the validity of the construct. Furthermore, the tendency to condense cultural differences into dichotomies may itself reflect Western heuristics for making sense of data rather than reflecting any true commonalities between groups (Sinha & Tripathi, 1994). In other words, either/or comparisons may be a specific preoccupation amongst scholars in the English-speaking Global North—a way of imposing order on data that do not necessarily conform to such clear-cut distinctions. This preoccupation with dualities may not universally characterise scientific practice (see Chapter 1). This in turn runs the risk of oversimplifying complex behaviour, often reducing groups into broad stereotypes that lead to good/bad comparisons.

Cross-cultural studies can provide illuminating insights into group behaviour. However, as a methodological practice, cross-cultural designs come with several assumptions about the causes and nature of group differences that should be introspected. Despite the genuine emphasis on the diversity and inclusivity of human experience, cross-cultural work has often reinforced the extant psychological canon. It has done this by adopting a particular epistemic stance that prioritises objectivity and experimental frameworks over phenomenological accounts of behaviour. This in turn has popularised the use of research questions, study designs and statistical methods that treat culture as a factor.

How Did Cross-Cultural Approaches Become Canonised?

As discussed in Chapter 1, psychology in the English-speaking Global North largely adopted the perspective of Enlightenment philosophers, that the goal of science was to systematically discover and describe the universal laws governing the natural world. Consequently, the scholarship of the day took on a reductive quality. By reducing complex and opaque mental processes to more simplistic and observable physiological ones, psychologists could test claims in a way that could be easily digested by scientists in other disciplines (Ellis & Stam, 2015). The story of psychology became one in which there is an empirical, objective, knowable reality that is the brain, and an ephemeral mind which was largely unknowable except through subjective means. Wilhelm Wundt, widely considered to be the founder of experimental psychology, characterised the discipline as one defined by this duality (Titchener, 1921). He claimed that both experimental (psycho-physical) methods and naturalistic observation were required to construct a complete science; the former could help uncover causal laws while the latter could be used to understand higher order mental operations. For Wundt, experimenta-tion was inappropriate for investigating cognitive and affective processes. He believed that these processes could only be interrogated using historical approaches to distil and describe cultural beliefs and collective practices. To this end, he sup-plemented his treatises on experimental psychology with extensive writings on the socio-historical context of psychological science (*Völkerpsychologie*) that championed the use of ethnographic data and phenomenological accounts of experience (Ellis & Stam, 2015).

The psychology that developed in the UK and USA in the 19th century adopted Wundt's empiricism and reconceived variability as individual differences that could be partitioned and explained using experimental and statistical methods. Ellis and Stam (2015) suggest that Wundt's socio-historical approach did not take root outside continental Europe because of a notable difference in cultural atti-tudes. In the German academic system, Wundt would have defended his science to an audience of philosophers to maintain the credibility of his work. In contrast, to obtain credentials or financial support, North American psychologists were more likely to defend their research to a mix of scholars and bureaucratic admin-istrators, who would translate the quality of their ideas into quantifiable metrics. Successful ideas were those whose results could be easily replicated, or where clear norms and behavioural parameters could be defined. British psychology blended these conventions with the new statistical methods developed to validate eugenic principles (see Chapter 2). The result was an epistemological shift, a psychological science that moved away from single-subject studies in favour of group-level com-parisons, where statistical regularities evidenced universal psychological laws.

In contrast to psychophysical psychology, without statistical backing or norma-tive frameworks, much of the psychological work on culture at the turn of the 20th century seemed lacking in rigour. Lonner (1974) characterises the cultural comparisons of the time as largely anecdotal, suggesting that the researchers undertaking such work were 'sabbatical opportunists who went on intellectual safaris about every seven years' (p. 2). One inference that can be drawn from this lack of systematicity is that researchers of the time viewed their methods as ade-quate for qualifying the behaviour of individuals perceived to be less sophisticated, rational, or complex than themselves. Detailed and thoughtful protocols were not necessary given the presumed inferiority of the participants. Observations were often intended to confirm eugenic ideas about population differences rather than generate or test new hypotheses about the behaviour and motivations of non-white, male, European people.

Figure 8.1 Ruth Benedict

Anthropologist Ruth Benedict (1887–1948) linked this problem both to the scientific imperialism of the English-speaking academic elite as well as cultural and scientific reactions to a century of evolutionary theory. She speculated that the need for humanity to perceive itself as singular and superior to other animal life had resulted in a peculiar cultural myopia amongst British and American scientists. This view was then exported and standardised as part of imperial projects, leading to an erroneous belief in the uniformity of human behaviour (Benedict, 1935). She argued that one of the philosophical justifications for studying 'primitive' peoples was an implicit awareness that under such a belief system, certain questions could no longer be introspected: 'The psychological consequences of this spread of white culture have been out of all proportion to the materialistic ...[giving that] culture a massive universality that we have long ceased to account for historically, and which we read off rather as necessary and inevitable' (p. 4). Although she espoused the value of cross-cultural approaches, Benedict recognised that in comparisons between Western cultures and 'small-scale' societies, researchers from the more dominant group experienced difficulties identifying their own traits and character-istics because they were considered settled fact. Benedict further linked this sense of white superiority and ethnocentrism to capitalist systems. She pointed to paral-lels between the inability of scientists to challenge Christian orthodoxy for long periods of Western history and the failure of her colleagues to think outside capital-ist incentive structures. In many ways, her writing on the transactional nature of academics presages the rise of the marketised education system (see Chapter 9).

Over the next century, psychology in the English-speaking Global North evolved into the study of abstract minds using formal models; if culture or context ever entered the picture, they were treated as external forces whose influence could be quantified and statistically evaluated. In this way, psychological research in the UK and USA gradually became WEIRDer and WEIRDer. Decades of global conflict and apartheid, however, made it untenable to ignore the ethnocentrism and cultural biases at the heart of much psychological research. When scientists in the 1960s started addressing the lack of representativeness in their scholarship they nonetheless adopted this individualistic framework that sought to treat culture as an independent factor (Ellis & Stam, 2015).

Formalisation of Cross-Cultural Studies

As a subdiscipline, cross-cultural psychology can trace its roots to post-war initiatives established to promote global collaboration, often with the goal of building a better world by better promoting human health, harmony and achievement. The research questions and methods that we might characterise as canonical to cross-cultural psychology were codified in the aftermath of World War II and against the backdrop of global civil rights movements. These initiatives were often applied in nature, addressing the mechanisms by which cultural, ethnic and racial factors might mediate, mask or otherwise modify assumed universals in human functioning (Adamopoulos & Lonner, 2001). They were supported by academic institutions as well as national and multinational governmental agencies and defence bodies. In 1966, for example, grant funding from UNESCO supported the founding of the International Union of Psychological Science, which in turn started the *International Journal of Psychology* as a flagship publication promoting cultural research. Training centres were established to facilitate multicultural exchanges in economic, military and academic domains. An early model for these collaborative hubs was the Centre for Cultural and Technical Interchange Between East and West established by the US Congress in 1960. To cite another illuminating example, a 1971 conference in Istanbul on the theme of 'mental tests' represented one of the first large-scale face-to-face meetings of cross-cultural researchers. Organised by Professor Hasan Tan (Middle East Technical University) and chaired by Lee Cronbach (who gave his name to Cronbach's alpha), the conference was supported by the NATO Advisory Panel on Human Factors. Significant effort was put into ensuring broad participation: funding from the Turkish Scientific and Technical Research Council as well as the US Social Science Research Council enabled scholars from 30 nations to attend the meeting.[2] Such meetings

---

[2]Sessions at the 1971 Istanbul conference centred on the theoretical and methodological basis of intelligence and aptitude tests. Discussants suggested that two-culture comparisons would be insufficient to understand the generalisability of these constructs. Despite this suggestion, the trend nonetheless dominated cross-cultural research in subsequent decades (Drenth, 2009).

codified the boundaries of the discipline through newsletters that eventually evolved into publications such as the *Journal of Cross-Cultural Psychology* (JCCP), and through directories of researchers that eventually transformed into professional bodies such as the International Association for Cross-Cultural Psychology (Adamopoulos & Lonner, 2001).

It is important to note that these early efforts at creating a research community prioritised diversity. There was a recognition that theoretical progress could not be made absent contributions from a broad community of researchers, participants, institutions and locales. Writing about the history and future of the field, Lonner (1974) identified that diversity was an issue of practical as well as ethical import, arguing that inclusive scholarship was a safeguard against predatory practices in which researchers take time, knowledge and resources from their participants without sharing anything of value with those communities. His description of these 'hit-and-run' researchers would find accord with contemporary accounts of 'helicopter science' wherein researchers descend on remote places for brief engagements that do not easily allow for reciprocal exchange or consensus-building with local communities. However, as cross-cultural approaches became dominant over time, the focus on representativeness and diversity was overshadowed by other priorities, such as establishing the legitimacy of the field as a 'hard' and therefore legitimate science. Bibliometric analysis from the last 50 years suggests that authors publishing in the *JCCP* tend to cite work in journals without a cultural focus, whereas the studies that most frequently cite *JCCP* authors tend to appear in applied journals, such as those focusing on counselling, psychometric validation, psychiatry, organisational psychology and business (Allik, 2012; Cretchley et al., 2010; Gabrenya & Glazer, 2022).

WHY DOES PSYCHOLOGY NEED TO THINK ABOUT WEIRDNESS?

As an acronym, WEIRD highlights several attributes of the university undergraduates who comprise the research samples in most published work. These attributes are arguably *atypical* when compared with the behaviour and beliefs of individuals from the majority of the world. Henrich and colleagues (2010) document how WEIRD participants are often outliers on a broad suite of tasks ranging from tests of IQ, through measures of spatial cognition, to decisions about cooperation and moral reasoning. As a collective, WEIRD people also serve as a template or norm against which all other groups are compared, whether for purposes of medical diagnosis, creation of standardised academic tests, or neuroimaging. Arguably, this tendency to extrapolate norms from a limited sample of human experience is responsible for some common myths in psychological science, such as the claim that human olfaction is very poor (see Focus Box 8.1).

Focus Box 8.1

Making Scents of Culture

You may have learned that human olfaction is the least developed of our sensory modalities. But where did this idea actually come from?

To address this question, we again turn to the work of Paul Broca. The idea that humans had minimal olfactory processing organs was driven in part by Broca's secularism: he sought to situate higher order cognitions in the brain rather than in a disembodied soul. This put Broca in direct conflict with the Catholic Church; his vocal and prolific endorsement of evolutionary theory further flaunted religious orthodoxy. To avoid closure of his lab, Broca made a concession to the Church by characterising human sensory abilities as unique and separate from those in the rest of the animal kingdom. Broca divided mammals into *osmatique* (organisms using smell as their principal sense) and *asnomatiques* (organisms without basic olfactory structures; McGann, 2017). Broca argued that human frontal lobes were enlarged because they housed free will. This came at the expense of the olfactory system and resulted in an olfactory bulb that was much smaller in humans than in other mammals. The subsequent characterisation of humans as 'non-smellers' became part of the psychological canon, so much so that by the 1920s, medical textbooks described human olfactory organs as practically vestigial (McGann, 2017)! Other researchers further reinforced the link between bestial drives and olfaction. In the 1890s, Fliess speculated that the nose was a sexual organ for women, and that menstrual pain could be eliminated by applying cocaine to 'genital spots' in the nose (Kern, 1974). Freud hypothesised that loss of olfaction in humans could thereby cause sexual repression and dysfunction, such as fetishes associated with taking excessive pleasure in smells (McGann, 2017).

The association between olfaction and carnality underpins racist assumptions made about human sensory capacities. In the early 1900s, English anthropologist, psychiatrist and neurologist W.H.R. Rivers (1864–1922) spearheaded a broad programme of cross-cultural research addressing the long-standing presumption that higher cognitive functions were associated with 'civil' society, whereas greater sensory acuity was associated with more 'primitive' peoples. Rivers was known for his methodological rigour. As director of the first two psychology laboratories in Britain he pioneered the use of double-blind studies to investigate the physiological and psychological effects of drugs (Slobodin, 1997). Individual differences in sensory capacities intrigued Rivers, and he published several works contrasting the sensory abilities of participants from England and the Toda people of Southern India. He presented participants with different solutions of camphor diluted with water and asked them to identify when they

(Continued)

could detect a change in the odour. Some participants might discriminate between samples not because of their sensitivity to different chemical concentrations, but because they had guessed the purpose of the experiment. In other words, some participants reasoned that the experimenters were expecting them to say that the solutions smelled differently. As a result, the Toda participants often made random guesses, which had the effect of making their judgements appear inaccurate. Rivers concluded that it would be difficult to 'attempt any exact comparison between the Todas and my English subjects [because] my own determinations of the thresholds, taken uncritically, would show the Toda to be inferior in the acuity of smell to the Englishmen, but this is certainly due in part, and perhaps altogether, to differences in the mode of making the judgments' (Rivers, 1905, p. 386). He further elaborated that 'any superiority of the savage in this as in other senses lies probably in his highly developed power of observation, in his practice in the discrimination and recognition of odours, and in his ability to assign a meaning to many of the smells he experiences' (p. 388). The preconceived notions that Rivers and his team held about the Toda participants were not confirmed; data painted a picture of the Toda people as individuals with reasoning skills and sensory abilities not unlike those of Englishmen.

Recent studies on olfaction in humans suggest that it is a very well-developed sensory capacity, with estimates suggesting that we can discriminate more than a trillion stimuli (Bushdid et al., 2014). Olfactory discrimination across species is correlated with the absolute volume of the olfactory bulb; humans have comparably greater volume than mice, hamsters, macaque monkeys and rats, suggesting that their sensory capacities are at least on par with these species (McGann, 2017). And intriguing neuropsychological work suggests that olfaction is possible absent this organ: healthy participants without olfactory bulbs can nonetheless detect, discriminate, identify and represent a normal range of odours (Weiss et al., 2020). Cross-cultural differences in olfaction do exist, though this seems to largely impact suprathreshold perception. In other words, culture may shape the ability to distinguish between odours and to correctly apply labels to these smells rather than influence the sensitivity with which individuals can detect odours in the environment (Oleszkiewicz et al., 2020).

That WEIRD individuals tend to look like statistical outliers holds true independent of the cultural contrasts under investigation. Whether comparing individualistic versus collectivistic groups or industrialised against 'traditional' or 'small-scale' societies, WEIRD individuals reliably appear outside average or typical responses. Highlighting the need for intracultural as well as cross-cultural approaches, Henrich and colleagues (2010) further document how the WEIRD participants drawn from predominantly affluent North American universities tend to be non-representative of the larger North American populace, including previous generations of their own families.

Why does this matter to psychological science? Below we identify some consequences of a reliance on WEIRD data and methods.

WEIRD Methods Are a Self-Fulfilling Prophecy

The WEIRD problem gained visibility in the late 2000s and early 2010s against the backdrop of larger conversations about replicability and generalisability in psychological science. Since then, numerous scholarly societies and journals have pledged to address issues of diversity and representativeness in their organisational practices (for a particularly conscientious example see Thomas, 2020). However, a decade of raising awareness has done little to change the structural dynamics at play. As of 2017, 11% of studies published in top-tier psychology journals did not specify any information about their participant samples, and estimates suggest that 80–95% of samples are still drawn from WEIRD samples (Apicella et al., 2020; Pollet & Saxton, 2019; Rad et al., 2018). Perhaps more striking is the observation that greater diversity and broadening of participant pools has done little to challenge the implicit assumption that WEIRD samples are the standard to which other groups should be compared. Buchanan and colleagues (2021) note that top-tier journals often require studies featuring non-white or non-Western samples to include white and/or Western comparison groups, whereas the inverse is rarely true. In the words of one minority ethnic researcher, studies comprising individuals from non-white, non-Western places are dismissed and rejected as 'some uninteresting data from a faraway country' (Bou Zeineddine et al., 2022, p. 333). This creates a recursive loop in which the substantial volume of knowledge generated about participants from WEIRD groups makes it easier to justify future studies with these participants, whereas the theoretical or methodological rationale for sampling participants from non-white or non-Western samples requires comparably greater justification.

The observations made of WEIRD participants also apply to the researchers conducting these studies. Resources and visibility of research are largely concentrated in North American and UK centres. In his initial survey, Arnett (2008) found proportionally more psychology citations orginate from institutions in the USA (70%) than in other sciences like chemistry (37%). This trend remains even in publications like the *Journal of Cross-Cultural Psychology*, where estimates suggest approximately 83% of studies originate from predominantly English-speaking nations like the USA, Canada, England, Australia and New Zealand (Allik, 2012). According to some estimates, 90% of publishing editors in psychology journals are white—a trend that typically extends to the scholars recruited to review papers as well as to grant review panels that facilitate the research in the first place (Buchanan et al., 2021). As a result, Black scholars in the USA receive funding at approximately half the rate of white scholars, and researchers of colour are much more likely to publish in less impactful 'specialty' or regional journals, which further reduces the visibility and citation rate of their work, especially amongst author networks anchored by white researchers (Bou Zeineddine et al., 2022; Buchanan et al., 2021). Collectively, these practices maintain the status quo of academic pipelines like grant attainment, publishing and graduate student recruitment, making it more difficult for researchers with divergent viewpoints and experiences to break into the discipline (see Chapter 9).

WEIRD Science Invalidates the Experience and Knowledge of Minoritised Groups

Overreliance on a narrow subset of participants (or indeed, on the narrow subset of predominantly white researchers in the Global North who study them) constrains the generation and development of new theories by canonising some ideas and approaches at the expense of others. This goes beyond questions of generalisability— it speaks to the beliefs we have as a scientific community about what constitutes 'good' evidence, which methods of inquiry are valid and what kinds of inferences can be drawn from the process of observing and testing natural phenomena.

These beliefs may be explicitly expressed, but they may also operate at a level of implicit awareness. In *Pedagogy of the Oppressed* (1970), Brazilian educator and philosopher Paulo Freire suggests that the sciences try to avoid this problem by conceptualising research as an objective, technical activity. However, conceiving science as a neutral enterprise is itself a value judgment, and couching it in these terms only serves to make this ideology invisible and therefore unassailable. The tendency to universalise white, WEIRD experiences has been described as a kind of epistemic violence—a systematic exclusion of racialised and minoritised others from the knowledge production process that often pathologises or brands as deviant their experiences (Readsura Decolonial Editorial Collective, 2022; see also Chapter 4).

Canham et al. (2021) characterise universities in the English-speaking Global North as 'structures of power that continuously reproduce themselves by claiming the sole right to define and to determine the nature of truth and what can be taught' (p. 197). They provide the following example:

> when I have asked colleagues to consider what an African perspective is
> and what it would mean for their area of teaching, I have been told that

there are no African perspectives on the brain for example. 'Because the brain is the brain is the brain!' The implication is a universalising discourse that sees cognition as one dimensional and Western. (p. 199)

This epistemic violence goes beyond the contents of knowledge and also characterises beliefs about how academia works. Minoritised scholars are placed in an impossible position when hired to represent 'diverse' views. Because of their identity alone they are seen as 'provocateurs' who intend to challenge the status quo; espousing non-canonical views about research or the academy often then results in conflict, bad feelings and dismissal. This essentially levies an emotional tax on minoritised scholars that is not imposed on their non-minoritised colleagues and which creates an unsustainable burden on those who remain in the system.

WEIRD Science Entrenches Colonial Power Structures

Broesch and colleagues (2020), in a critique of the WEIRD framework, note that highlighting what makes this particular group of participants atypical inadvertently reinforces a 'West versus the rest' mentality. This runs the risk of reproducing the same extractive, colonial practices that lead to the marginalisation of minoritised groups in the first place.

Readers who engage with the WEIRD literature will note the importance of evolutionary theory to this domain of scholarship. In this perspective, developing and testing questions about kinship, economic exchange and cooperation is best facilitated by comparing Western, industrialised societies with those so-called 'traditional' or 'small-scale' societies that occupy areas that are ecologically similar to those inhabited by early modern humans. This results in several potential complications.

The first complication is ethical. Most non-WEIRD samples recruited to test such theories are drawn from Indigenous communities, often from low- and middle-income countries in the Global South (Broesch et al., 2020). The practices and social organisation of such communities are often romanticised as existing outside of contemporary life; time-capsules of what life may have been like before the advent of agriculture and widespread trade. However, in practice these groups have often been subject to significant pressures in the form of colonialism and globalisation. They may be ecologically, socially, economically or politically marginalised. The power differential between researchers and those they research is heightened when we consider that the majority of cross-cultural research is implemented in English or other colonial languages, and often in collaboration with institutions (such as universities, governments or aid organisations) with their own colonial, sexist or racist histories and agendas (Broesch et al., 2020).

The second complication is theoretical. In assuming an idealised reality for non-WEIRD populations, researchers may fail to adequately test the questions they purport to address. We cannot in good conscience say that a group of nomadic foragers possess the same motivations and behavioural repertoires as hunter–gatherer communities thousands of years ago. To say that these groups have identical psychologies is to ignore the many years of cultural and environmental changes that likely made certain behaviours relevant in the past irrelevant now and vice versa (Broesch et al., 2020). A good example of this comes from studies of economic reasoning, where small-scale societies are often presumed to represent the psychologies that would have been present at the dawn of reciprocal exchange (see Chapter 3 for additional critique of this framing). If people from these communities share in ways that are collaborative, it might be tempting to infer that this supports evolutionary claims about the origins of reciprocity. However, it might also be the case that researchers have inadvertently picked up on more contemporary beliefs or constraints that drive the same behaviour. Thus, without deep knowledge of communities, the conclusions researchers draw may highlight group differences that are nonetheless unattributable to the factors that have been hypothesised as relevant.

Structural issues also impact on teaching and knowledge exchange activities. Canham et al. (2021) argue that the historical perspective in the Global North has been one in which colonies possess the raw material that is data (material resources, but also culture) and Euro-Americans possess science, the means of making sense of that data. Much of that sense-making happens in educational contexts. Universities in the English-speaking Global North developed and proliferated in a system that claimed the sole right to determine what constitutes truth and appropriate ways of communicating those truths about nature. Course materials, pedagogical styles and community outreach projects often reproduce these power structures. The result is a canonised way of knowing that is not value-neutral and that often makes transhistorical, universalistic claims about what constitutes good science practice. Consequently, Canham and colleagues describe the decolonial project as one that calls for 'epistemic disobedience' to dismantle extractive relationships so that minoritised individuals are seen as the producers rather than the objects of knowledge (2021, p. 195).

WEIRD Science Generates Extractive Economies of Knowledge

Finally, the findings and knowledge generated by WEIRD science are not the only exports of this system. Its structures, value systems and underlying assumptions are also communicated to participants and to the scientific and social community at large. This can create a conflict between WEIRD science and local ways of knowing. Ideas and practices from the WEIRD canon that are initially replicated and accepted may eventually be rejected when they do not fit local contexts. This often leads to problem-oriented research that focuses on local issues or in a blending of Indigenous and WEIRD approaches, both of which tend to be relegated to niche, specialty publications.

Extraction may also characterise the activities that WEIRD scholars undertake to disseminate their work. Although well-intentioned, outreach and impact activities may take on a paternalistic tone when they purport to teach participants about themselves or their context. This is a *deficit model*, one in which it is presumed that the participants from whom the knowledge is drawn do not themselves possess this knowing (see also Chapter 10). It assumes that some information, skill or ability is lacking and that this can be corrected by sharing the information that has been generated by research activities. In contrast, community-centred approaches are those in which participants help to define the parameters of the research question, which allows for a more authentic exchange of knowledge and experience.

WHAT NEXT?

Calls to address the lack of representation in psychological science have been with the discipline since its inception. The WEIRD acronym acts as shorthand for identifying the kinds of people who may be over-represented in research and what attributes might make them atypical compared to the majority of people in the world. This way of dichotomising psychology into WEIRD and non-WEIRD camps invites a cross-cultural approach, one in which culture and context are treated as explanatory factors rather than aspects of experience that are core to personhood. This chapter has documented the consequences of WEIRD science, and how cross-cultural approaches have sometimes inadvertently entrenched WEIRD perspectives. The question we now pose is how to move forward.

Recognising the history of WEIRD science and identifying its pitfalls is not a palliative for what ails contemporary psychology. In some ways, the WEIRD acronym is a red herring, identifying attributes that we might infer are responsible for the atypical behaviours noted in WEIRD groups (Downey, 2010). However, is being Western, educated, industrialised, rich and democratic really what makes individuals from these groups so atypical? Cultural anthropologists often point to physical characteristics, such as stature (height and weight), activity level (caloric consumption and expenditure) and gender displays as important hallmarks of cultural differences (Downey, 2010). Rather than assuming cultural differences stem from these WEIRD attributes, researchers might consider factors that are more relevant to their research questions when posing group contrasts (Broesch et al., 2020). For example, wealth undoubtedly changes the ways in which individuals act in their environs, but a contrast between 'rich' and 'poor' potentially simplifies and obscures elements of those experiences that hold the most explanatory power, such as relative social mobility, class, materialism or consumerism (Downey, 2010). Furthermore, just because we treat race, culture and ethnicity as classifiers, that does not mean the classifier itself is meaningful to those groups of people. Engaging in community-centred approaches can ensure that the factors under investigation are relevant to researchers and the participants themselves.

Adopting a cross-cultural approach has become the principal method by which researchers attempt to 'de-WEIRD' their scholarship by sampling from outside the pool of university undergraduates. Such cross-cultural frameworks often tend to treat cultural attributes as fixed and monolithic. This may be true for some ways of grouping people, but not others. Considering the relative homogeneity and heterogeneity of groups is important—how fixed versus fluid are the social categories we think might underpin behaviour? In his formalisation of the individualism–collectivism model of culture, Triandis (1989) suggested that such labels may only capture 40% of a given population! Scholars using binary cross-cultural comparisons to address the limits of WEIRD science should proceed with caution, as such dichotomies may risk creating false homogeneity. For example, Western populations can live in small-scale settings. The UK is full of numerous villages with small populations, where people tend to eat, live and work locally, and where true anonymity is difficult to find. To say these people who live in small villages in Scotland and those who live in central London are all 'Western' in the same way might obscure important nuances in how these people experience the world. For some kinds of questions, cross-cultural approaches may therefore be less informative than intra-cultural comparison.

De-WEIRDing psychology makes for a more representative science, but does not necessarily solve some of the epistemological tensions identified in this chapter. It does not resolve the debate between camps that see culture as extraneous to cognition—an independent variable that can be used to explain 'noise' in behaviour—and camps that see culture as integral to and inseparable from human experience. To some extent this is a debate about whether examining culture is a means by which we can better understand human behaviour, or the behaviour in and of itself. This is a philosophical distinction with important ethical and pragmatic consequences. These two camps take different approaches to how research should be conducted and the extent to which the research questions and tools themselves can be developed apart from a given cultural context. Without considering these issues, researchers and their backing institutions run the risk of perpetuating the problems they seek to redress by adopting a method that is incompatible with their stated goals.

With all this in mind, below are some recommendations for addressing the problems of WEIRD science. Many of the suggestions below are drawn from excellent guidance by Raman (2023) and Broesch and colleagues (2020):

1   Know your community. Do the hard work of understanding the places you will work and the people with whom you hope to collaborate. Do not expect others to educate you about their communities, and do not expect to passively receive such knowledge.
2   Consider your approach. Not all questions lend themselves to cross-cultural approaches, but all questions are embedded in a particular cultural context. Researchers, teachers and participants bring their own values, assumptions and beliefs to the classroom or to an experiment. Consider not just how the research is valuable to you, but how the project might be useful for the community.
3   Acknowledge multiple kinds of expertise, including those that traditionally do not fall into the realm of what we value as 'objective' scientific method. Be willing to learn from others and take their knowledge seriously, even if it is non-traditional in form.
4   Recognise Indigenous autonomy and sovereignty and do not work where you are not welcome, or where you have not done the work to build relationships and trust with communities.
5   Rethink how impact and knowledge dissemination work within academia as well as the communities with whom we work to avoid extractive models of scholarship. Consider participatory models of collaboration that allow participants/communities to feed into the process of hypothesis generation, data analysis, data interpretation and peer review.
6   When engaging in field work, hire local individuals and provide supportive training. Compensate all team members appropriately, including non-academics and undergraduate research assistants.
7   Practise 'citational justice' and include *all* members of your research team who contribute to a project. This includes non-academics who support field work by acting as community contacts, assisting with translations and aiding with participant recruitment or procurement of resources (Raman, 2023).
8   Where relevant, return things that have been taken from the community. This could include biological samples, artefacts, photographs and documents. Where resources may need to be altered or destroyed (as in the example of biological samples), ask community representatives for their perspective on the most respectful way of handling these tasks.

9 Cultivate cultural competency as part of conversations surrounding research and teaching ethics. Consideration of local values and customs should inform not just research practices, but also the discrete outputs of a research project, be they artefacts, papers or other metrics. Eugenia Zuroski (2020) provides an excellent exercise to help scholars position themselves (and think about the importance of that positionality) here: https://maifeminism.com/where-do-you-know-from-an-exercise-in-placing-ourselves-together-in-the-classroom/.

10 Adopt community-centred and transdisciplinary models of scholarship that emphasise co-creation of knowledge; researchers and teachers are not entitled to co-opt the experiences of the people with whom they work. Avoid models of scholarship that treat knowledge and experience as transactional, products to be consumed rather than collaboratively created.

The aim of this chapter has been to tell a story about the ethnocentric biases inherent to psychology as it is practised in the English-speaking Global North. It tells a story about how these biases emerged over the history of the discipline, in many regards mirroring and reinforcing traditional power structures. Neither the dominance of cross-cultural approaches in mainstream psychology, nor the recent emphasis on overturning WEIRD science are, on their own, enough to move psychology past its colonial roots. Cultural psychology and cross-cultural psychology may both offer opportunities to diversify psychological scholarship, but only if we also consider the larger context in which this science operates. Greater inclusivity cannot be achieved by replicating the same models of capitalist research focused on white individuals in the English-speaking Global North that has historically dominated the field. Our intention in shining a light on this aspect of the psychological canon is not to discourage researchers and teachers from embarking on cultural work, but rather to emphasise the need for conscientiousness. Constructive and informed exchange between scholars and communities offers opportunities to create a new, collaborative canon.

FURTHER READING

Broesch, T., et al. (2020). Navigating cross-cultural research: Methodological and ethical considerations. *Proceedings of the Royal Society B: Biological Sciences,* *287*(1935), 20201245. https://doi.org/10.1098/rspb.2020.1245 [journal article]

This paper, with 20 authors, provides a critical appraisal of where psychology stands after a decade of WEIRD science; it also shares insightful guidance on conducting ethical cross-cultural research.

Raman, S. (2023). What it means to practise values-based research. *Nature* [Online ahead of print]. https://doi.org/10.1038/d41586-023-01878-1 [journal article]

This interview with biologist Spoorthy Raman describes how anticolonial and feminist science can be put into practice for researchers who do not work with human participants.

Downey, G. (2010). We agree it's WEIRD, but is it WEIRD enough? neuroanthropology.net. https://neuroanthropology.net/2010/07/10/we-agree-its-weird-but-is-it-weird-enough/ [web page]

An analysis of post-WEIRD psychology written from the perspective of a cultural anthropologist.

9

#NOTALLUNIVERSITIES

HOW HIGHER EDUCATION PERPETUATES THE INEQUITIES IT CLAIMS TO ELIMINATE

Universities are central to much of what we have written about in this book. They provide venues for academic research and the preparation of academic papers, and are the last formal education establishments attended by many. Beyond their importance to scholarship, they are also perceived as hotbeds of liberal values and anti-establishment protest. As examples of their canonisation in this regard, we often speak of their involvement in the popular American protest against the Vietnam war, the French riots of May 1968 and as the battleground for the early 21st century obsession with 'cancel culture'. With this in mind, it is no surprise that modern universities of the Global North have embraced 'on-brand' progressive values of diversity and inclusion. If they hadn't, this book would simply not have been commissioned. But how consistent are these seemingly contemporary values with the principles that have underpinned university life through the ages? Here, we seek to understand what a university does when it embraces efforts aimed at promoting diversity and inclusion.

Deviating from the approach we have taken in previous chapters focusing on disciplinary issues within psychology and neuroscience, in this chapter we broaden our scope to academia in general. Where relevant, we do draw on examples from our field, so as to situate what we discuss in a familiar setting. Nonetheless, this chapter could likely appear in a text critically examining the canon in *any* field. Although our focus as psychologists is on the study of mind and behaviour, we will demonstrate that this does not give our own thoughts and behaviours immunity from the pressures of contemporary study and work in higher education.

INSTITUTIONS FOR THE TRANSMISSION OF 'USEFUL KNOWLEDGE'

Two texts that would shape Western thought on higher education were written in the 1800s. Prussian Philosopher Wilhelm von Humboldt wrote of universities as institutions based on three principles: 'unity of research and teaching, freedom of teaching, and academic self-governance' (Boulton & Lucas, 2011, p. 2506). Some years later, English theologian John Henry Newman put forward his philosophy of university education as primarily a 'place of teaching universal knowledge' rather than 'scientific and philosophical discovery' (Newman, 1852, p. ix). Whilst the two disagreed on the place of research, they were united on the importance of students, and of teaching them. Regardless of their views on whether knowledge was generated at university, both agreed that they should be places at which it was passed on.

Two hundred years later, what do students at institutions that have developed in the shadow of these philosophies believe to be the purpose of their university educations? In a study conducted across six European countries, 295 students identified three key purposes: attaining employment, achieving personal growth and improving society (Brooks et al., 2021). It seems significant to us that these students have identified that their learning has value to them, and that this value is not intrinsic but extrinsic—to help with their goals for work and earnings, their development as people and their capacity to contribute to society. Whilst it would be easy to state here that this is emblematic of a shift away from the liberal educational values, it is entirely rational for students to hope their education will end up being useful. This rationality was evident in the study sample too, with those enrolled at university in nations with the greatest fees (such as the UK) viewing the effects on their employment chances as most important.

Modern day universities, then, are institutions that educate students who want 'useful knowledge' (Burns, 1986). What comprises useful knowledge depends on who you ask, but in the broadest possible terms, it is knowledge that provides benefit to those who have it, and the situations they find themselves in. In this way, knowledge has been commodified—governments can speak of the knowledge-based economy and we understand that they are referring to a financial system in which industrial production has given way to intellectual production as the primary driver of economic growth. As major distributors of knowledge, universities are increasingly seeing themselves as having a responsibility to distribute this commodity in a manner consistent with their values. This responsibility brings with it some tensions though, especially as values like equality, diversity and inclusion were thought about very differently when Humboldt and Newman were laying the groundwork for the structures that underpin the modern university.

THE POWER TO RECEIVE KNOWLEDGE

Universities operate on principles that are notionally 'meritocratic'. When it comes to teaching, we are told that the smartest, hardest working students demonstrate their aptitude for learning in their school-leaving qualifications and gain entrance to the most prestigious universities. Once at university, the most capable students gain the best grades, and leave with the best degree classifications.

Secondary School Attainment

This meritocratic admissions process is situated in, and deeply affected by, societal inequality. Whilst the objective standards of university entry sound fair—e.g. the entry requirements for a subject at Oxford University might be one A* and two As at A-level (or equivalent), and the same fees are charged to UK students as at any other institution—scratch beneath the surface and this fairness breaks down. Whilst UK universities do have the same set tuition fees for UK students, UK secondary or high schools do not. Broadly speaking, state secondary education is tax-payer funded and free at the point of access for all, whilst private secondary education is funded through fees paid by parents of students. In 2021/2 the average annual spend on a single pupil within the state education system was just over £7000, compared to average annual fees (minus bursaries) of just under £14,000 in the UK private education system (Sibieta, 2021). It would be an inefficient school indeed that could not translate at least some of the near-doubled potential for expenditure per pupil into better academic outcomes, and this is borne out in the 58% of top A* grades at A level awarded at private schools in 2022 compared to only 38% at state schools (Mason, 2022). Those with the means and inclination to buy private secondary education open doors for their children to university, and beyond.

University Attainment

Once at university, societal inequity continues to influence attainment. In the absence of recent data comparing state and privately educated students, we present the effects of socioeconomic status. When indexed according to current and past levels of participation in higher education, students from areas with the greatest participation achieved first or upper second class degrees at a rate of 89%, compared to 81% for those from areas with the lowest participation (2020/1 data from English universities; Bolton & Lewis, 2023). (It should be stated that the vagaries of socioeconomic indexes likely mask far greater attainment gaps according to more specific criteria. For example, Black students graduate with the top degree classifications at a rate of 69% compared to 87% for their white peers.) These differences carry over into future wealth, with increasing childhood socioeconomic status associated with increasing graduate income at age 30 (Britton et al., 2021). Whilst a university education adds to income across the board, it does so unevenly. It adds 6% and 27% to state-educated men's and women's earnings respectively, and 29% and 36% to privately educated men's and women's earnings.

As to *why* these differences should be present, Britton and colleagues speculate that 'elite social networks' (p. 55) explain the uplift to income that privately educated men get as a result of their degrees. These elite social networks are started at school, and consolidated through closed university societies, balls and exclusive events for the 'right' sorts of people at the 'right' sorts of university. They contribute to a higher education system that, despite its best intentions, fails to level societal inequities, and actually amplifies them. That this amplification occurs within a supposedly egalitarian university system legitimises class and gender power differentials as borne of merit, masking the 'old boys' network' underpinning it. Evidently all students receive useful knowledge, but the most privileged students find more useful ways to use it.

THE POWER TO CREATE AND PUBLISH KNOWLEDGE
Grants

When it comes to those employed by universities to generate and teach useful knowledge, we are told similar stories about meritocratic systems that underpin opportunities within higher education, typically from the perspective of how research is evaluated. Grant applications are assessed by panels of scientists so that research funding can be allocated to the best proposals. Scientific papers are reviewed by teams of researchers as part of a peer-review process, to see whether or not they should be published in the most esteemed journals. This culminates in researchers building track-records of success that earn them promotion and recognition by academic societies and award panels.

The assumption of quality leading to success forms the foundation for faith in the system. But how much should we trust that, for example, the 'best' grant applications are awarded the highest scores, and therefore most likely to be funded? Jerrim and de Vries (2023) analysed the peer-review consistency of over 6000 grant proposals submitted to the Economic and Social Research Council (ESRC), a UK funding body with a remit that includes psychology research. They found negligible correlations (topping out at 0.2) between pairs of reviewers' scores. They then examined the distributions of scores assigned by two different sorts of reviewer—those who were *nominated* and those who were *independent*. Nominated reviewers are selected by the authors of grant applications. Independent reviewers are not selected by the authors, but assigned as part of the review process. The independence or lack thereof of the two types of reviewer is evident in the scores they gave grants. Nominated reviewers gave top ratings 59% of the time, whilst independent reviewers did so only 17% of the time. If we consider these two findings together, in such a noisy system where there is little agreement on what constitutes quality, the reward for being part of a network of researchers who may think favourably of each others' work translates into a greater likelihood of having your research funded. Put another way, proposals from researchers without large lab-group cohorts to suggest as reviewers, or who were not afforded the opportunity to build networks at national and international conferences, will be at a disadvantage. Just as the networks that well-connected students build at university benefit them later in life, the same appears to be true for scientists with large and well-respected family trees (see Chapter 1).

Publications and Citations

These potential biases are reproduced more or less explicitly in the publication process. On the more explicit side is the journal *Proceedings of the National Academy of Sciences* (*PNAS*), a highly esteemed multidisciplinary outlet that published papers from a range of sciences including psychology and neuroscience. *PNAS* offers two routes to publication, 'direct' or 'contributed' submissions. Both routes require the paper to undergo peer review, where an editor solicits evaluations of the paper from reviewers, on the basis of which they make the decision to publish or reject the work. The difference lies in the independence of the reviewers. Direct submission reviewers are determined by the editor. Contributed submission reviewers, on the other hand, are determined, with some editorial oversight, by the authors themselves. Whilst there are additional procedures designed to increase confidence in contributed submission review (reviewers are evaluated for appropriateness, the papers may also be sent to additional independent reviewers), it remains the case that contributed submissions gain the benefit of bypassing fully independent review, presumably affording the same advantages as those outlined for grant review (with agreement from historic data showing these papers to be less well cited overall than direct submissions; Davis, 2016). And who is allowed to use the contributed submission route? Members of the National Academy of Sciences, a prestigious learned society of scientists whose new members are elected by majority vote participated in by existing members. Once again, it is not hard to see how academic reputation, lineage and networks help those with privilege to compound their advantage—no accident when it comes to learned societies, as we discuss later.

It is easy to point the finger at one journal's practices and argue that its failings characterise the entire industry. But what truth is there to this given that the majority of journals do not offer authors the opportunity to pick their reviewers? Smith and colleagues (2023) ran a meta-analysis—a statistical analysis by which the results of multiple studies are combined to answer a research question—to interrogate whether peer-review outcomes differ according to author demographics. Across more than 300,000 papers, submitted to over 600 journals in the biological sciences, they found that authors with assumed female gender had a greater likelihood of rejection at some stages of the peer-review process than those with assumed male gender. They found similar disadvantages for authors based in Asia compared to those based in Europe, North America and Oceania, and authors based in nations whose primary language is not English. The reasons for these disparities may differ from those characterising the reviewer bias in *PNAS*, but they build a picture of publishing practices that are hostile to those who do not represent the historic status quo.

And so, biases compound at every stage. Even the practice of citing well-known papers in the field, to situate one's own work within the canon, pushes citations to established individuals and ideas. Not only does this have consequences for who gets cited, but it consolidates intellectual power to a small number of researchers. These academic power-brokers have been identified as key players in 'invisible colleges' (Quiñones-Vidal et al., 2004, p. 443), with evidence from articles published in the *Journal of Personality and Social Psychology* that they build publication networks in the form of clusters of psychologists who work with them and not their competitors.

The consolidation of intellectual power through the practices of citing established individuals and ideas, and the formation of 'invisible colleges', further compound the advantage of those with established networks, and therefore status, in the field. This feedback loop perpetuates the existing power structures within academia, leaving little room for new voices and ideas.

Learned Societies

Learned societies, with their own governance structures, membership criteria and funding, are a formalised manifestation of the 'invisible college'. Membership acts as a marker of prestige, signalling the member's credentials in ways that are readily accepted by promotion committees, with consequent financial advantage. That said, they also come with baggage like the potential for cronyism—the perpetuation of the old boys' club through procedures that consider diversity as secondary to the pursuit of excellence. This baggage and its consequence for diverse representation is increasingly considered to be an unfortunate throwback of how learned societies originated (Roscoe, 2022), but it would be naïve to consider that it has always been considered this way. In an article titled 'Positive Eugenics', Fisher wrote of the importance of professional bodies being able to select their own members 'to exclude all inferior types, who would lower both the standard of living and the level of professional status' (Fisher, 1917, p. 207). Whilst this may have been important to differentiate physicians from 'quacks' (p. 209), the 'positive' aspect of the eugenic philosophy that the professional society satisfied for Fisher came in the form of 'advantageous prospects [offered] to the sons of its members' so as to mitigate against 'the large proportion of "new blood" which enters the professions in every generation, [which is] inferior to the professional families of longstanding' (p. 210). The leg-up that an exclusive society offers then, is *meant to* advantage the family and associates of its members.

Networks of scientists can grease the wheels for each other to navigate securing grants, publishing and gaining professional advantage, thereby denying those opportunities to those on the outside. Given their obsession with middle-class professionals, is it any wonder then that universities were once heralded by eugenicists as the perfect testing grounds for positive eugenics? (Indeed, Galton's fictional eugenic Utopia Kantsaywhere [1910] was a settlement administered by a university.) It is certainly not the case that modern day university decision-making is wholly determined according to these cronyistic, nepotistic principles, but it is true that the structures that facilitated these biases have not been dismantled but merely reoriented, with some attempts made to correct the problems that they lead to. Indeed, many view an inherent incompatibility within the idea of *decolonising* higher education. These are colonial organisations, and it would be foolish to think that we could remove the power and incentive structures and be left with anything we would recognise as a university.

THE SHAPERS OF USEFUL KNOWLEDGE

If universities are still inherently colonial organisations, who are the imperial powers they serve? Within the modern higher education market, power inevitably flows through the money that keeps universities operational. According to the Higher Education Statistics Agency (HESA, 2023b), in 2021 UK universities received over half of their income from student fees, with the remainder divided primarily between government funding and funding from research grants.

Given the financial power that students collectively have, it is no surprise that universities should increasingly align their provision to that requested by students. As we have already seen, students paying fees desire to benefit financially from their investment in their education. In order to do so, they must be able to contribute to organisations that value their 'graduate attributes',[1] such as entrepreneurism, being effective leaders and team-workers. And commercial organisations *do* view these graduates as valuable. In 2000, the European Union set out its Lisbon Strategy—a ten-year economic plan that positioned universities as key drivers of financial growth through, amongst other things, the development of a skilled workforce (European Commission, 2006). But, graduate attributes do not form the core learning within degree subjects such as psychology (even if we may learn about them in organisational psychology modules). We therefore run the risk of de-prioritising the primary purpose of any programme of degree study, to learn how to think in that domain and elevating the secondary qualities that result from deep engagement in the subject (Boulton & Lucas, 2011). At the very least, we create a schism between what many university lecturers believe they should be training their students in, and what many fee-paying students believe they should be trained in.

Also part of the Lisbon Strategy was harnessing university-generated knowledge innovation. Whilst obvious examples include industrial partnerships and spun-out businesses, a more insidious way in which this agenda has affected all research, even psychological research that we don't typically think of as lending itself to commercial or industrial exploitation, is in the UK's 'impact agenda'. UK researchers are required by government funding agencies, in every grant application they submit, to propose how they will achieve economic, social and cultural impact with their research. This consideration has embedded itself into the research environment to such an extent that it has also been added to the Research Excellence Framework (REF)—a subject-specific evaluation of each university's research output that helps determine how much government funding each university receives. Whilst defenders of the impact agenda argue that it ensures that research is relevant, and more immediately beneficial to the tax-payers funding it, critics argue that it commodifies research according to current societal values, discouraging research with less obvious immediate impact, despite its potential long-term value (Boulton & Lucas, 2011). In any case, the successful implementation of the impact

---

[1]Graduate attributes represent the knowledge, skills and abilities that UK universities are increasingly emphasising as being trained in their graduates over the course of their degree programmes.

agenda on university research demonstrates that the academic self-governance Humboldt envisioned has been diluted somewhat.[2] Whilst academics have ideas of what constitutes *important* research, businesses, governments and funding bodies have their own on what constitutes *useful* and *fundable* research.

DIVERSIFYING PARTICIPATION IN AN INEQUITABLE SYSTEM

As higher education becomes increasingly commodified, universities inevitably face the pressure of maintaining financial stability amidst the turbulence of market forces. Under such conditions the priority shifts to preserving assets whilst reducing liabilities, thus ensuring future security. Students and donors contribute to universities' assets in the form of tuition fees, gifts and legacies, while academic staff add to liabilities through salaries, pensions and benefits—although this is offset by the grant income they secure. Consequently, there has been a growing trend in the UK to increase student numbers, particularly targeting international students who pay markedly higher tuition fees than domestic students, while simultaneously curbing the costs associated with teaching them (Collini, 2017). This incentive to minimise liabilities has led to increased job insecurity for staff on short-term contracts, a reliance on casualised labour to fill teaching gaps and the adoption of a 'do what you love' mantra that justifies the erosion of working conditions based on the idea that no other job offers the intellectual freedom once associated with a career in academia (before the sector became so commodified; Tokumitsu, 2014).

Though many academics quite rightly decry changes to the university labour market, as university workers ourselves we are no strangers to the culture of casualised work. Over a decade before much of the reform to UK higher education began in the 1980s, British-Polish sociologist Stanislav Andreski lamented a consequence of encouraging research-led teaching as offering an 'opportunity to recruit cheap (and in a way forced) labour for the captains of the research industry' (1973, p. 187). Whilst paid internship schemes are increasingly supported by universities, unpaid internships still offer an alternative route to gaining laboratory experience and the resultant increased likelihood of finding a career in science, exclusively for those with financial security in the early stages of their career.

---

[2]And this is before we consider requirements such as the need to comply with the UK government's *Prevent Agenda* (reporting students who oppose fundamental 'British values'), and monitoring attendance at lectures of students on certain overseas visas. These requirements have been described as Islamophobic, and potentially discriminatory by the University and College Union (2013, 2021).

After all, what harm is there in making progress on research whilst offering someone who is on campus over the summer an opportunity to gain valuable research experience? The harm is done to those who have had to leave campus because they need to work a summer job or care for their dependants, whose academic CVs suffer in comparison. If academics do not have the integrity to consistently interrogate the practices they encourage in their own laboratories in the same way they interrogate the working conditions imposed on them by university management, what hope is there of achieving the goals of equality, diversity and inclusion that most would say they support?

This is the crux of the problem with universities' efforts to encourage equality, diversity and inclusion. Whether they invest in widening access schemes to increase admissions of students from non-traditional backgrounds, or promote staff from ethnically minoritised and under-represented groups to senior academic and administrative positions, the university remains a marketised and extractive seat of power that is biased towards serving those with privilege. Increasing the diversity of those participating in inequitable systems does not dismantle the inequity—it merely gives it the veneer of meritocratic fairness that allows the inequity to persist, and leads more people on the outside into thinking that they just weren't good enough to succeed.

PSYCHOLOGICAL TOOLS FOR THE MOLLIFICATION OF THE MASSES

Although psychology research may appear tangential to many broader issues within higher education, certain psychological concepts and interventions have gained prominence as tools for managing the workforce. Grit, resilience, mindfulness and implicit bias training have been championed by higher education managers as ways of dealing with overwhelming workloads, burnout and structural racism.

The concepts of grit and resilience are sometimes used interchangeably, but are personality constructs with distinct psychological literatures. Grit is defined as an individual's combination of passion and perseverance towards long-term goals (Hochanadel & Finamore, 2015). Resilience was originally investigated in the context of child development, and is the individual's ability to adapt and bounce back from setbacks, adversity and stress (Luthar et al., 2000). Development of both has been associated with having a 'growth mindset'—the belief that one's abilities and intelligence can be developed and improved through effort and perseverance. Their growing prominence as workplace interventions is supported by a range of studies, many involving trainee medics, which suggest they may protect against burnout (e.g. Galaiya et al., 2020). What is interesting from our perspective is that they often form an educational institution's response to increasing rates of workplace stress, mental ill-health and burnout in staff and students.

Mindfulness training refers to a range of interventions that encourage present-moment awareness and non-judgemental attention to one's thoughts and feelings (Dawson et al., 2020). These practices may be derivative of meditation, yoga or controlled breathing, and are also offered to staff and students in response to growing concerns about mental health. Like grit and resilience, mindfulness centres the discussion on an individual's capacity to cope with their circumstances. The problem with these constructs and interventions is that they avoid addressing the systemic and cultural causes of stress, and place the blame on the individual (Chamorro-Premuzic & Lusk, 2017; Mehta, 2015). The idea that managers should oversee unmanageable and even toxic workplace cultures by telling people who cannot cope that it is *their* responsibility to be more resilient and take more mindful care of themselves is an astounding sleight of hand—one that is made possible by the heavy demand for jobs in the sector, and competitive admission to the most sought after institutions.

Another institutional response widely adopted since the 2020 murder of George Floyd and subsequent #blacklivesmatter protests is the unconscious bias awareness intervention. This intervention derives from the implicit association test, often referred to by its initialism, the IAT. The IAT measures the unconscious biases that people hold based on how they associate positive and negative attributes with people varying along a range of demographic characteristics (e.g. race and gender; see https://implicit.harvard.edu/implicit/takeatest.html for a range of online IATs; Banaji & Greenwald, 2013). Whilst there is good evidence that IATs, and unconscious bias awareness interventions, reveal the biases that people hold, there is little evidence to suggest that mere awareness of these biases does anything to remedy them (Green & Hagiwara, 2020). Furthermore, the normative adoption of these interventions, the overwhelming prevalence of implicit biases against minoritised groups and the consequent take-home message that '[w]e are all *affected by* [emphasis added] unconscious bias' (Frith, 2015, p. 2) has had the effect of normalising and excusing the perpetuation of inequity. According to Tate and Page (2018), in the case of racial inequity, this has shifted the conversation away from racism and towards a blameless, ethereal prejudice that *acts upon* good people. This is discussed at length in Grzanka and Cole's (2021) excellent article 'An argument for bad psychology', with the authors concluding that bias training once again absolves the institution from having to deal with the structural racism it perpetuates.

In conclusion, our critique is not aimed at disputing the research foundations of these constructs and interventions. Instead, we take issue with the transfer of structural problems to the individual. As psychologists, we must be cautious about serving our own desires to feel useful, and to produce impactful research. It is crucial we remain vigilant and avoid allowing our tools to create a mere illusion of change while failing to address the underlying systems and cultures that perpetuate inequity.

─Focus Box 9.1─

What's Wrong with Open Science and Reproducibility?

The open science and reproducibility movements in psychology are a response to concerns about the accessibility and replicability of psychological research (Open Science Collaboration, 2012). Proponents aim to make the scientific process more transparent, accessible and reproducible by promoting open practices such as sharing data and materials, publishing findings in open-access formats (i.e. so that no subscription or payment is required to access a journal article) and pre-registering research plans. These aims are fundamentally agreeable, yet the movements have faced criticism as perpetuating extant inequalities in academia under the guise of encouraging best practice.

Criticisms include the culture adopted by the proponents of these movements, and the assumed privilege they manifest. Condescending, aggressive policing of what does and does not constitute 'good' science according to the principles of openness gave rise to the #bropenscience hashtag (Whitaker & Guest, 2020). Meanwhile, the additional work needed to engage in every aspect of good practice, as prescribed by the 'bros', suggests endeavours that are primarily targeted at those who work at institutions that give their researchers the time to do this. On top of this, the money required to publish in open formats (article processing charges, the fees publishers charge to make articles free to readers, range from hundreds to thousands of pounds) means that it is very easy to perceive full adherence to current scientific best practice as magnifying the privileges that already exist within the research sector. Whilst open science and reproducibility are intended to be inclusive movements, for some the impression is that they are run by an exclusionary network, dogmatically proselytising the new, unattainable rules.

Criticism of the culture within these movements might be dismissed as tone policing, but there is evidence to suggest that it has an impact on the diversity of those participating in the field. Murphy and colleagues (2020) ran a semantic analysis of both the open science and reproducibility literatures, finding greater pro-sociality indicated by the language used in the former compared to the latter. They also found that women were more likely to occupy prominent authorship positions in open science than in reproducibility papers. Though it is problematic to infer causality here, it is reasonable to hypothesise that exclusive and hostile language poses a barrier to participation that disproportionally affects those who are already marginalised.

A final observation is that open science and reproducibility formalise sets of procedures which, if complied with, indicate adherence to good practice. This technocratic approach can be useful, but it also diverts thinking away from *why* it is necessary to formalise these procedures at all (Grzanka & Cole, 2021). In focusing on how we conduct good research in spite of the incentive structures that have pushed many in psychology away from this practice, we run the risk of legitimising the unrealistic demands placed on researchers to *publish or perish*.

WHAT NEXT?

Universities are built upon foundations of structural inequity. How then should we think about dismantling the academic systems that reflect and perpetuate societal inequity, without dismantling the very idea of the university itself? From a pessimistic perspective, this is just not possible. Universities exist because they confer exclusive credentials on those privileged enough to attend them. Moreover, they magnify inequities by legitimising visible and invisible social networks, and co-opting the minoritised into structural exploitation, all whilst presenting the illusion of a commitment to equality and diversity. From a more optimistic perspective, universities can take an active role in dismantling structural inequity by starting with their own systems. They can engage in profound cultural transformation to empower and uplift those they have marginalised, but only if they acknowledge their participation in this marginalisation, and engage honestly with the process of rectifying its consequences. This reckoning requires an admission of culpability, and a radical departure from what has made them successful for many hundreds of years. But how might this be done?

In *Black Skin, White Masks* (1952), Frantz Fanon wrote:

We are convinced that it would be of enormous interest to discover a black literature or architecture from the third century before Christ. We would be overjoyed to learn of the existence of a correspondence between some black philosopher and Plato. But we can absolutely not see how this

> fact would change the lives of eight-year-old kids working in the cane field of Martinique or Guadeloupe. (p. 205)

He identifies the problems with many of the curriculum decolonisation efforts that are currently so fashionable in universities. What is the point of what we refer to as decolonisation if it does not have any *impact* on the lives of the colonised? True decolonisation in higher education must involve giving voice to those who have been oppressed, and supporting their efforts to secure reparations for their colonisation, even if that means admitting that one has participated in exploitation, and ceding power, wealth and status that has been gained because of it.

What might this transformation entail? It involves institutions of the Global North forging partnerships with nations and institutions that have been previously exploited. And not just through patriarchal, 'recolonial' partnerships that involve a one-way transfer of knowledge from the status-rich to the status-poor, but a two-way respect and understanding of what each institution can learn from the other. This will likely necessitate a radical overhaul of the systems of thought (see Chapter 1), and standards of evidence, that are so often prized and policed within institutions of the Global North (Grzanka & Cole, 2021). Drawing once again on Eugenia Zuroski's 'Where do you know from?' (2020), we should not only acknowledge the abstract value in non-traditional academic knowledge, but recognise the value it holds *for us*. This value may not manifest in the extractive, profitable forms we are used to, but perhaps it will come in the form of repairing our relationships through active participation in the emancipation of those we have oppressed. There is value in social justice.

To truly commit to social justice, universities must ensure consistency in their local actions. They must commit to fair working conditions, and equitable treatment of students of all backgrounds. They must end exploitative working relationships at all levels, including between research group leaders and their students, employees and interns. They must genuinely strive to eliminate sources of bias that disadvantage the minoritised, even if that means that many within their ranks also lose privilege. Furthermore, universities must be transparent about what their true priorities are, so that employees do not become so overstretched that burnout becomes unavoidable. Mondragon University in Spain offers an interesting example of this final point. As a co-operative, university workers receive a share of the organisation's surplus, and the university's teaching and research priorities are explicitly focused on supporting local companies and institutions (Winn, 2015). Whilst this explicitly entrepreneurial, marketised focus does not appeal to everyone, co-operative members are in no doubt about the university's aims and how their efforts contribute to achieving them.

Universities hold the power to confront structural, societal and global inequity. But using this power to create a truly inclusive higher education system—a teaching and research sector that is *useful* and *impactful* towards achieving social justice—demands honesty and the willingness to share this power. Nonetheless, by engaging in such transformative action, universities would back up their vocal commitment to equality, diversity and inclusion, with tangible efforts that foster meaningful change.

FURTHER READING

Sandel, M. J. (2020). *The tyranny of merit: What's become of the common good?* Penguin Books. [book]

A comprehensive critique of the ideal of meritocracy. Sandel makes a compelling case that true meritocracy cannot be achieved and, in its current form, perpetuates inequality and undermines the common good.

Grzanka, P. R., & Cole, E. R. (2021). An argument for bad psychology: Disciplinary disruption, public engagement, and social transformation. *American Psychologist, 76*(8), 1334. https://doi.org/10.1037/amp0000853 [journal article]

A radical argument that embracing some aspects of 'bad' practice in psychology will lead to a more inclusive, more reflexive discipline.

Tokumitsu, M. (2014). In the name of love. *Jacobin.* https://jacobin.com/2014/01/in-the-name-of-love/ [magazine article]

A critique of the mantra 'do what you love' as perpetuating inequality and exploitation by disguising wage labour as vocational.

10

CONCLUSION

Why write a book about the stories that have shaped psychology? Here we offer a reflection on the common threads that bind the narratives we have chosen for this book. They concern not just psychology's impact on society, but also the way in which society has impacted psychology. As part of this reflection, we consider what equalities work means for the future of our discipline. We then close the book with a series of questions that often arise when we speak with colleagues about our work, and our answers to them. Although unconventional, this presentation is inspired by Bernard Coard's coalition-building work (1971/2021) and bell hooks' use of transcribed interviews (1994). We encourage readers to pose these and related questions in their own circles to see what perspectives arise.

THE BIG PICTURE

The critical approach taken here offers our understanding of how and why certain people, perspectives and processes have become canonical to the field as we know it today. Across the different stories we have traced here, commonalities emerge. These themes all speak to the ways in which power structures created and maintain the beliefs we see as central to psychology. In brief, eugenic theories about innate differences in traits and abilities formed the basis of a psychological science grounded in the objective, systematic measurement of individual differences. Where these individual differences were generalised to entire groups of people, psychology often reinforced power structures that disenfranchised and disempowered minoritised persons. This legacy influenced—and continues to shape—the kind of knowledge produced by psychologists as well as the kind of individuals who are allowed to participate in knowledge-making in the first place.

Eugenics and the Ordering of the World

Many of the ideas that have influenced psychology are a reaction to eugenic theories that redefined scientific and social discourse in the 1800s. From the adoption of statistical formulae (Chapter 2) and technologies (Chapter 5) to intelligence testing (Chapter 3), theories of social stratification and hierarchy lie at the heart of many of our psychological tools and methods. The intended purpose of these instruments was to provide a seemingly objective way of segregating different elements of the population—whether along lines of gender (Chapter 6), race (Chapter 7) or other marker of class, culture or ability (Chapters 4 and 8). Many scientist proponents of eugenics viewed it as an engine of meritocracy that could improve educational outcomes and social mobility within Britain, the United States and their colonies (Linstrum, 2016; Regmi, 2023). In other instances, the application of eugenics was clearly intended to suppress minoritised groups, either erasing them from public life or characterising their experiences as aberrant (Albee, 1996). In either case, the preoccupation with genetics and evolution stemmed from a larger cultural context in which industrialisation, colonialism and systems of economic exploitation all demanded—and justified—ways of naturalising group differences and white, patriarchal power structures. Eugenic thought provided a seemingly objective way to explain social inequality in ways that removed responsibility and moral culpability from individuals at the top of power structures. Disparities in status, wealth and power were viewed as consequences of differences in intrinsic abilities or traits, such as intelligence, personality and mental health. As a discipline, psychologists invented or refined tools to provide reliable ways of quantifying these differences; in some cases, they also invented or refined theories explaining how such measurable differences were innate and invariant properties of individuals that represented meaningful genetic differences between races, classes and genders of people. In other words, many canonical theories and tools of psychological science were developed to order the world and defend this social hierarchy (Lewontin et al., 1993). In positioning itself as a science, psychology has legitimised tools and processes reinforcing the belief that white, male, straight and able-bodied perspectives are the universal referent against which all other behaviour is understood and, in some cases, pathologised.

The Cult of Individualism

The influence of eugenics reveals a tension in how the psychology of the Global North conceives individuals and individualism. As the scientific study of individualised minds, psychology has grappled with ways of explaining how atomised behaviour results in collective action. From neurons to crowds, the challenge has been to explain how the rules that govern individual action apply or extend to larger groups. As a result, psychology has often focused on the more tractable problem of understanding individual traits or mechanisms that explain behaviour. Mirroring this unit of analysis, historical analyses of psychology have also tended to focus on influential individuals.

The focus on individual agency has, at times, been transformative—we can see, for example, how emphasis on personal autonomy led to revolutionary changes in child welfare and the British educational system (Chapter 3). We can also understand how viewing people as individuals (rather than representatives of a given group) is critical to compassionate and culturally sensitive mental health care (Chapter 4). However, this emphasis on individuality also leads to outcomes that are not always beneficial. One consequence of the individualistic perspective is that the psychology of the Global North has often been decontextualised, investigating mental processes apart from the contexts or environs in which they arise. We can see evidence of this in the way that we rarely acknowledge the eugenic origins of statistics or the racialised phrenological roots of brain imaging (Chapters 2 and 5), or in the way that many mental health conditions are often attributed to individual shortcomings rather than more complex societal factors (see Chapters 4 and 6). As a result, our historical understanding of psychology is often incomplete, our theories impoverished and reductionist. The selective focus on persons to the exclusion of processes similarly limits our efforts to diversify psychology and the larger higher education system (Chapter 9).

Objectivity and Psychological Gatekeeping

Throughout the book, we hope we have made clear that there are countless ways in which the story of our discipline could be framed. The canonical thinkers and perspectives we know from textbooks were, without question, influential in psychology. However, in treating that knowledge as definitive, we may overlook or dismiss alternative ideas, approaches and figures. This form of gatekeeping limits our knowledge by constraining the kinds of data we consider useful as well as the kinds of persons we view as authoritative (for example, within WEIRD psychology; Chapter 8).

Moving beyond such gatekeeping requires change on multiple levels, as we will argue later in this chapter. It may even require us to rethink whether psychology is a science and, fundamentally, what defines a science (see Chapter 1). Questioning canonical persons, perspectives and processes has the potential to be threatening and disruptive because it challenges us to confront the political and ethical assumptions that underpin a science we would like to view as contextless and impartial (Birhane & Guest, 2021; Mignolo, 2007). Science often presents itself as ever-advancing and progressive, a systematic way of getting closer to 'the truth' of natural phenomena. What we hope we have made clear here is that this story is only partially correct. There are many instances where the field advanced not because of its objectivity and rationality, but because of its usefulness in political, economic, or military contexts (Harding, 1993). Many of the stories in this book highlight how psychology developed in the context of coloniality.

When the process of systematically testing claims occurs without consideration of such social forces, psychology suffers from the ostrich problem: we hide our heads in the sand for fear that admission of biases and errors will lead to the perception that not enough has been done to redress them (Harding, 1993). Not only does this paranoia about the past shape our science in the present, but it hampers any future efforts in the larger educational ecosystem to create truly inclusive scholarship. In Chapter 9, for example, we see that universities reproduce coloniality by supporting neoliberal, marketised systems of education.

Coloniality suppresses the subjectivity and silences the history of minoritised persons, all in the name of modernity, objectivity, rationality and universality. As we noted in our positioning statement, although we are critical of the way psychological science is practised and understood in the Global North, our critique is nonetheless grounded in dominant systems of thinking. To truly move beyond the gatekeeping inherent to our current scientific practice, we need to embrace new ways of thinking about science that allow suppressed and repressed people to reauthor their histories and regain control over knowledge production (Martín-Baró, 1994).

In what follows, we explore different models for engaging in critical reflections about psychology with an eye toward reframing and restructuring the process of pursuing, creating and disseminating knowledge. Our goal is to highlight approaches that we encountered in the process of writing this book, noting where they may help to modify or transform the psychological canon.

TRANSFORMING THE PSYCHOLOGICAL CANON

In the preceding chapters, we presented several examples of how scholarship can extend, modify, or transform an existing canon into a body of work that better represents a diversity of thought and human experience. These strategies range from those that are more incremental in scope, adding to the existing canon without substantially challenging its core tenets, to those that are more radical in nature, seeking to redefine how scholarship is conducted. Below we briefly describe and evaluate four approaches; we would point interested readers to an excellent paper by Crawford and Marecek (1989), whose analysis of women in psychology provided the inspiration and structure for our observations here.

The Eminent Individuals Approach

Throughout the book, we have seen multiple instances of historians of psychology centring their narratives on exceptional, eminent individuals. Consider the example of academic lineage in Chapter 1 and Galton's own analysis of the 'great men' of science summarised in Chapter 3. This is a relatively intuitive way of understanding a discipline: It builds on our propensity to think in terms of dualities, such as heroes and villains, or theories and counter-theories. As such, the 'eminent individuals' approach to addressing the psychological canon seeks to expand the scope of who is considered an exceptional, influential scholar. The goal of the approach is to diversify the canon by identifying the contribution of scholars whose work may have been overlooked. Examples of this practice in action might include 'diversity months' in which the contributions of groups of minoritised scholars are celebrated, or in recent widespread efforts for lecturers to diversify the authorship of their course reading lists. It also encompasses actions such as the creation of special interest groups (like the Psychology of Women section of the British Psychological Association; see Chapter 6) and institutional frameworks (like Advanced HE's Race Equality Charter and Athena Swan Charter) that are intended to amplify the accomplishments of talented, minoritised individuals. The goal of this approach is to improve the psychological canon by making it more representative and enabling a greater diversity of scholars to participate in knowledge production. One benefit of this approach is that it underscores the systemic nature of the barriers faced by minoritised people. In emphasising the stories of exceptional people who succeeded despite these barriers, the 'eminent individuals' approach candidly details how other talented scholars never achieve canonicity or fame because of these same obstacles. One drawback to this approach, however, is that it still treats the individual as the unit of analysis best suited for addressing equalities work. It does not present a sustained critique of the societal power structures that oppress minoritised persons and perspectives or that codify majority positions into the canon.

The Deficit Model Approach

Institutions and organisations undertaking equalities work often adopt what we have referred to elsewhere in the book as the deficit model (see Chapters 8 and 9 for examples). In this approach, differences in experiences that stem from minoritised characteristics represent problems that should be fixed. Take the example of intelligence testing described in Chapter 7. A deficit model approach might ask why Black children tend to have lower performance on standardised aptitude measures compared to their white counterparts. The assumption here is that some trait or characteristic of the individual—in this case, race—places them at a relative disadvantage compared to individuals from the cultural majority group. One benefit of such frameworks is that they make apparent disparities of experience and outcome that should be redressed, for example by dedicating resources to students and schools in need of additional support. We also appreciate this approach for the way it recognises how behaviour that is categorised as anomalous or pathological often stems from complex social rather than biological factors. In focusing on the experience of everyday people (rather than eminent individuals) the approach is more representative and ecologically relevant. However, the deficit model is not without drawbacks. The approach treats dominant groups as the de facto standard by which all behaviour is evaluated and deemed to be good or bad (Crawford & Marecek, 1989). This does not effectively challenge the core assumption that the experiences of the dominant group are typical and should be treated as normative. The links between identity and deficit are associative rather than causal in nature; they are usually established by identifying some demographic feature (like gender or sexual orientation) and examining how it correlates with certain outcomes in genetic distribution, hormonal functioning, brain structures, health outcomes, or test performance. In isolating individual traits or characteristics as responsible for differential behaviour or treatment, the deficit model also runs into problems when the outcomes faced by minoritised persons are complex, multiple and intersecting (Grzanka, 2020). For example, the deficit model often reduces individuals to a single dimension rather than considering the intersecting ways in which other identities might influence experiences of marginalisation and empowerment (e.g., Black women facing different workplace challenges than Black men and white women; see Chapter 6). Actions to expand the canon or to address workplace diversity will therefore be limited if they only conceptualise difference as negative and as limited to single aspects of identity.

The Psychology of X Approach

A critique that we raised about white feminism in Chapter 6 is that it is often reductionistic and treats all women as a homogenous group whose experiences of discrimination are likewise uniform. The 'psychology of X' approach seeks to overcome the limits of this framework by reconceiving differences in terms of process or social roles (Crawford & Marecek, 1989). For example, efforts to broaden the canon by focusing on the psychology of sexuality may focus less on labels and more on how queer experiences impact scholarship. This approach allows for a more dynamic understanding of minoritised identities and experiences, including the fact that identities often change over time and depending on context. We can reframe narratives about eminent individuals to highlight how the same person can experience both privilege and marginalisation depending on how they operate within a power structure (see Focus Box 1.1 in Chapter 1). A drawback of this approach is that it assumes that all members of a given group identify with that aspect of their identity, when in fact it may not be relevant to them at all. It is also methodologically difficult to measure identity as performative or a process rather than a stable demographic feature. As a result, we may overlook narratives or individuals that reject or ignore the power structures and processes that interest us. For example, Begeny and colleagues (2020) document how beliefs about identity are often the strongest predictor of prejudiced behaviour; they find that female managers who do not believe gender discrimination is a problem are equally likely to perpetuate gender bias as male managers. It is therefore critical allow for both acceptance of and resistance to the aspects of diversity that we hope to incorporate into the canon.

The Transformation Approach

The final approach we describe here focuses on normative practices and interrogates the philosophical assumptions at the core of a discipline. In other words, it takes a critical lens to the canonical perspectives and processes that define a field in order to understand its canon. An example from our work here is to reassess what we mean by 'objectivity' when we position psychology as a natural science. Examining the meaning and history of objectivity reveals much about our assumptions about truth and its correspondence to the natural world (Harding, 1995). Psychology's conflation of objectivity with impartiality and mechanistic measurement is at the heart of our belief that certain methods—such as statistical inference or neuroimaging (see Chapters 2 and 5)—are free from bias and therefore more reliable tools than other forms of investigation. As we hope to have demonstrated, there are many reasons to doubt that experimentation is free from social influence; furthermore, social influence is not necessarily an ill that should be expunged from all research. According to Crawford and Marecek, claims of objectivity only serve to 'disguise the politics of meaning' (1989, p. 158). The transformation approach to revising the canon advocates for transparency and positionality—for the researcher to openly reflect on their relationship to their work. The transformation approach also advocates for minoritised persons to be treated as the experts on their own experience. A re-examination of the stories in our canon is an important part of this process of liberation and reclamation; it allows minoritised people to recover historical memory and share this knowledge with others in a way that builds community and shared understanding (Martín-Baró, 1994). Interrogation of the systems that silence and oppress minoritised persons opens the door to developing new psychological theories that are responsive to the groups they represent and may result in the creation of more culturally appropriate services and tools (Singh, 2016). The major downside to this approach is that it is time-consuming and frequently discomforting, particularly for colleagues who perceive such exercises as the imposition of politics into value-neutral science. In response to this point we share the following observation: 'Because psychology is a cultural institution, doing psychological research is inevitably a political act' (Crawford & Marecek, 1989). Self-scrutiny may be uncomfortable, particularly when and where we are confronted with our participation in a system that has harmed others. But acknowledging this harm—and trying to reconstruct the discipline in ways that avoid further harm—is the very least we can do as citizens and scholars. A transformative approach to understanding the canon is also exciting, in that it gives us an opportunity to imagine what a new science could look like.

In the final part of this chapter we turn our attention to the kinds of questions we frequently encounter when discussing our work. Our intention in doing so is not to pre-empt critique, but rather to encourage reflection and dialogue. It is our attempt to document how we engaged in the approaches detailed above, and how we have since made sense of our discipline.

WHAT NEXT? Q&A

Q. What are the origins of the book?

A. The book has its roots in a second-year undergraduate statistics course that AOC gave at St Andrews. He noticed that the audience's (and his own) attention would wane over the course of an hour-long lecture and attempted to counteract this. He introduced brief interludes in which he shifted the focus from statistics, to the people behind them. Originally a homage to the likes of Fisher, Pearson and Gosset, over years this changed to a more critical examination of why he had been drawn to talk about these people and not others. Yes, their stories were interesting, but so too were the reasons we revere them and not others. This change in approach, from uncritical presentation of the 'great men' of statistics, to a reflexive examination of how AOC had ignored the structures these statisticians had established and maintained, would form the backbone of the book proposal.

ER became interested in the themes of this book during her graduate training. As a white and queer person, she frequently discussed her personal experiences of discrimination with a colleague who was Black. In these conversations it became apparent that what ER viewed as coalition-building was, in fact, the opposite: rather than finding commonality, ER negated her colleague's views and treated their experiences as interchangeable and homogenous in ways that were not accurate or helpful. This was a painful process, but it led ER to recognise that the same tensions might be playing out in her research. Over the next few years, she engaged with colleagues about how equalities work could intersect with cross-cultural research. This formed the basis of a series of lectures she presented to undergraduate and postgraduate students at St Andrews.

In writing this book, we have tried to maintain this reflexivity, picking ideas and people that represent the canon, and attempting to understand how the canon was established, and how it perpetuates. We do not claim that the people or ideas we have chosen represent the entirety of the canon, nor that our interpretations of its origins are the *truth*. What we do hope we have shown is that there are many explanations for why modern psychology looks the way it does, and that only one, deficient explanation involves people and ideas rising within a perfect meritocracy. In these explorations, we also hope to have chosen interesting enough stories that the readers' (and the authors') attention is maintained long enough to have learned something worth sharing with others.

Q. Was writing this book a decolonial project?

A. There are decolonial aspects to the project, particularly our representations of how some have attempted to redress the power imbalances in their fields. But the majority of what we are doing is to simply understand the origins of our discipline, and of course much of that is rooted in the colonial histories of Britain and the United States of America.

We would certainly characterise our efforts as antiracist and antisexist, and as an attempt to address the legacy of coloniality in our field. However, decolonial has become a qualifier to describe a host of initiatives that broadly seek to diversify academic practice; *decolonisation* in higher education has become a metaphor despite the reminder from Tuck and Yang (2012). Decolonisation, according to scholars like Fanon, is inherently violent. It requires violence to overthrow the violence enacted by the colonisers and we (like all those who use the term as a metaphor) are not proposing anything like this. We are acting from seats of privilege and proposing changes within the bounds of the established systems of power to the ways in which we do things. Further, we as authors, in how we embody our identities, do not represent the colonially oppressed. It is not our place to be decolonisers, nor would we expect to remain enfranchised were successful decolonisation to take place.

Q. Who is this book for?

A. All who are interested in psychology, including, but not limited to, students, researchers and teachers. We hope practitioners, clinicians and colleagues in adjacent fields may also find it thought-provoking.

Q. How did you write this book (e.g., why did you pick these stories to tell)?

A. We read a great deal to find stories and situations that interested us, that resonated with our own experiences and would allow us to represent the points we make authentically. We also wanted to find opportunities to revisit the origins of stories we *thought* we knew. We settled on the narratives in this book because we thought they formed an interlocking picture of our discipline—it was exciting to see how names, persons and places who appeared in one chapter often appeared in others. We think that makes the point about canonicity nicely.

Q. What topics are missing?

A. Lots. This is not a comprehensive account of the narratives that have shaped psychology. Nor does it comprehensively address that many groups have been marginalised by psychology and psychologists. It is a jumping off point for your own exploration of the disciplines you care about.

Some topics—such as sexuality and disability—we addressed as they pertain to other identities, stories and histories. We did so not because these topics are unimportant in their own right, but because we thought this editorial choice helped make for a stronger, clearer story about power. For example, there is much to say about the ways in which psychology has been complicit in the criminalisation and ill-treatment of queer people (see Chapter 4 for a brief overview). But ideas about gender and gender essentialism also obviously impact how people experience, perform and identify with sexuality (see Chapter 6). The concept of *being* queer (i.e., *identifying* as LGBTQIA+) is a relatively recent historical development (Halperin, 2002). Some evidence suggests that in Victorian Britain social norms were organised around gender identity rather than sexual orientation; expressions of queer desire were largely tolerated as long as they did not also flaunt stereotypical gender expressions (Marcus, 2007). In this instance, we thought it told a stronger story to focus on the issue of gender essentialism as a way of raising the many kinds of inequalities that stem from that choice.

Q. Should understanding this critical approach be core or supplemental to a curriculum?

A. Definitely not supplemental. That said, mandating study of this approach as a core, but separate module in a curriculum would miss the point we have made in this book. We suggest that our approach should be integrated into all core teaching so that this is acknowledged throughout the curriculum. We need to understand *why* we are learning what we learn as we learn it so that we do not have the option of distilling the ideas we are learning away from their socio-political context and origins. In our view, the same is true of all EDI (equality, diversity and inclusion) efforts—mainstream so that they are everyone's responsibility, rather than ghettoising to specialists. This requires resourcing and training—of course it does!—so maybe this has to be staged, but ultimately all those involved in the business of delivering psychology education need to be exposed to this, regardless of inherent interest in EDI.

Q. Would adopting these ideas/approaches make psychology less of a science?

A. Would you be asking whether integrating understanding of Fisher and Galton into statistics education would make it any less of a mathematical discipline? No. Indeed, it is a requirement of the British Psychological Association that psychology undergraduates learn about the origins of the discipline. Why should *this* sort of learning be more of a problem for the scientific credentials of psychology than what is currently taught? This probably speaks to an insecurity that psychologists have about their entitlement to the trappings of being considered a science (funding structures, research contract staff, equipment resources) than it has to any meaningful change in status. Indeed, one of the threads we trace throughout the book is how psychology has consistently attempted to 'harden' its reputation by incorporating methods and technology from other disciplines, particularly in the experimental sciences.

Why should understanding the origins of a science have any bearing on whether it be considered a science at all? An answer to this rhetorical question probably lies in the preoccupation with objectivity and how this seems to go hand in hand with decontextualisation.

Q. I'm a neuroscientist; does this book apply to me?

A. If Hogben, the zoologist whose animal model is now a staple in numerous neuroscience labs, could acknowledge his own privilege and advocate for social justice (as detailed in Chapter 2), then all bench scientists should similarly recognise and act on their capacity to do the same. Throughout the book we have attempted to show how technology has often been used to reinforce power structures and hierarchies by concentrating expertise and resources in the hands of a select few. Investigating the origins of these tools can offer a powerful insight into the systems of power and philosophical assumptions that guide research practice (see, for example, Chapter 2 on statistics, Chapter 5 on brain imaging and Chapter 7 on Coard's 'weapons of mass suppression'). In addition to interrogating the gadgets and analyses we employ, we might also consider the history of the model organisms and cell cultures we use. (An example we did not detail here is the story of Henrietta Lacks, a Black woman whose cancer cells were harvested without her knowledge and developed into one of the most widely used cell lines in biomedical research; Skloot, 2011). Researchers working in institutions built on land and resources stolen from Indigenous people may similarly consider how that fact impacts the way they practise their scholarship (Raman, 2023).

As described in Chapter 8, there are many steps that researchers can take to engage with communities in the process of developing research questions and implementing research protocols. This applies to research with non-human populations, as in the instance of researchers who investigate the biological basis of neurodegenerative diseases or drug therapies. In collaborating with individuals who suffer from Parkinson's disease, for example, new insights may be generated that could impact research protocol. In addition, all researchers—whether they work with humans, spinal cords, or artificial intelligences—have an obligation to reflect on how their work will be utilised by funders and disseminated to the broader public. This raises numerous questions about power and power relationships that we would all do well to consider.

We would also note that all privilege is political. One is undoubtedly privileged (in some respects) if one is plying one's trade as a researcher of any discipline, particularly in a university setting. We urge researchers to consider the kinds of gatekeeping described throughout the book (though particularly in Chapters 6 and 9) that prevent certain kinds of researchers from participating in the process of knowledge creation.

Q. Does participation in equality and inclusion efforts (like awards charters, or diversifying curricula) work?

A. At time of writing, both of us are leading efforts to apply for equalities charters. In our experience, the answer to this question very much depends on the spirit in which the organisation enters into EDI efforts. If it is just with a view to obtaining a credential, then it works to raise awareness of what 'ought to be done', but it does little to change the culture of an environment (indeed it can be detrimental in that it yields an outcome that devalues the associated credential). If it is engaged with in the spirit of culture change—not 'what do we need to do to get the credential?' but 'what do we need to do to make our education and work environments better for our students and staff?' then yes, this stands a much better chance of working. Of course, this needs to be reflected in practice, with traditional metrics (data from surveys etc.) combined with measures that characterise lived experience of culture.

Q. What response do you have to those who say this is 'woke' agitating?

A. Those arguments usually come from people who are unwilling to recognise that privilege and power have always played a role in science and scholarship. This may be because they themselves have benefitted from privilege, and they do not wish this fact to denigrate their achievements. This may be because they would rather view their work as apolitical: things are simpler that way. In any case, we would ask them to look at the sources we have documented in our work. Read the documents we are responding to, especially those we are reacting against, and consider whether they represent ideas that they would consider acceptable. Also consider whether the authors of those documents thought that their science was separate from their political and societal power—they did not. So how do they, the reader separated from the original context by decades, even centuries, know better than the authors?

Q. What response do you have to people who say systemic change is not possible?

A. Fisher recognised that societal and political change was possible when he lobbied the British government for eugenic policies that reflected his political ideals. He very nearly achieved this change. Horrific instantiations of eugenic policies were implemented across the world, led by a social movement supported by scientists. Why have we become so pessimistic about our capacity for systemic change now?

Q. How do we organise for change?

A. We spread stories. We mainstream and integrate these ideas into our work, rather than ghettoising them into an EDI-focused lecture or workshop. We acknowledge and dismantle the power that we wield to oppress others (however kindly given as internships, or precarious contracts etc.) as an example of how we would like the power that oppresses us to be dismantled.

CONCLUDING THOUGHTS

In closing, we believe that ours is a discipline that wields the power to perpetuate harm, but also to confront and rectify the very injustices with which it has been entangled. As a discipline, psychology has supported oppressive systems that have historically silenced the voices of marginalised people. And as a discipline, we now face an opportunity to redress injustices and offer a platform for marginalised perspectives. This restorative work can only be done, however, by confronting the history of our field and understanding the legacy of this history for contemporary practice. This requires openness to learning, to embracing discomfort, to admitting when and where we have been complicit in promoting inequity, and to reappraising our own scholarship. The act of unravelling the historical impact of colonialism on psychology is not a passive one. It is an ongoing act of reclamation. Our critical reflections on the narratives that shape psychology offer an invitation to confront our past, interrogate our present and reimagine a psychology that honours the rich diversity of human experience.

REFERENCES

Ackerknecht, E. H., & Rosenberg, C. E. (2016). *A short history of medicine*. Johns Hopkins University Press.

Adamopoulos, J., & Lonner, W. J. (2001). Culture and psychology at a crossroad: Historical perspective and theoretical analysis. In D. Matsumoto (Ed.), *The handbook of culture and psychology* (pp. 11–35). Oxford University Press.

Adams, C. E., Awad, G. A., Rathbone, J., Thornley, B., & Soares-Weiser, K. (2014). Chlorpromazine versus placebo for schizophrenia. *Cochrane Database of Systematic Reviews, 1*. https://doi.org/10.1002/14651858.CD000284.pub3

Adams, G., Estrada-Villalta, S., & Gómez Ordóñez, L. H. (2018). The modernity/coloniality of being: Hegemonic psychology as intercultural relations. *International Journal of Intercultural Relations, 62*, 13–22. https://doi.org/10.1016/j.ijintrel.2017.06.006

ADHD-200. (2011). The ADHD-200 Sample. Retrieved from http://fcon_1000.projects.nitrc.org/indi/adhd200/

Albee, G. W. (1996). The psychological origins of the white male patriarchy. *Journal of Primary Prevention, 17*(1), 75–97. https://doi.org/10.1007/BF02262739

Allik, J. (2012). Bibliometric analysis of the Journal of Cross-Cultural Psychology during the first ten years of the new millennium. *Journal of Cross-Cultural Psychology, 44*(4), 657–667. https://doi.org/10.1177/0022022112461941

American Psychiatric Association. (1952). *Diagnostic and statistical manual of mental disorders* (1st ed., DSM-I). American Psychiatric Association.

American Psychiatric Association. (1968). *Diagnostic and statistical manual of mental disorders* (2nd ed., DSM-II). American Psychiatric Association.

American Psychiatric Association. (1973). *Diagnostic and statistical manual of mental disorders* (2nd ed., DSM-II 6th printing). American Psychiatric Association.

American Psychiatric Association. (1980). *Diagnostic and statistical manual of mental disorders* (3rd ed., DSM-III). American Psychiatric Association.

American Psychiatric Association. (2022). *Diagnostic and statistical manual of mental disorders* (5th revised ed., DSM-5TR). American Psychiatric Association.

American Psychological Association. (2020). *Publication manual of the American Psychological Association* (7th ed.) American Psychological Association.

American Psychological Association. (2023). Objectivity. Retrieved from https://dictionary.apa.org/objectivity

Anderson, J. E. (1956). Child development: An historical perspective. *Child Development, 27*(2), 181–196. https://doi.org/10.2307/1126088

Andreasen, N. C., Grove, W. M., Shapiro, R. W., Keller, M. B., Hirschfeld, R. M., & McDonald-Scott, P. (1981). Reliability of lifetime diagnosis: A multicenter collaborative perspective. *Archives of General Psychiatry*, *38*(4), 400–405. https://doi.org/10.1001/archpsyc.1981.01780290034003

Andreski, S. (1973). *Social sciences as sorcery*. St Martin's Press.

Anker, P. (2004). The politics of ecology in South Africa on the radical left. *Journal of the History of Biology*, *37*(2), 303–331. http://www.jstor.org/stable/4331876

Apicella, C., Norenzayan, A., & Henrich, J. (2020). Beyond WEIRD: A review of the last decade and a look ahead to the global laboratory of the future. *Evolution and Human Behavior*, *41*(5), 319–329. https://doi.org/10.1016/j.evolhumbehav.2020.07.015

Arnett, J. J. (2008). The neglected 95%: Why American psychology needs to become less American. *American Psychologist*, *63*(7), 602–614. https://doi.org/10.1037/0003-066X.63.7.602

Ashmore, M., Brown, S. D., & Macmillan, K. (2005). Lost in the Mall with Mesmer and Wundt: Demarcations and demonstrations in the psychologies. *Science, Technology, & Human Values*, *30*(1), 76–110. https://doi.org/10.1177/0162243904270716

Ballweg, M. L., Drury, C., Cowley, T., McCleary, K. K., & Veasley, C. (2010). *Chronic pain in women: Neglect, dismissal, and discrimination*. Overlapping Conditions Alliance. Retrieved from https://tmj.org/wp-content/uploads/2022/01/CECPW_Policy-Recommendations.pdf

Banaji, M. R., & Greenwald, A. G. (2013). *Blindspot: Hidden biases of good people*. Delacorte Press.

Bancel, N., David, T., & Thomas, D. (Eds.). (2014). *The invention of race: Scientific and popular representations* (1st ed.). Routledge.

Bartlett, C., Doyal, L., Ebrahim, S., Davey, P., Bachmann, M., Egger, M., & Dieppe, P. (2005). The causes and effects of socio-demographic exclusions from clinical trials. *Health Technology Assessment*, *9*(38). https://doi.org/10.3310/hta9380

Battle-Baptiste, W., & Rusert, B. (2018). *W. E. B. Du Bois's data portraits: Visualising Black America*. Princeton Architectural Press.

Bayes, T., & Price. (1763). LII. An essay towards solving a problem in the doctrine of chances. By the late Rev. Mr. Bayes, F. R. S. communicated by Mr. Price, in a letter to John Canton, A. M. F. R. S. *Philosophical Transactions of the Royal Society of London*, *53*, 370–418. https://doi.org/10.1098/rstl.1763.0053

Beaulieu, A. (2001). Voxels in the brain: Neuroscience, informatics and changing notions of objectivity. *Social Studies of Science*, *31*(5), 635–680.

Beck, H. P., Levinson, S., & Irons, G. (2009). Finding Little Albert: A journey to John B. Watson's infant laboratory. *American Psychologist*, *64*(7), 605–614. https://doi.org/10.1037/a0017234

Becker, J. B., Arnold, A. P., Berkley, K. J., Blaustein, J. D., Eckel, L. A., Hampson, E., Herman, J. P., Marts, S., Sadee, W., Steiner, M., Taylor, J., & Young, E. (2005).

Strategies and methods for research on sex differences in brain and behavior. *Endocrinology, 146*(4), 1650–1673. https://doi.org/10.1210/en.2004-1142

Begeny, C. T., Ryan, M. K., Moss-Racusin, C. A., & Ravetz, G. (2020). In some professions, women have become well represented, yet gender bias persists—perpetuated by those who think it is not happening. *Science Advances, 6*(26), eaba7814. https://doi.org/10.1126/sciadv.aba7814

Belgrave, F. Z., & Allison, K. W. (2018). *African American psychology: From Africa to America.* Sage Publications.

Benedict, R. (1935). *Patterns of culture.* Routledge & Kegan Paul.

Benjamin, L. T. (1980). Women in psychology: Biography and autobiography. *Psychology of Women Quarterly, 5*(1), 140–144. https://doi.org/10.1111/j.1471-6402.1981.tb01040.x

Benjamin, L. T. (2000). The psychology laboratory at the turn of the 20th century. *American Psychologist, 55*(3), 318–321. https://doi.org/10.1037/0003-066X.55.3.318

Benschop, R. (1998). What is a tachistoscope? Historical explorations of an instrument. *Science in Context, 11*(1), 23–50. https://doi.org/10.1017/S0269889700002908

Berrios, G. E. (1990). Alzheimer's disease: A conceptual history. *International Journal of Geriatric Psychiatry, 5*(6), 355–365. https://doi.org/10.1002/gps.930050603

Berrios, G. E., & Hauser, R. (1988). The early development of Kraepelin's ideas on classification: A conceptual history. *Psychological Medicine, 18*(4), 813–821. https://doi.org/10.1017/s0033291700009740

Bhatia, S., & Priya, K. R. (2021). Coloniality and psychology: From silencing to re-centering marginalized voices in postcolonial times. *Review of General Psychology, 25*(4), 422–436. https://doi.org/10.1177/10892680211046507

Bhattacharya, A. (2022). *The man from the future: The visionary life of John von Neumann.* W. W. Norton.

Bills, A. G. (1938). Changing views of psychology as science. *Psychological Review, 45*(5), 377–394. https://doi.org/10.1037/h0062515

Birhane, A., & Guest, O. (2021). Towards decolonising computational sciences. *Kvinder, Køn & Forskning, 29*(1), 60–73. https://doi.org/10.7146/kkf.v29i2.124899

Black, E. (2003, November 9). Eugenics and the Nazis – the California connection. *SFGATE.* Retrieved from www.sfgate.com/opinion/article/Eugenics-and-the-Nazis-the-California-2549771.php

Blashfield, R. K., Keeley, J. W., Flanagan, E. H., & Miles, S. R. (2014). The cycle of classification: DSM-I through DSM-5. *Annual Review of Clinical Psychology, 10*(1), 25–51. https://doi.org/10.1146/annurev-clinpsy-032813-153639

Blickenstaff, J. C. (2005). Women and science careers: Leaky pipeline or gender filter? *Gender and Education, 17*(4), 369–386. https://doi.org/10.1080/09540250500145072

Bloch, M. N. (1991). Critical science and the history of child development's influence on early education research. *Early Education and Development, 2*(2), 95–108. https://doi.org/10.1207/s15566935eed0202_2

Bodmer, W., Bailey, R. A., Charlesworth, B., Eyre-Walker, A., Farewell, V., Mead, A., & Senn, S. (2021). The outstanding scientist, R.A. Fisher: His views on eugenics and race. *Heredity*, *126*(4), 565–576. https://doi.org/10.1038/s41437-020-00394-6

Bolton, P., & Lewis, J. (2023). *Equality of access and outcomes in higher education in England*. Retrieved from https://commonslibrary.parliament.uk/research-briefings/cbp-9195/

Boring, E. G. (1929). *A history of experimental psychology*. Appleton-Century.

Bou Zeineddine, F., Saab, R., Lášticová, B., Kende, A., & Ayanian, A. H. (2022). 'Some uninteresting data from a faraway country': Inequity and coloniality in international social psychological publications. *Journal of Social Issues*, *78*(2), 320–345. https://doi.org/10.1111/josi.12481

Boulton, G., & Lucas, C. (2011). What are universities for? *Chinese Science Bulletin*, *56*(23), 2506–2517. https://doi.org/10.1007/s11434-011-4608-7

Box, J. F. (1978). *R. A. Fisher: The life of a scientist*. Wiley.

Boyd, R. W., Lindo, E. G., Weeks, L. D., & McLemore, M. R. (2020). *On racism: A new standard for publishing on racial health inequities*. Retrieved from www.healthaffairs.org/content/forefront/racism-new-standard-publishing-racial-health-inequities

Bradley, B. S. (1989). *Visions of infancy*. Polity/Blackwell.

Brame, K. D. (2021). *Kenneth B. Clark*. Black listed culture. Retrieved from https://blacklistedculture.com/kenneth-b-clark/

Brett, M., Johnsrude, I. S., & Owen, A. M. (2002). The problem of functional localization in the human brain. *Nature Reviews Neuroscience*, *3*(3), 243–249. https://doi.org/10.1038/nrn756

Britton, J., Dearden, L., & Waltmann, B. (2021). *The returns to undergraduate degrees by socio-economic group and ethnicity*. Retrieved from https://ifs.org.uk/publications/returns-undergraduate-degrees-socio-economic-group-and-ethnicity

Broesch, T., Crittenden, A. N., Beheim, B. A., Blackwell, A. D., Bunce, J. A., Colleran, H., Hagel, K., Kline, M., McElreath, R., Nelson, R. G., Pisor, A. C., Prall, S., Pretelli, I., Purzycki, B., Quinn, E. A., Ross, C., Scelza, B., Starkweather, K., Stieglitz, J., & Mulder, M. B. (2020). Navigating cross-cultural research: methodological and ethical considerations. *Proceedings of the Royal Society B: Biological Sciences*, *287*(1935), 20201245. https://doi.org/10.1098/rspb.2020.1245

Brooks, R., Gupta, A., Jayadeva, S., & Abrahams, J. (2021). Students' views about the purpose of higher education: A comparative analysis of six European countries. *Higher Education Research & Development*, *40*(7), 1375–1388. https://doi.org/10.1080/07294360.2020.1830039

Brown, B. A., Long, H. L., Weitz, T. A., & Milliken, N. (2001). Challenges of recruitment: Focus groups with research study recruiters. *Women & Health*, *31*(2–3), 153–166. https://doi.org/10.1300/J013v31n02_08

Brown, E. N., & Borovina, D. L. (2021). The Trinity high-explosive implosion system: The foundation for precision explosive applications. *Nuclear Technology*, *207*(sup1), S204–S221. https://doi.org/10.1080/00295450.2021.1913954

Bruner, J. (1991). Self-making and world-making. *Journal of Aesthetic Education*, *25*(1), 67–78. https://doi.org/10.2307/3333092

Buchanan, N. T., Perez, M., Prinstein, M. J., & Thurston, I. B. (2021). Upending racism in psychological science: Strategies to change how science is conducted, reported, reviewed, and disseminated. *American Psychologist*, *76*(7), 1097–1112. https://doi.org/10.1037/amp0000905

Burawoy, M. (2005). For public sociology. *American Sociological Review*, *70*(1), 4–28. https://doi.org/10.1177/000312240507000102

Burman, E. (1994). *Deconstructing developmental psychology*. Routledge.

Burman, E. (2019). Child as method: Implications for decolonising educational research. *International Studies in Sociology of Education*, *28*(1), 4–26. https://doi.org/10.1080/09620214.2017.1412266

Burns, J. (1986). From 'polite learning' to 'useful knowledge'. *History Today*, *36*(4), 21–29.

Bushdid, C., Magnasco, M. O., Vosshall, L. B., & Keller, A. (2014). Humans can discriminate more than 1 trillion olfactory stimuli. *Science*, *343*(6177), 1370–1372. https://doi.org/10.1126/science.1249168

Campbell, L. G., Mehtani, S., Dozier, M. E., & Rinehart, J. (2013). Gender-heterogeneous working groups produce higher quality science. *PLoS ONE*, *8*(10), e79147. https://doi.org/10.1371/journal.pone.0079147

Canham, H., Baloyi, L., & Segalo, P. (2021). Disrupting the psychology canon? Exploring African-centered decolonial pedagogy. In G. Stevens & C. C. Sonn (Eds.), *Decoloniality and epistemic justice in contemporary community psychology* (pp. 193–212). Springer International Publishing. https://doi.org/10.1007/978-3-030-72220-3_11

Capshew, J. H. (1992). Psychologists on site: A reconnaissance of the historiography of the laboratory. *American Psychologist*, *47*(2), 132–142. https://doi.org/10.1037/0003-066X.47.2.132

Cardel, M. I., Dean, N., & Montoya-Williams, D. (2020). Preventing a secondary epidemic of lost early career scientists. effects of Covid-19 pandemic on women with children. *Annals of the American Thoracic Society*, *17*(11), 1366–1370. https://doi.org/10.1513/AnnalsATS.202006-589IP

Carmichael-Murphy, P., & Danquah, A. (2022). *Hidden histories: Black in psychology*. University of Manchester. https://gmhigher.ac.uk/resources/hidden-histories-black-in-psychology/

Caron, S. M. (1998). Birth control and the Black community in the 1960s: Genocide or power politics? *Journal of Social History*, *31*(3), 545–569. https://doi.org/10.1353/jsh/31.3.545

Cartwright, S. A. (1851). Diseases and peculiarities of the Negro race. In J. D. B. De Bow (Ed.), *De Bow's review of the Southern and Western states* (Vol. 11, pp. 331–336).

Ceci, S. J., Ginther, D. K., Kahn, S., & Williams, W. M. (2014). Women in academic science: A changing landscape. *Psychological Science in the Public Interest, 15*(3), 75–141. https://doi.org/10.1177/1529100614541236

Chamorro-Premuzic, T., & Lusk, D. (2017). *The dark side of resilience.* Retrieved from https://hbr.org/2017/08/the-dark-side-of-resilience

Chesterton, G. K. (1922). *Eugenics and other evils.* Cassell.

Chodoff, P. (1974). The diagnosis of hysteria: An overview. *American Journal of Psychiatry, 131*(10), 1073–1078.

Chrisler, J. C., & McHugh, M. C. (2011). Waves of feminist psychology in the United States: Politics and perspectives. In A. Rutherford, R. Capdevila, V. Undurti, & I. Palmary (Eds.), *Handbook of international feminisms: perspectives on psychology, women, culture, and rights* (pp. 37–58). Springer New York. https://doi.org/10.1007/978-1-4419-9869-9_3

Christopher, J. C., & Hickinbottom, S. (2008). Positive psychology, ethnocentrism, and the disguised ideology of individualism. *Theory & Psychology, 18*(5), 563–589. https://doi.org/10.1177/0959354308093396

Clark, A. E., D'Ambrosio, C., & Zhu, R. (2021). Job quality and workplace gender diversity in Europe. *Journal of Economic Behavior & Organization, 183*, 420–432. https://doi.org/10.1016/j.jebo.2021.01.012

Clark, K. B., & Clark, M. P. (1950). Emotional factors in racial identification and preference in Negro children. *Journal of Negro Education, 19*, 341–350. https://doi.org/10.2307/2966491

Cleghorn, E. (2021). *Unwell women: A journey of medicine and myth in a man-made world.* Weidenfeld & Nicolson.

Coard, B. (1971/2021). *How the West Indian child is made educationally sub-normal in the British school system* (5th ed.). McDermott Publishing.

Cohen, I. B. (1984). Florence Nightingale. *Scientific American, 250*(3), 128–137. http://www.jstor.org/stable/24969329

Collini, S. (2017). *Speaking of universities.* Verso.

Colman, A. M. (2016). Race differences in IQ: Hans Eysenck's contribution to the debate in the light of subsequent research. *Personality and Individual Differences, 103*, 182–189. https://doi.org/10.1016/j.paid.2016.04.050

Comas-Díaz, L., & Rivera, E. T. (Eds.). (2020). *Liberation psychology: Theory, method, practice, and social justice.* American Psychological Association. http://www.jstor.org/stable/j.ctv1chs1sn.

Combe, G. (1828). *The constitution of man considered in relation to external objects.* John Anderson.

Commission for Racial Equality. (1988). *Medical school admissions: Report of a formal investigation into St. George's Hospital Medical School.* Commission for Racial Equality.

Commission on Race and Ethnic Disparities. (2021). *The Report of the Commission on Race and Ethnic Disparities.* Retrieved from www.gov.uk/government/publications/the-report-of-the-commission-on-race-and-ethnic-disparities

Cosgrove, K. P., Mazure, C. M., & Staley, J. K. (2007). Evolving knowledge of sex differences in brain structure, function, and chemistry. *Biological Psychiatry, 62*(8), 847-855. https://doi.org/10.1016/j.biopsych.2007.03.001

Cosgrove, L., & Vaswani, A. (2019). The influence of pharmaceutical companies and restoring integrity to psychiatric research and practice. In S. Steingard (Ed.), *Critical psychiatry: Controversies and clinical implications* (pp. 71–96). Springer International Publishing. https://doi.org/10.1007/978-3-030-02732-2_3

Costall, A. (2006). 'Introspectionism' and the mythical origins of scientific psychology. *Consciousness and Cognition, 15*(4), 634–654. https://doi.org/10.1016/j.concog.2006.09.008

Cotton, H. A. (1921). *The defective delinquent and insane: The relation of focal infections to their causation, treatment and prevention*. Princeton University Press. https://doi.org/10.1037/10799-000

Cotton, H. A. (1923). The relation of chronic sepsis to the so-called functional mental disorders. *Journal of Mental Science, 69*(287), 434–465. https://doi.org/10.1192/bjp.69.287.434

Cox, D. R. (2001). Biometrika: The first 100 years. *Biometrika, 88*(1), 3–11. http://www.jstor.org/stable/2673673

Cramblet Alvarez, L. D., Jones, K. N., Walljasper-Schuyler, C., Trujillo, M., Weiser, M. A., Rodriguez, J. L., Ringler, R. L., & Leach, J. L. (2019). Psychology's hidden figures: Undergraduate psychology majors' (in)ability to recognize our diverse pioneers. *Psi Chi Journal of Psychological Research, 24*(2). https://doi.org/10.24839/2325-7342.JN24.2.84

Crawford, M., & Marecek, J. (1989). Psychology reconstructs the female: 1968–1988. *Psychology of Women Quarterly, 13*(2), 147–165. https://doi.org/10.1111/j.1471-6402.1989.tb00993.x

Cretchley, J., Rooney, D., & Gallois, C. (2010). Mapping a 40-year history with Leximancer: Themes and concepts in the journal of cross-cultural psychology. *Journal of Cross-Cultural Psychology, 41*(3), 318–328. https://doi.org/10.1177/0022022110366105

Crispin, J. (2018). Beyond Goop and evil: The curious feminist logic of Gwyneth Paltrow's self-care empire. *The Baffler, 41*, 42–49.

Cumming, G. (2014). The new statistics: Why and how. *Psychological Science, 25*(1), 7–29. https://doi.org/10.1177/0956797613504966

Curtis, A. (2021). *Can't get you out of my head* (TV Series). BBC.

Curtis, M. E., & Glaser, R. (1981). Changing conceptions of intelligence. *Review of Research in Education, 9*, 111–148. https://doi.org/10.2307/1167184

Dahan, O. (2021). The birthing brain: A lacuna in neuroscience. *Brain and Cognition, 150*, 105722. https://doi.org/10.1016/j.bandc.2021.105722

Dain, N. (1989). Critics and dissenters: Reflections on 'anti-psychiatry' in the United States. *Journal of the History of the Behavioral Sciences, 25*(1), 3–25. https://doi.org/10.1002/1520-6696(198901)25:1<3::AID-JHBS2300250102>3.0.CO;2-G

Danziger, K. (2006). Universalism and Indigenization in the history of modern psychology. In C. B. Adrian (Ed.), *Internationalizing the history of psychology* (pp. 208–225). New York University Press. https://doi.org/10.18574/nyu/9780814739082.003.0015

Darwin, C. (1859). *On the origin of species by means of natural selection, or The preservation of favoured races in the struggle for life.* John Murray.

Darwin, C. (1877). A biographical sketch of an infant. *Mind, os-2*(7), 285–294. https://doi.org/10.1093/mind/os-2.7.285

Daston, L., & Galison, P. (2007). *Objectivity.* Zone Books.

Davatzikos, C. (2009). Computational neuroanatomy using shape transformations. In I. N. Bankman (Ed.), *Handbook of medical image processing and analysis* (2nd ed.) (pp. 293–304). Academic Press.

David, H. A. (2009). Karl Pearson—the scientific life in a statistical age by Theodore M. Porter: A review. *International Statistical Review/Revue Internationale de Statistique, 77*(1), 30–39. http://www.jstor.org/stable/27919688

David, S. V., & Hayden, B. Y. (2012). Neurotree: A collaborative, graphical database of the academic genealogy of neuroscience. *PLoS ONE, 7*(10), e46608. https://doi.org/10.1371/journal.pone.0046608

Davis, G. (2012). The most deadly disease of asylumdom: General paralysis of the insane and Scottish psychiatry, c.1840–1940. *Journal of the Royal College of Physicians of Edinburgh, 42*(3), 266–273. https://doi.org/10.4997/jrcpe.2012.316

Davis, P. M. (2016). Comparing the citation performance of PNAS papers by submission track. *bioRxiv*, 036616. https://doi.org/10.1101/036616

Dawson, A. F., Brown, W. W., Anderson, J., Datta, B., Donald, J. N., Hong, K., Allan, S., Mole, T. B., Jones, P. B., & Galante, J. (2020). Mindfulness-based interventions for university students: A systematic review and meta-analysis of randomised controlled trials. *Applied Psychology: Health and Well-Being, 12*(2), 384–410. https://doi.org/10.1111/aphw.12188

de Candolle, A. (1885). *Histoire des sciences et des savants depuis deux siècles: précédée et suivie d'autres études sur des sujets scientifiques en particulier sur l'hérédité et la sélection dans l'espèce humaine.* H. Georg. https://doi.org/10.5962/bhl.title.29432

de Ronde, W., Pols, H. A. P., van Leeuwen, J. P. T. M., & de Jong, F. H. (2003). The importance of oestrogens in males. *Clinical Endocrinology, 58*, 529–542. https://doi.org/10.1046/j.1365-2265.2003.01669.x

DelViscio, J. (2017). *The man with the most famous brain in science.* Retrieved from www.statnews.com/2017/08/02/colin-holmes-famous-brain-science/

Demertzi, A., Liew, C., Ledoux, D., Bruno, M.-A., Sharpe, M., Laureys, S., & Zeman, A. (2009). Dualism persists in the science of mind. *Annals of the New York Academy of Sciences, 1157*(1), 1–9. https://doi.org/10.1111/j.1749-6632.2008.04117.x

Dennis, W. (1954). Bibliographies of eminent psychologists. *American Psychologist, 9*(1), 35–36. https://doi.org/10.1037/h0060842

Diener, E., Oishi, S., & Park, J. (2014). An incomplete list of eminent psychologists of the modern era. *Archives of Scientific Psychology*, *2*(1), 20–31. https://doi.org/10.1037/arc0000006

Douglas, E. T. (1969). *Margaret Sanger: Pioneer of the future*. Holt, Rinehart and Winston.

Downey, G. (2010, July 10). We agree it's WEIRD, but is it WEIRD enough? neuroanthropology.net. Retrieved from https://neuroanthropology.net/2010/07/10/we-agree-its-weird-but-is-it-weird-enough/

Drenth, P. J. D. (2009). The 1971 Istanbul Conference: First face-to-face meeting of many cross-cultural psychologists. *Online Readings in Psychology and Culture*, *1*(1). https://doi.org/10.9707/2307-0919.1005

Drescher, J. (2015). Out of DSM: Depathologizing homosexuality. *Behavioral Sciences*, *5*(4), 565–575. https://doi.org/10.3390/bs5040565

Du Bois, W. E. B. (1932). Black folk and birth control. *Birth Control Review*, *16*(6), 166–167.

DuBois, Z., & Shattuck-Heidorn, H. (2020). Challenging the binary: Gender/sex and the bio-logistics of normalcy. *American Journal of Human Biology*, *33*, e23623. https://doi.org/10.1002/ajhb.23623

Duckworth, A. L., Peterson, C., Matthews, M. D., & Kelly, D. R. (2007). Grit: Perseverance and passion for long-term goals. *Journal of Personality and Social Psychology*, *92*, 1087–1101. https://doi.org/10.1037/0022-3514.92.6.1087

dvgrn. (2013, November 23). Re: Geminoid Challenge [Comment on the online forum post Geminoid Challenge]. ConwayLife.com. Retrieved from https://conwaylife.com/forums/viewtopic.php?f=2&t=1006&p=9917#p9901

Eagly, A. H., & Riger, S. (2014). Feminism and psychology: Critiques of methods and epistemology. *American Psychologist*, *69*(7), 685–702. https://doi.org/10.1037/a0037372

Eaton, A. A., Grzanka, P. R., Schlehofer, M. M., & Silka, L. (2021). Public psychology: Introduction to the special issue. *American Psychologist*, *76*(8), 1209–1216. https://doi.org/10.1037/amp0000933

Edmiston, E. K., & Juster, R. P. (2022). Refining research and representation of sexual and gender diversity in neuroscience. *Biological psychiatry: Cognitive Neuroscience and Neuroimaging*, *7*, 1251–1257. https://doi.org/10.1016/j.bpsc.2022.07.007

Ellis, B. D., & Stam, H. J. (2015). Crisis? What crisis? Cross-cultural psychology's appropriation of cultural psychology. *Culture & Psychology*, *21*, 293–317. https://doi.org/10.1177/1354067X15601198

Engel, G. L. (1977). The need for a new medical model: A challenge for biomedicine. *Science*, *196*(4286), 129–136. https://doi.org/10.1126/science.847460

Epstein, R. (2016). The empty brain. *Aeon*. Retrieved from https://aeon.co/essays/your-brain-does-not-process-information-and-it-is-not-a-computer

Equality Challenge Unit. (2017, April 5). ASSET 2016: experiences of gender equality in STEMM academia and their intersections with ethnicity, sexual orientation, disability and age. *AdvanceHE*. Retrieved from www.advance-he. ac.uk/knowledge-hub/asset-2016.

Ericksen, R. P. (2012). *Complicity in the Holocaust: Churches and universities in Nazi Germany*. Cambridge University Press. https://doi.org/10.1017/ CBO9781139059602

Erickson, P. (1981). The anthropology of Charles Caldwell, M.D. *Isis*, *72*(2), 252–256. http://www.jstor.org/stable/230972

European Commission. (2006). *Delivering on the modernisation agenda for universities: Education, research and innovation (COM 208)*. Retrieved from https://eur-lex.europa.eu/legal-content/EN/TXT/PDF/?uri=CELEX:52006DC0208 &from=EN.

Eysenck, H. J. (1971). *The IQ argument: Race, intelligence and education*. Library Press.

Fancher, R. E. (1983). Alphonse de Candolle, Francis Galton, and the early history of the nature–nurture controversy. *Journal of the History of the Behavioral Sciences*, *19*(4), 341–352. https://doi.org/10.1002/1520-6696(198310)19:4<341::AID-JHBS2300190403>3.0.CO;2-7

Fanon, F. (1952). *Black skin, white masks* (R. Philcox, Trans.). Penguin.

Fanon, F. (1961). *The wretched of the earth* (C. Farrington, Trans.). Penguin.

Farran, S. (2010). Pacific perspectives: Fa'afafine and Fakaleiti in Samoa and Tonga: People between worlds. *Liverpool Law Review*, *31*(1), 13–28. https://doi. org/10.1007/s10991-010-9070-0

Fausto-Sterling, A. (2005). The bare bones of sex: Part 1—Sex and Gender. *Signs: Journal of Women in Culture and Society*, *30*, 1491–1527. https://doi. org/10.1086/424932

Filon, L. N. G., Yule, G. U., Westergaard, H., Greenwood, M., & Pearson, K. (1934). *Speeches delivered at a dinner held in University College, London in honour of Professor Karl Pearson 23 April 1934*. Privately Printed at the University Press.

Fisher, R. A. (1917). Positive eugenics. *The Eugenics Review*, *9*(3), 206.

Fisher, R. A. (1918). The correlation between relatives on the supposition of Mendelian inheritance. *Transactions of the Royal Society of Edinburgh*, *52*(2), 399–433. https://doi.org/10.1017/S0080456800012163

Fisher, R. A. (1925). *Statistical methods for research workers* (11th ed. rev.). Edinburgh.

Fisher, R. A. (1930). *The genetical theory of natural selection*. Clarendon Press. https:// doi.org/10.5962/bhl.title.27468

FKF Applied Research. (2007). Home page. Retrieved from https://web.archive.org/ web/20070630221550/http://www.fkfappliedresearch.com/

Foucault, M. (1965). *Madness and civilization: A history of insanity in the age of reason*. Pantheon Books.

Freeden, M. (1979). Eugenics and progressive thought: A study in ideological affinity. *The Historical Journal*, *22*(3), 645–671. http://www.jstor.org/ stable/2638658

Freire, P. (1970). *Pedagogy of the oppressed*. Herder and Herder.

Frith, U. (2015). Unconscious bias. The Royal Society. Retrieved from https://royalsociety.org/~/media/policy/publications/2015/unconscious-bias-briefing-2015.pdf

Gabrenya, W., & Glazer, S. (2022). Bridging 50 years of theoretical and applied cross-cultural psychology: Contributions of IACCP and JCCP. *Journal of Cross-Cultural Psychology, 53*(7–8), 752–788. https://doi.org/10.1177/00220221221110874

Galaiya, R., Kinross, J., & Arulampalam, T. (2020). Factors associated with burnout syndrome in surgeons: A systematic review. *Annals of the Royal College of Surgeons of England, 102*(6), 401–407. https://doi.org/10.1308/rcsann.2020.0040

Galton, F. (1869). *Hereditary genius: An inquiry into its laws and consequences*. Macmillan and Co. https://doi.org/10.1037/13474-000

Galton, F. S. (1874). *English men of science: Their nature and nurture*. Macmillan and Co. www.biodiversitylibrary.org/item/73240

Galton, F. (1883). *Inquiries into human faculty and its development*. Macmillan and Co. https://doi.org/10.1037/14178-000

Galton, F. (1885). On the anthropometric laboratory at the late international health exhibition. *Journal of the Anthropological Institute of Great Britain and Ireland, 14*, 205–221. https://doi.org/10.2307/2841978

Galton, F. (1886). Regression towards mediocrity in hereditary stature. *Journal of the Anthropological Institute of Great Britain and Ireland, 15*, 246–263. https://doi.org/10.2307/2841583

Galton, F. (1888). Co-relations and their measurement, chiefly from anthropometric data. *Proceedings of the Royal Society of London, 45*, 135–145. http://www.jstor.org/stable/114860

Galton, F. (1889). On the principle and methods of assigning marks for bodily efficiency. *British Association Report*, 474–477.

Galton, F. (1907). *Probability, the foundation of eugenics: The Herbert Spencer lecture delivered on June 5, 1907*. Clarendon Press.

Galton, F. (c. 1910). *The Eugenic College of Kantsaywhere* (unpublished novel held in and digitised by the Galton Archive at UCL). https://ucl.primo.exlibrisgroup.com/permalink/44UCL_INST/5apqbq/alma9931472632604761

Gardner, M. (1970). The fantastic combinations of John Conway's new solitaire game 'life'. *Scientific American, 223*(4), 120–123. http://www.jstor.org/stable/24927642

Gelb, S. A. (1986). Henry H. Goddard and the immigrants, 1910–1917: The studies and their social context. *Journal of the History of the Behavioral Sciences, 22*(4), 324–332. https://doi.org/10.1002/1520-6696(198610)22:4<324::AID-JHBS2300220404>3.0.CO;2-Y

Gelfand, S. D. (2016). Using insights from applied moral psychology to promote ethical behavior among engineering students and professional engineers. *Science and Engineering Ethics, 22*(5), 1513–1534. https://doi.org/10.1007/s11948-015-9721-6

Geraci, L., Balsis, S., & Busch, A. J. B. (2015). Gender and the h index in psychology. *Scientometrics, 105*(3), 2023–2034. https://doi.org/10.1007/s11192-015-1757-5

Gibson, B., Robbins, E., & Rochat, P. (2015). White bias in 3–7-year-old children across cultures. *Journal of Cognition and Culture, 15*(3–4), 344–373. https://doi.org/10.1163/15685373-12342155

Gibson, N. C., & Beneduce, R. (2017). *Frantz Fanon, psychiatry and politics*. Rowman & Littlefield International.

Glomb, K., Rué Queralt, J., Pascucci, D., Defferrard, M., Tourbier, S., Carboni, M., Rubega, M., Vulliémoz, S., Plomp, G., & Hagmann, P. (2020). Connectome spectral analysis to track EEG task dynamics on a subsecond scale. *NeuroImage, 221*, 117137. https://doi.org/10.1016/j.neuroimage.2020.117137

Goddard, H. H. (1917). Mental tests and the immigrant. *Journal of Delinquency, 11*(5), 243–277.

Goddard, H. H. (1919). *Psychology of the normal and subnormal*. Dodd, Mead and Company.

Golly SourceForge (2021). Retrieved from https://golly.sourceforge.net/

Goode, J. (2023). Mamie Phipps Clark. *Current Biology, 33*(7), R243–R246. https://doi.org/10.1016/j.cub.2023.02.068

Goodenough, F. L. (1926). A new approach to the measurement of the intelligence of young children. *The Pedagogical Seminary and Journal of Genetic Psychology, 33*(2), 185–211. https://doi.org/10.1080/08856559.1926.10532353

Goodenough, F. L. (1928). Studies in the psychology of children's drawings. *Psychological Bulletin, 25*(5), 272–283. https://doi.org/10.1037/h0071049

Goodey, C. F. (2011). *A history of intelligence and 'intellectual disability': The shaping of psychology in early modern Europe*. Routledge.

Gordon, E. W. (1992). Human diversity, cultural hegemony, and the integrity of the academic canon. *Journal of Negro Education, 61*(3), 405–418. https://doi.org/10.2307/2295257

Gosset, W. S. (1947). *Students' collected papers, edited by E. S. Pearson and John Wishart; with a foreword by Launce McMullen*. Biometrika Office, University College.

Gottlieb, G. (2007). Probabilistic epigenesis. *Developmental Science, 10*(1), 1–11. https://doi.org/10.1111/j.1467-7687.2007.00556.x

Granger, D. A., Shirtcliff, E. A., Booth, A., Kivlighan, K. T., & Schwartz, E. B. (2004). The 'trouble' with salivary testosterone. *Psychoneuroendocrinology, 29*, 1229–1240. https://doi.org/10.1016/j.psyneuen.2004.02.005

Green, C. S., & Bavelier, D. (2008). Exercising your brain: A review of human brain plasticity and training-induced learning. *Psychology and Aging, 23*(4), 692–701. https://doi.org/10.1037/a0014345

Green, T. L., & Hagiwara, N. (2020). The problem with implicit bias training. *Scientific American*. Retrieved from www.scientificamerican.com/article/the-problem-with-implicit-bias-training/

Greenblatt, S. H. (1995). Phrenology in the science and culture of the 19th century. *Neurosurgery, 37*(4), 790–804; discussion 804–795. https://doi.org/10.1227/00006123-199510000-00025

Gross, D., & Schäfer, G. (2011). Egas Moniz (1874–1955) and the 'invention' of modern psychosurgery: A historical and ethical reanalysis under special consideration of Portuguese original sources. *Neurosurgical Focus, 30*(2), E8. https://doi.org/10.3171/2010.10.Focus10214

Grzanka, P. R. (2020). From buzzword to critical psychology: An invitation to take intersectionality seriously. *Women & Therapy, 43*(3–4), 244–261. https://doi.org/10.1080/02703149.2020.1729473

Grzanka, P. R., & Cole, E. R. (2021). An argument for bad psychology: Disciplinary disruption, public engagement, and social transformation. *American Psychologist, 76*(8), 1334. https://doi.org/10.1037/amp0000853

Haeckel, E. (2009). *The riddle of the universe at the close of the nineteenth century.* Cambridge University Press.

Haggbloom, S. J., Warnick, R., Warnick, J. E., Jones, V. K., Yarbrough, G. L., Russell, T. M., Borecky, C. M., McGahhey, R., Powell, J. L., Beavers, J., & Monte, E. (2002). The 100 most eminent psychologists of the 20th century. *Review of General Psychology, 6*(2), 139–152. https://doi.org/10.1037/1089-2680.6.2.139

Halperin, D. M. (2002). *How to do the history of homosexuality.* University of Chicago Press.

Halvorsrud, K., Nazroo, J., Otis, M., Brown Hajdukova, E., & Bhui, K. (2019). Ethnic inequalities in the incidence of diagnosis of severe mental illness in England: A systematic review and new meta-analyses for non-affective and affective psychoses. *Social Psychiatry and Psychiatric Epidemiology, 54*(11), 1311–1323. https://doi.org/10.1007/s00127-019-01758-y

Hammer, B. (2007, May 28). FKF seeks new funding for its mind-delving scans. *Washington Business Journal.* Retrieved from www.bizjournals.com/washington/stories/2007/05/28/story6.html

Harding, S. G. (1993). Introduction: Eurocentric scientific illiteracy—a challenge for the world community. In S. G. Harding (Ed.), *The 'racial' economy of science: Toward a democratic future* (pp. 1–29). Indiana University Press.

Harding, S. (1995). 'Strong objectivity': A response to the new objectivity question. *Synthese, 104*(3), 331–349. https://doi.org/10.1007/BF01064504

Harper, D. J. (2013). On the persistence of psychiatric diagnosis: Moving beyond a zombie classification system. *Feminism & Psychology, 23*(1), 78–85. https://doi.org/10.1177/0959353512467970

Harris, A. (1959). Florence L. Goodenough, 1886–1959. *Child Development, 30*(3), 305–306.

Harris, B. (1979). Whatever happened to little Albert? *American Psychologist, 34*(2), 151–160. https://doi.org/10.1037/0003-066X.34.2.151

Hecht, J. M. (2003). *The end of the soul: Scientific modernity, atheism, and anthropology in France.* Columbia University Press.

Hedges, E. R. (1973). Afterword. In *The Yellow Wall-Paper by Charlotte Perkins Gilman* (pp. 37–68). The Feminist Press.

Heikkilä, M. (2023). OpenAI's hunger for data is coming back to bite it. Retrieved from www.technologyreview.com/2023/04/19/1071789/openais-hunger-for-data-is-coming-back-to-bite-it/

Henrich, J., Heine, S. J., & Norenzayan, A. (2010). The weirdest people in the world? *Behavioral and Brain Sciences, 33*(2–3), 61–83. https://doi.org/10.1017/S0140525X0999152X

HESA (Higher Education Statistics Agency). (2023a). What are their salaries? Retrieved 9 August 2023 from www.hesa.ac.uk/data-and-analysis/staff/salaries

HESA (Higher Education Statistics Agency). (2023b). HE finance data. Retrieved 19 March 2023 from www.hesa.ac.uk/data-and-analysis/finances/uk-he-finances-2019-20

Heywood, J. (2001). *A history of childhood*. Polity Press.

Hines, M. (2020). Neuroscience and sex/gender: Looking back and forward. *Journal of Neuroscience, 40*(1), 37–43. https://doi.org/10.1523/jneurosci.0750-19.2019

Hochanadel, A., & Finamore, D. (2015). Fixed and growth mindset in education and how grit helps students persist in the face of adversity. *Journal of International Education Research, 11*, 47. https://doi.org/10.19030/jier.v11i1.9099

Hoekzema, E., Barba-Muller, E., Pozzobon, C., Picado, M., Lucco, F., Garcia-Garcia, D., Soliva, J. C., Tobena, A., Desco, M., Crone, E. A., Ballesteros, A., Carmona, S., & Vilarroya, O. (2017). *Nature Neuroscience, 20*, 287–296. https://doi.org/10.1038/nn.4458

Hogben, L. (1919). Modern heredity and social science. *Socialist Review, 16*, 147–156.

Hogben, L., Charles, E., & Slome, D. (1931). Studies on the pituitary: VIII. The relation of the pituitary gland to calcium metabolism and ovarian function in xenopus. *Journal of Experimental Biology, 8*(4), 345–354. https://doi.org/10.1242/jeb.8.4.345

Hogben, M., & Waterman, C. K. (1997). Are all of your students represented in their textbooks? A content analysis of coverage of diversity issues in introductory psychology textbooks. *Teaching of Psychology, 24*(2), 95–100. https://doi.org/10.1207/s15328023top2402_3

Hollingworth, L. S. (1914). Variability as related to sex differences in achievement: A critique. *American Journal of Sociology, 19*(4), 510–530. https://doi.org/10.1086/212287

Hollingworth, L. S. (1916). Social devices for impelling women to bear and rear children. *American Journal of Sociology, 22*(1), 19–29. https://doi.org/10.1086/212572

Holmes, C. J., Hoge, R., Collins, L., Woods, R., Toga, A. W., & Evans, A. C. (1998). Enhancement of MR images using registration for signal averaging. *Journal of Computer Assisted Tomography, 22*(2). https://doi.org/10.1097/00004728-199803000-00032

Hooker, E. (1957). The adjustment of the male overt homosexual. *Journal of Projective Techniques, 21*(1), 18–31. https://doi.org/10.1080/08853126. 1957.10380742

hooks, b. (1994). *Teaching to transgress: Education as the practice of freedom.* Routledge. https://doi.org/10.3366/para.1994.17.3.270

Horwitz, J. (2021). The Facebook files. *Wall Street Journal.* Retrieved from www.wsj. com/articles/the-facebook-files-11631713039

Hudson, B. (2017). The poor child's nurse. Wellcome Collection. Retrieved from https://wellcomecollection.org/articles/WckzzigAACe3DJPD

Huettel, S. A., Song, A. W., & McCarthy, G. (2009). *Functional magnetic resonance imaging.* Oxford University Press.

Hunter, S. (2019). *Hijras and the legacy of British colonial rule in India.* Retrieved from https://blogs.lse.ac.uk/gender/2019/06/17/hijras-and-the-legacy-of-british-colonial-rule-in-india/

Hyde, J. S., Bigler, R. S., Joel, D., Tate, C. C., & Van Anders, S. M. (2019). The future of sex and gender in psychology: Five challenges to the gender binary. *American Psychologist, 74*(2), 171–193. https://doi.org/10.1037/amp0000307

Iacoboni, M., Freedman, J., Kaplan, J., Freedman, T., Knapp, B., & Fitzgerald, K. (2007, November 11). This is your brain on politics. *New York Times.* Retrieved from www.nytimes.com/2007/11/11/opinion/11freedman.html

Jack, P. (2022). Equal Pay Day 2022: What is the gender pay gap at my university? *Times Higher Education.* Retrieved from www.timeshighereducation.com/news/equal-pay-day-2022-what-gender-pay-gap-my-university

Jamison, R. N., Butler, S. F., Budman, S. H., Edwards, R. R., & Wasan, A. D. (2010). Gender differences in risk factors for aberrant prescription opioid use. *Journal of Pain, 11*(4), 312–320. https://doi.org/10.1016/j.jpain.2009.07.016

Jansen, J. C., Osterhammel, J., & Riemer, J. (2017). *Decolonization: A short history.* Princeton University Press.

Jensen, A. (1969). How much can we boost IQ and scholastic achievement. *Harvard Educational Review, 39*(1), 1–123. https://doi.org/10.17763/haer.39.1.l3u15956627424k7

Jensen, C. C. (1928, August). *The ways of behaviorism/Psychological care of infant and child.* [Review] *The Atlantic.*

Jerrim, J., & de Vries, R. (2023). Are peer reviews of grant proposals reliable? An analysis of Economic and Social Research Council (ESRC) funding applications. *Social Science Journal, 60*(1), 91–109. https://doi.org/10.1080/03623319.2020.172 8506

Joel, D. (2021). Beyond the binary: Rethinking sex and the brain. *Neuroscience & Biobehavioural Reviews, 122,* 165–175. https://doi.org/10.1016/j.neubiorev.2020.11.018

Joel, D., & Yankelevitch-Yahav, R. (2014). Reconceptualizing sex, brain and psychopathology: Interaction, interaction, interaction. *British Journal of Pharmacology, 171*(20), 4620–4635. https://doi.org/10.1111/bph.12732

Johnson, J., Madill, A., Koutsopoulou, G. Z., Brown, C., & Harris, R. (2020). Tackling gender imbalance in psychology. *The Psychologist*. Retrieved from www. bps.org.uk/psychologist/tackling-gender-imbalance-psychology

Jolly, J. L. (2010). Florence L. Goodenough: Portrait of a psychologist. *Roeper Review*, *32*(2), 98–105. https://doi.org/10.1080/02783191003587884

Kalinke, U., Barouch, D. H., Rizzi, R., Lagkadinou, E., Türeci, Ö., Pather, S., & Neels, P. (2022). Clinical development and approval of COVID-19 vaccines. *Expert Review of Vaccines*, 1–11. https://doi.org/10.1080/1476058 4.2022.2042257

Kamin, L. J. (1974). *The science and politics of IQ*. Lawrence Erlbaum.

Karter, J. M., & Kamens, S. R. (2019). Toward conceptual competence in psychiatric diagnosis: An ecological model for critiques of the DSM. In S. Steingard (Ed.), *Critical psychiatry: Controversies and clinical implications* (pp. 17–69). Springer International Publishing. https://doi.org/10.1007/978-3-030-02732-2_2

Kaufman, A. S. (2009). *IQ testing 101*. Springer Publishing Company.

Keller, E. F. (1985). *Reflections on gender and science*. Yale University Press.

Keller, E. F. (2003). *A feeling for the organism: The life and work of Barbara McClintock* (10th ed.). Henry Holt and Company.

Kellner, C. H., Greenberg, R. M., Murrough, J. W., Bryson, E. O., Briggs, M. C., & Pasculli, R. M. (2012). ECT in treatment-resistant depression. *American Journal of Psychiatry*, *169*(12), 1238–1244. https://doi.org/10.1176/appi. ajp.2012.12050648

Kelly, J. (2014). *Sigmund Freud: The phrases you use without realising it*. Retrieved from www.bbc.co.uk/news/magazine-29251040

Kern, S. (1974). Olfactory ontology and scented harmonies: On the history of smell. *Journal of Popular Culture*, *VII*(4), 816–824. https://doi.org/10.1111/j.0022-3840.1974.0704_816.x

Keynes, J. M. (1937). Some consequences of a declining population. *Eugenics Review*, *29*, 13–17.

Khanna, R. (2003). *Dark continents: Psychoanalysis and colonialism*. Duke University Press. https://doi.org/10.1215/9780822384588

Kinsey, A. C., Pomeroy, W. B., & Martin, C. E. (1949). Sexual behavior in the human male. *Journal of Nervous and Mental Disease*, *109*(3), 283. https://doi. org/10.1097/00005053-194903000-00016

Kinsey, A. C., Pomeroy, W. B., Martin, C. E., & Gebhard, P. H. (1953). *Sexual behavior in the human female*. Saunders.

Klee, E. (1985). *Dokumente zur 'Euthanasie'*. Fischer Taschenbuch.

Kloos, B., Hill, J., Thomas, E., Wandersman, A., Elias, M. J., & Dalton, J. H. (2012). *Community psychology*. Cengage Learning.

Klukoff, H., Kanani, H., Gaglione, C., & Alexander, A. (2021). Toward an abolitionist practice of psychology: Reimagining psychology's relationship with the criminal justice system. *Journal of Humanistic Psychology*, *61*(4), 451–469. https://doi.org/10.1177/00221678211015755

Koren, M. (2013). B.F. Skinner: The man who taught pigeons to play ping-pong and rats to pull levers. *Smithsonian Magazine*. Retrieved from www.smithsonianmag.com/science-nature/bf-skinner-the-man-who-taught-pigeons-to-play-ping-pong-and-rats-to-pull-levers-5363946/

Krukowski, R. A., Jagsi, R., & Cardel, M. I. (2021). Academic productivity differences by gender and child age in science, technology, engineering, mathematics, and medicine faculty during the COVID-19 pandemic. *Journal of Women's Health*, *30*(3), 341–347. https://doi.org/10.1089/jwh.2020.8710

Kruskal, W. (1980). The significance of Fisher: A review of R.A. Fisher: The Life of a Scientist. *Journal of the American Statistical Association*, *75*(372), 1019–1030. https://doi.org/10.2307/2287199

Kubrick, S. (1968). *2001: A space odyssey* Metro-Goldwyn-Mayer Corp.

Kuhlmann, F. (1912). A revision of the Binet-Simon system for measuring the intelligence of children. *Journal of Psycho-Asthenics Monograph Supplements*, *1*(1), 1–41.

Kumar, M. (2011). (Re)Locating the feminist standpoint in the practice of psychology today: A case of India. In A. Rutherford, R. Capdevila, V. Undurti, & I. Palmary (Eds.), *Handbook of international feminisms: Perspectives on psychology, women, culture, and rights* (pp. 175–193). Springer New York. https://doi.org/10.1007/978-1-4419-9869-9_9

Kurtiş, T., & Adams, G. (2015). Decolonizing liberation: Toward a transnational feminist psychology. *Journal of Social and Political Psychology*, *3*(1), 388–413. https://doi.org/10.5964/jspp.v3i1.326

Larivière, V., Ni, C., Gingras, Y., Cronin, B., & Sugimoto, C. R. (2013). Bibliometrics: Global gender disparities in science. *Nature*, *504*(7479), 211–213. https://doi.org/10.1038/504211a

Lewontin, R. C., Rose, S., & Kamin, L. J. (1993). IQ: The rank ordering of the world. In S. G. Harding (Ed.), *The 'Racial' economy of science: Toward a democratic future* (pp. 142–160). Indiana University Press.

Liening, S. H., Stanton, S. J., Saini, E. K., & Schultheiss, O. C. (2010). Salivary testosterone, cortisol, and progesterone: Two-week stability, interhormone correlations, and effects of time of day, menstrual cycle, and oral contraceptive use on steroid hormone levels. *Physiology & Behaviour*, *99*, 8–16. https://doi.org/10.1016/j.physbeh.2009.10.001

Lindqvist, A., Sendén, M. G., & Renström, E. A. (2021). What is gender, anyway: A review of the options for operationalising gender. *Psychology & Sexuality*, *12*(4), 332–344. https://doi.org/10.1080/19419899.2020.1729844

Linnaeus, C. (1735). *Systema naturæ, sive regna tria naturæ systematice proposita per classes, ordines, genera, & species*. Theodor Haak.

Linnaeus, C. (1737). *Critica botanica*. Conrad Wishoff.

Linstrum, E. (2016). *Ruling minds: Psychology in the British Empire*. Harvard University Press.

Locke, J. (1690/1997). *An essay concerning human understanding*. Penguin.

Lonner, W. J. (1974). The past, present, and future of cross-cultural psychology. 54th Annual Convention of the Western Psychological Association, San Francisco, California.

López-Muñoz, F., Ucha-Udabe, R., & Alamo, C. (2005). The history of barbiturates a century after their clinical introduction. *Neuropsychiatric Disease and Treatment, 1*(4), 329–343.

Louçã, F. (2009). Emancipation through interaction – how eugenics and statistics converged and diverged. *Journal of the History of Biology, 42*, 649–684. https://doi.org/10.1007/s10739-008-9167-7

Lugones, M. (2016). The coloniality of gender. In W. Harcourt (Ed.), *The Palgrave handbook of gender and development: Critical engagements in feminist theory and practice* (pp. 13–33). Palgrave Macmillan UK. https://doi.org/10.1007/978-1-137-38273-3_2

Luthar, S. S., Cicchetti, D., & Becker, B. (2000). The construct of resilience: A critical evaluation and guidelines for future work. *Child Development, 71*(3), 543–562. https://doi.org/10.1111/1467-8624.00164

MacKenzie, D. A. (1981). *Statistics in Britain, 1865–1930: The social construction of scientific knowledge*. Edinburgh University Press.

Maguire, E. A., Gadian, D. G., Johnsrude, I. S., Good, C. D., Ashburner, J., Frackowiak, R. S. J., & Frith, C. D. (2000). Navigation-related structural change in the hippocampi of taxi drivers. *Proceedings of the National Academy of Sciences, 97*(8), 4398–4403. https://doi.org/10.1073/pnas.070039597

Malane, R. A. (2005). *Sex in mind: The gendered brain in nineteenth-century literature and mental sciences*. Peter Lang.

Mamlouk, G. M., Dorris, D. M., Barrett, L. R., & Meitzen, J. (2020). Sex bias and omission in neuroscience research is influenced by research model and journal, but not reported NIH funding. *Frontiers in Neuroendocrinology, 57*, 100835. https://doi.org/10.1016/j.yfrne.2020.100835

Manzo, L. K. C., & Minello, A. (2020). Mothers, childcare duties, and remote working under COVID-19 lockdown in Italy: Cultivating communities of care. *Dialogues in Human Geography, 10*(2), 120–123. https://doi.org/10.1177/2043820620934268

Marcus, S. (2007). *Between women: Friendship, desire, and marriage in Victorian England*. Princeton University Press. https://doi.org/10.1515/9781400830855

Martín-Baró, I. (1994). *Writings for a liberation psychology*. Harvard University Press.

Martinez-Garcia, M., Paternina-Die, M., Desco, M., Vilarroya, O., & Carmona, S. (2021). *Frontiers in Global Women's Health, 2*, 742775. https://doi.org/10.3389/fgwh.2021.742775

Mason, C. (2022). A levels 2022: Top grades fall at private schools. Retrieved from www.tes.com/magazine/news/secondary/levels-2022-top-grades-fall-private-schools

Massa, M. G., Aghi, K., & Hill, M. (2023). Deconstructing sex: Strategies for undoing binary thinking in neuroendocrinology and behavior. *Hormones and Behavior, 156*, 105441. https://doi.org/10.1016/j.yhbeh.2023.105441

Matchock, R. L., Dorn, L. D., & Susman, E. J. (2007). Diurnal and seasonal cortisol, testosterone, and DHEA rhythms in boys and girls during puberty. *Chronobiology International, 24*, 969–990. https://doi.org/10.1080/07420520701649471

Mayes, R., & Horwitz, A. V. (2005). DSM-III and the revolution in the classification of mental illness. *Journal of the History of the Behavioral Sciences, 41*(3), 249–267. https://doi.org/10.1002/jhbs.20103

Mazziotta, J. C., Woods, R., Iacoboni, M., Sicotte, N., Yaden, K., Tran, M., Bean, C., Kaplan, J., & Toga, A. W. (2009). The myth of the normal, average human brain—The ICBM experience: (1) Subject screening and eligibility. *NeuroImage, 44*(3), 914–922. https://doi.org/10.1016/j.neuroimage.2008.07.062

McGann, J. P. (2017). Poor human olfaction is a 19th-century myth. *Science, 356*(6338), eaam7263. https://doi.org/10.1126/science.aam7263

McGrayne, S. B. (2011). *The theory that would not die: How Bayes' rule cracked the enigma code, hunted down Russian submarines, & emerged triumphant from two centuries of controversy.* Yale University Press.

McNeill, L. (2017). How a psychologist's work on race identity helped overturn school segregation in 1950s America. *Smithsonian Magazine*. Retrieved from www.smithsonianmag.com/science-nature/psychologist-work-racial-identity-helped-overturn-school-segregation-180966934/

Mehta, J. (2015, April 27). The problem with grit. *Education Week*. Retrieved from www.edweek.org/education/opinion-the-problem-with-grit/2015/04

Menon, S. S., & Krishnamurthy, K. (2019). A comparison of static and dynamic functional connectivities for identifying subjects and biological sex using intrinsic individual brain connectivity. *Scientific Reports, 9*(1), 5729. https://doi.org/10.1038/s41598-019-42090-4

Metzl, J. M. (2010). *The protest psychosis: How schizophrenia became a Black disease.* Beacon Press.

Micale, M. S. (1989). Hysteria and its historiography: A review of past and present writings (I). *History of Science, 27*(3), 223–261. https://doi.org/10.1177/007327538902700301

Mignolo, W. D. (2007). DELINKING. *Cultural Studies, 21*(2–3), 449–514. https://doi.org/10.1080/09502380601162647

Moncrieff, J. (2018). Research on a 'drug-centred' approach to psychiatric drug treatment: Assessing the impact of mental and behavioural alterations produced by psychiatric drugs. *Epidemiology and Psychiatric Sciences, 27*(2), 133–140. https://doi.org/10.1017/s2045796017000555

Moncrieff, J. (2019). An alternative approach to drug treatment in psychiatry. In S. Steingard (Ed.), *Critical psychiatry: Controversies and clinical implications* (pp. 97–111). Springer International Publishing. https://doi.org/10.1007/978-3-030-02732-2_4

Moncrieff, J., & Steingard, S. (2019). What is critical psychiatry? In S. Steingard (Ed.), *Critical psychiatry: Controversies and clinical implications* (pp. 1–15). Springer International Publishing. https://doi.org/10.1007/978-3-030-02732-2_1

Morgenroth, T., & Ryan, M. K. (2020). The effects of gender trouble: An integrative theoretical framework of the perpetuation and disruption of the gender/sex binary. *Perspectives on Psychological Science, 16*(6), 1113–1142. https://doi.org/10.1177/1745691620902442

Morgenthau, H. J. (1964). Modern science and political power. *Columbia Law Review, 64*(8), 1386–1409. https://doi.org/10.2307/1120764

Morris, D. B. (1991). *Culture of pain.* University of California Press.

Mowrer, W. M. C. (1933). Intelligence scales for preschool children. *Child Development, 4*(4), 318–322. https://doi.org/10.2307/1125771

Moxham, N., & Fyfe, A. (2018). The Royal Society and the prehistory of peer review, 1665–1965. *The Historical Journal, 61*(4), 863–889. https://doi.org/10.1017/S0018246X17000334

Mülberger, A. (2020). Biographies of a scientific subject: The intelligence test. In *Oxford research encyclopedia.* Oxford University Press.

Murphy, F. C., Bishop, D. V. M., & Sigala, N. (2014). Women scientists in psychology – time for action. *The Psychologist, 27*(12), 918–922.

Murphy, G. (1929). *An historical introduction to modern psychology.* Harcourt, Brace.

Murphy, M. C., Mejia, A. F., Mejia, J., Yan, X., Cheryan, S., Dasgupta, N., Destin, M., Fryberg, S. A., Garcia, J. A., Haines, E. L., Harackiewicz, J. M., Ledgerwood, A., Moss-Racusin, C. A., Park, L. E., Perry, S. P., Ratliff, K. A., Rattan, A., Sanchez, D. T., Savani, K., . . . Pestilli, F. (2020). Open science, communal culture, and women's participation in the movement to improve science. *Proceedings of the National Academy of Sciences, 117*(39), 24154–24164. https://doi.org/10.1073/pnas.1921320117

National Institutes of Health Office of Research on Women's Health. (2018). History of women's participation in clinical research. Retrieved from https://orwh.od.nih.gov/toolkit/recruitment/history

Newbronner, E., Glendinning, C., Atkin, K., & Wadman, R. (2019). The health and quality of life of Thalidomide survivors as they age – evidence from a UK survey. *PLoS ONE, 14*(1), e0210222. https://doi.org/10.1371/journal.pone.0210222

Newman, J. H. (1852). *The idea of a university defined and illustrated in nine discourses delivered to the Catholics of Dublin.* Project Gutenberg. www.gutenberg.org/files/24526/24526-pdf.pdf

Nguyen, T. V., McCracken, J., Ducharme, S., Botteron, K. N., Mahabir, M., Johnson, W., Israel, M., Evans, A. C., & Karama, S. (2013). Testosterone-related cortical maturation across childhood and adolescence. *Cerebral Cortex, 23*, 1424–1432. https://doi.org/10.1093/cercor/bhs125

Nuffield Trust. (2023). Enoch Powell – Address to the National Association of Mental Health Annual Conference, 9 March 1961. Retrieved from www.

nuffieldtrust.org.uk/health-and-social-care-explained/the-history-of-the-nhs/
enoch-powell-address-to-the-national-association-of-mental-health-annual-
conference-9-march-1961

O'Neil, C. (2016). *Weapons of math destruction: How big data increases inequality and threatens democracy.* Crown Books.

O'Reilly, R. (2022). *Qualifications price index 2021.* Retrieved from www.gov.uk/
government/publications/qualifications-price-index-2021/qualifications-
price-index-2021

Odic, D., & Wojcik, E. H. (2020). The publication gender gap in psychology.
American Psychologist, 75(1), 92–103. https://doi.org/10.1037/amp0000480

Oettel, M., & Mukhopadhyay, A. K. (2004). Progesterone: The forgotten hormone
in men? *The Aging Male, 7,* 236–257. https://doi.org/10.1080/1368553
0400004199

Office for National Statistics. (2022). Gender pay gap in the UK: 2022. Retrieved
from www.ons.gov.uk/employmentandlabourmarket/peopleinwork/
earningsandworkinghours/bulletins/genderpaygapintheuk/2022

Olbert, C. M., Nagendra, A., & Buck, B. (2018). Meta-analysis of Black vs. White
racial disparity in schizophrenia diagnosis in the United States: Do structured
assessments attenuate racial disparities? *Journal of Abnormal Psychology, 127*(1),
104–115. https://doi.org/10.1037/abn0000309

Oleszkiewicz, A., Alizadeh, R., Altundag, A., Chen, B., Corrai, A., Fanari, R.,
Farhadi, M., Gupta, N., Habel, R., & Hudson, R. (2020). Global study of
variability in olfactory sensitivity. *Behavioral Neuroscience, 134*(5), 394–406.
https://doi.org/10.1037/bne0000378

Open Science Collaboration. (2012). An open, large-scale, collaborative effort to
estimate the reproducibility of psychological science. *Perspectives on
Psychological Science, 7*(6), 657–660. https://doi.org/10.1177/1745691612462588

Orchard, E. R., Rutherford, H. J. V., Holmes, A. J., & Jamadar, S. D. (2023). Matrescence:
Lifetime impact of motherhood on cognition and the brain. *Trends in Cognitive
Sciences, 27,* 302–316. https://doi.org/10.1016/j.tics.2022.12.002

Oudshoorn, N. (1994). *Beyond the natural body: An archaeology of sex hormones.*
Routledge.

Paludi, M. A., & Strayer, L. A. (1985). What's in an author's name? Differential
evaluations of performance as a function of author's name. *Sex Roles: A Journal
of Research, 12*(3–4), 353–361. https://doi.org/10.1007/BF00287601

Pearce, J. M. S. (2009). Marie-Jean-Pierre Flourens (1794–1867) and cortical
localization. *European Neurology, 61*(5), 311–314. https://doi.org/10.1159/000206858

Pearl, R., & Pearl, M. D. (1909). Data on variation in the comb of the domestic
fowl. *Biometrika, 6*(4), 420–432. https://doi.org/10.1093/biomet/6.4.420

Pearson, E. S., Plackett, R. L., & Barnard, G. A. (1990). *Student: A statistical biography
of William Sealy Gosset.* Clarendon Press; Oxford University Press.

Pearson, K. (1892). *The grammar of science.* Scott.

Pearson, K. (1895). Note on regression and inheritance in the case of two parents. *Proceedings of the Royal Society of London, 58*(347–352), 240–242. https://doi.org/10.1098/rspl.1895.0041

Pearson, K. (1896). Mathematical contributions to the theory of evolution. III. Regression, heredity, and panmixia. *Philosophical Transactions of the Royal Society of London. Series A, Containing Papers of a Mathematical or Physical Character, 187*, 253–318. https://doi.org/10.1098/rsta.1896.0007

Pearson, K. (1900). On the criterion that a given system of deviations from the probable in the case of a correlated system of variables is such that it can be reasonably supposed to have arisen from random sampling. *The London, Edinburgh, and Dublin Philosophical Magazine and Journal of Science, 50*(302), 157–175. https://doi.org/10.1080/14786440009463897

Pearson, K. (1903). The law of ancestral heredity. *Biometrika, 2*(2), 211–228. https://doi.org/10.1093/biomet/2.2.211

Pearson, K. (1909). Note on the skin-colour of the crosses between negro and white. *Biometrika, 6*(4), 348–353. https://doi.org/10.1093/biomet/6.4.348

Pearson, K., Fisher, R. A., & Inman, H. F. (1994). Karl Pearson and R. A. Fisher on statistical tests: A 1935 exchange from nature. *The American Statistician, 48*(1), 2–11. https://doi.org/10.2307/2685077

Pérez-Álvarez, M. (2018). Psychology as a science of subject and comportment, beyond the mind and behavior. *Integrative Psychological and Behavioral Science, 52*(1), 25–51. https://doi.org/10.1007/s12124-017-9408-4

Persson, S., & Pownall, M. (2021). Can open science be a tool to dismantle claims of hardwired brain sex differences? Opportunities and challenges for feminist researchers. *Psychology of Women Quarterly, 45*(4), 493–504. https://doi.org/10.1177/03616843211037613

Pinter, R. (1933). The feebleminded child. In C. Murchison (Ed.), *A handbook of child psychology*. Clark University Press.

Pintner, R. (1927). Intelligence tests. *Psychological Bulletin, 24*(7), 391–408. https://doi.org/10.1037/h0072717

Planned Parenthood. (2021). Opposition claims about Margaret Sanger. Retrieved from www.plannedparenthood.org/uploads/filer_public/cc/2e/cc2e84f2-126f-41a5-a24b-43e093c47b2c/210414-sanger-opposition-claims-p01.pdf

Platt, J. R. (1964). Strong inference: Certain systematic methods of scientific thinking may produce much more rapid progress than others. *Science, 146*(3642), 347–353. https://doi.org/10.1126/science.146.3642.347

Poldrack, R. A. (2011). Inferring mental states from neuroimaging data: From reverse inference to large-scale decoding. *Neuron, 72*(5), 692–697. https://doi.org/10.1016/j.neuron.2011.11.001

Pollet, T. V., & Saxton, T. K. (2019). How diverse are the samples used in the journals 'Evolution & Human Behavior' and 'Evolutionary Psychology'? *Evolutionary Psychological Science, 5*(3), 357–368. https://doi.org/10.1007/s40806-019-00192-2

Poortinga, Y. H. (2016). Integration of basic controversies in cross-cultural psychology. *Psychology and Developing Societies, 28*(2), 161–182. https://doi.org/10.1177/0971333616657169

Poskett, J. (2019). *Materials of the mind: Phrenology, race, and the global history of science, 1815–1920.* University of Chicago Press.

Procter, J. (2004). *Stuart Hall.* Routledge.

Proctor, R. W., & Evans, R. (2014). E. B. Titchener, women psychologists, and the experimentalists. *American Journal of Psychology, 127*(4), 501–526. https://doi.org/10.5406/amerjpsyc.127.4.0501

Quiñones-Vidal, E., Loźpez-García, J. J., Peñarañda-Ortega, M., & Tortosa-Gil, F. (2004). The nature of social and personality psychology as reflected in JPSP, 1965–2000. *Journal of Personality and Social Psychology, 86*, 435–452. https://doi.org/10.1037/0022-3514.86.3.435

Rad, M. S., Martingano, A. J., & Ginges, J. (2018). Toward a psychology of *Homo sapiens*: Making psychological science more representative of the human population. *Proceedings of the National Academy of Sciences, 115*(45), 11401–11405. https://doi.org/10.1073/pnas.1721165115

Radke, H. (2018). The magic bullet: How a drug called Miltown ushered in an age of pill-popping for anxious Americans. Retrieved from www.topic.com/the-magic-bullet

Raman, S. (2023). What it means to practise values-based research. *Nature* [Online ahead of print]. https://doi.org/10.1038/d41586-023-01878-1

Read, J. (2005). The bio-bio-bio model of madness. *The Psychologist, 18*, 596–597.

Read, J., Harrop, C., Geekie, J., & Renton, J. (2018). An audit of ECT in England 2011–2015: Usage, demographics, and adherence to guidelines and legislation. *Psychology and Psychotherapy: Theory, Research and Practice, 91*(3), 263–277. https://doi.org/10.1111/papt.12160

Readsura Decolonial Editorial Collective. (2022). Psychology as a site for decolonial analysis. *Journal of Social Issues, 78*(2), 255–277. https://doi.org/10.1111/josi.12524

Regmi, K. D. (2023). Decolonising meritocratic higher education: Key challenges and directions for change. *Globalisation, Societies and Education*, 1–18. https://doi.org/10.1080/14767724.2023.2210516

Riggs, D. W., & Walker, G. A. (2006). Queer(y)ing rights: Psychology, liberal individualism and colonisation. *Australian Psychologist, 41*(2), 95–103. https://doi.org/10.1080/00050060600578846

Rippon, G., Jordan-Young, R., Kaiser, A., & Fine, C. (2014). Recommendations for sex/gender neuroimaging research: Key principles and implications for research design, analysis, and interpretation [Review]. *Frontiers in Human Neuroscience, 8*. https://doi.org/10.3389/fnhum.2014.00650

Rivers, W. H. R. (1905). Observations on the senses of the Todas. *British Journal of Psychology, 1*(4), 321–396. https://doi.org/10.1111/j.2044-8295.1905.tb00164.x

Robcis, C. (2020). Frantz Fanon, institutional psychotherapy, and the decolonization of psychiatry. *Journal of the History of Ideas, 81*(2), 303–325. https://doi.org/10.1353/jhi.2020.0009

Roberts, D. E. (1993). Racism and patriarchy in the meaning of motherhood. *Journal of Gender and the Law*, *1*(1), 1–38.

Roberts, N. (2004). Character in the mind: Citizenship, education and psychology in Britain, 1880–1914. *History of Education*, *33*(2), 177–197. https://doi.org/10.10 80/00467600410001648779

Robertson, I. H., & Murre, J. M. J. (1999). Rehabilitation of brain damage: Brain plasticity and principles of guided recovery. *Psychological Bulletin*, *125*(5), 544–575. https://doi.org/10.1037/0033-2909.125.5.544

Rogers, K. B. (1997). The lifelong productivity of Terman's original women researcher. Annual Meeting of the American Educational Research Association, Chicago, Illinois.

Roget, P. M. (1824). 'Cranioscopy'. In *Encyclopedia Britannica* (Supplement to 4th, 5th and 6th ed.). Archibald Constable and Company.

Roland, P. E., Graufelds, C. J., Wáhlin, J., Ingelman, L., Andersson, M., Ledberg, A., Pedersen, J., Åkerman, S., Dabringhaus, A., & Zilles, K. (1994). Human brain atlas: For high-resolution functional and anatomical mapping. *Human Brain Mapping*, *1*(3), 173–184. https://doi.org/10.1002/hbm.460010303

Ronson, J. (2011). The kids are not alright. *New Scientist*, *210*(2815), 44–47. https://doi.org/10.1016/S0262-4079(11)61329-8

Roscoe, J. (2022). For learned societies, diversity, equity, and inclusion should be a central focus. Retrieved from https://blogs.lse.ac.uk/impactofsocialsciences/2022/07/05/for-learned-societies-diversity-equity-and-inclusion-should-be-a-central-focus/

Rose, N. (1985). *The psychological complex: Psychology, politics, and society in England 1869–1939*. Routledge & Kegan Paul.

Rosenblatt, F. (1958). The perceptron: A probabilistic model for information storage and organization in the brain. *Psychological Review*, *65*(6), 386–408. https://doi.org/10.1037/h0042519

Rosenhan, D. L. (1973). On being sane in insane places. *Science*, *179*, 250–258. https://doi.org/10.1126/science.179.4070.250

Roth, P. L., Bevier, C. A., Bobko, P., Switzer III, F. S., & Tyler, P. (2001). Ethnic group differences in cognitive ability in employment and educational settings: A meta-analysis. *Personnel Psychology*, *54*, 297–330. https://doi.org/10.1111/j.1744-6570.2001.tb00094.x

Rousseau, J. J. (1762/1979). *Émile, ou de l'Éducation*. Basic Books.

Rutherford, A. (2015). Maintaining masculinity in mid-twentieth-century American psychology: Edwin Boring, scientific eminence, and the 'woman problem'. *Osiris*, *30*(1), 250–271. https://doi.org/10.1086/683022

Sacks, O. (1985). *The man who mistook his wife for a hat and other clinical tales*. Summit Books.

Salsburg, D. (2002). *The lady tasting tea: How statistics revolutionized science in the twentieth century*. Henry Holt and Company.

Salter, P., & Adams, G. (2013). Toward a critical race psychology. *Social and Personality Psychology Compass, 7*, 781–793. https://doi.org/10.1111/spc3.12068

Sandel, M. J. (2020). *The tyranny of merit: What's become of the common good?* Penguin Books.

Sanger, M. (1939). Letter from Margaret Sanger to Dr C. J. Gamble, December 10, 1939. Smith Libraries Exhibits. Retrieved from https://libex.smith.edu/omeka/items/show/495

Sanz, V. (2017). No way out of the binary: A critical history of the scientific production of sex. *Signs: Journal of Women in Culture and Society, 43*, 1–27. https://doi.org/10.1086/692517

Schoenherr, J. R. (2017). Prestige technology in the evolution and social organization of early psychological science. *Theory & Psychology, 27*(1), 6–33. https://doi.org/10.1177/0959354316677076

Schulz, S. L. (2017). The informed consent model of transgender care: An alternative to the diagnosis of gender dysphoria. *Journal of Humanistic Psychology, 58*(1), 72–92. https://doi.org/10.1177/0022167817745217

Schwarz, K. A., & Pfister, R. (2016). Scientific psychology in the 18th century: A historical rediscovery. *Perspectives on Psychological Science, 11*(3), 399–407. https://doi.org/10.1177/1745691616635601

Science and Technology Committee. (2014). Women in scientific careers: Sixth Report of Session 2013–14. Retrieved from https://publications.parliament.uk/pa/cm201314/cmselect/cmsctech/701/701.pdf

Scottish Parliament. (2022). Gender Recognition Reform (Scotland) Bill. Retrieved from www.parliament.scot/bills-and-laws/bills/gender-recognition-reform-scotland-bill/stage-3

Scull, A. (2015). *Madness in civilization: A cultural history of insanity, from the Bible to Freud, from the madhouse to modern medicine.* Princeton University Press.

Seal, H. L. (1967). Studies in the history of probability and statistics. XV The historical development of the Gauss linear model. *Biometrika, 54*(1–2), 1–24. https://doi.org/10.1093/biomet/54.1-2.1

Sears, R. R. (1975). Your ancients revisited: A history of child development. In E. M. Hetherington (Ed.), *Review of Child Development Research* (pp. 67–70). University of Chicago Press.

Sharfstein, S. (2005). Big Pharma and American psychiatry: The good, the bad, and the ugly. *Psychiatric News, 40*(16), 1–34. https://doi.org/10.1176/pn.40.16.00400003

Shorter, E. (2009). History of electroconvulsive therapy. In C. M. Swartz (Ed.), *Electroconvulsive and neuromodulation therapies* (pp. 167–179). Cambridge University Press.

Sibieta, L. (2021, October). The growing gap between state school and private school spending. *IFS.* Retrieved from https://ifs.org.uk/articles/growing-gap-between-state-school-and-private-school-spending

Sidhu, G., Asgarian, N., Greiner, R., & Brown, M. (2012). Kernel Principal Component Analysis for dimensionality reduction in fMRI-based diagnosis of ADHD. *Frontiers in Systems Neuroscience, 6*, 74. https://doi.org/10.3389/fnsys.2012.00074

Singh, A. A. (2016). Moving from affirmation to liberation in psychological practice with transgender and gender nonconforming clients. *American Psychologist, 71*(8), 755–762. https://doi.org/10.1037/amp0000106

Sinha, D., & Tripathi, R. C. (1994). Individualism in a collectivist culture: A case of coexistence of opposites. In *Individualism and collectivism: Theory, method, and applications.* (pp. 123–136). Sage Publications.

Skinner, B. F. (1948). *Walden Two*. Macmillan.

Skloot, R. (2011). *The immortal life of Henrietta Lacks.* Broadway Paperbacks.

Slobodin, R. (1997). *W.H.R. Rivers: Pioneer anthropologist, psychiatrist of The Ghost Road.* Sutton.

Smidt, S. (2006). *The developing child in the 21st century: A global perspective on child development.* Routledge.

Smith, N. W. (1974). The ancient background to Greek psychology and some implications for today. *The Psychological Record, 24*(3), 309–324. https://doi.org/10.1007/BF03394249

Smith, O. M., Davis, K. L., Pizza, R. B., Waterman, R., Dobson, K. C., Foster, B., Jarvey, J. C., Jones, L. N., Leuenberger, W., Nourn, N., Conway, E. E., Fiser, C. M., Hansen, Z. A., Hristova, A., Mack, C., Saunders, A. N., Utley, O. J., Young, M. L., & Davis, C. L. (2023). Peer review perpetuates barriers for historically excluded groups. *Nature Ecology & Evolution, 7*, 512–523. https://doi.org/10.1038/s41559-023-01999-w

Smyth, M. M. (2001). Certainty and uncertainty sciences: Marking the boundaries of psychology in introductory textbooks. *Social Studies of Science, 31*(3), 389–416. https://doi.org/10.1177/030631201031003003

Snedecor, G. W. (1934). *Calculation and interpretation of analysis of variance and covariance.* Collegiate Press. https://doi.org/10.1037/13308-000

Spatig-Amerikaner, A. (2012). *Unequal education: Federal loophole enables lower spending on students of color.* Center for American Progress. Retrieved from https://cdn.uncf.org/wp-content/uploads/PDFs/UnequalEduation.pdf

Speaker, S. L. (1997). From 'happiness pills' to 'national nightmare': Changing cultural assessment of minor tranquilizers in America, 1955–1980. *Journal of the History of Medicine and Allied Sciences, 52*(3), 338–376. https://doi.org/10.1093/jhmas/52.3.338

Spearman, C. (1904). The proof and measurement of association between two things. *The American Journal of Psychology, 15*(1), 72–101. https://doi.org/10.2307/1412159

Spitzer, R. L., & Fleiss, J. L. (1974). A re-analysis of the reliability of psychiatric diagnosis. *The British Journal of Psychiatry, 125*(587), 341–347. https://doi.org/10.1192/bjp.125.4.341

Stannus, H. S. (1913). Anomalies of pigmentation among natives of Nyasaland: A contribution to the study of albinism. *Biometrika, 9*(3/4), 333–365. https://doi.org/10.2307/2331897

Staum, M. S. (2011). *Nature and nurture in French social sciences, 1859–1914 and beyond.* McGill-Queen's University Press.

Steingard, S. (2019). A path to the future for psychiatry. In S. Steingard (Ed.), *Critical psychiatry: Controversies and clinical implications* (pp. 207–220). Springer International Publishing. https://doi.org/10.1007/978-3-030-02732-2_9

Stephan, P. E. (1996). The economics of science. *Journal of Economic Literature, 34*(3), 1199–1235. http://www.jstor.org/stable/2729500

Sternberg, R. J., Grigorenko, E. L., & Kidd, K. K. (2005). Intelligence, race, and genetics. *American Psychologist, 60*(1), 46–59. https://doi.org/10.1037/0003-066X.60.1.46

Stetson, C. P. (1892). The yellow wall-paper: A story. *The New England Magazine, 11*(5), 647–656.

Stone, P. K., & Sanders, L. (2021). *Bodies and lives in Victorian England: Science, sexuality, and the affliction of being female.* Routledge. https://doi.org/10.4324/9780429398735

Student. (1908). The probable error of a mean. *Biometrika, 6*(1), 1–25. https://doi.org/10.2307/2331554

Swartz, S. (2022). *Psychoanalysis and colonialism: A contemporary introduction.* Routledge.

Tampa, M., Sarbu, I., Matei, C., Benea, V., & Georgescu, S. R. (2014). Brief history of syphilis. *Journal of Medicine and Life, 7*(1), 4–10.

Tasca, C., Rapetti, M., Carta, M. G., & Fadda, B. (2012). Women and hysteria in the history of mental health. *Clinical Practice & Epidemiology in Mental Health, 8*(1), 110–119. https://doi.org/10.2174/1745017901208010110

Tate, S. A., & Page, D. (2018). Whiteliness and institutional racism: Hiding behind (un)conscious bias. *Ethics and Education, 13*(1), 141–155. https://doi.org/10.1080/17449642.2018.1428718

Tauber, A. I. (2022). *The triumph of uncertainty: Science and self in the postmodern age.* Central European University Press. https://doi.org/10.1515/9789633865828

Teigen, K. H. (2002). One hundred years of laws in psychology. *American Journal of Psychology, 115*(1), 103–118. https://doi.org/10.2307/1423676

Terman, L. (1928). Introduction. In G. M. Whipple (Ed.), *National Society for the Study of Education, 27th Yearbook, Part I.* Public School Publishing.

Thelen, E. (2005). Dynamic systems theory and the complexity of change. *Psychoanalytic Dialogues, 15*(2), 255–283. https://doi.org/10.1080/10481881509348831

Thomas, A. (2020). Why diverse perspectives matter for Memory & Cognition. *Memory & Cognition, 48*(2), 173–175. https://doi.org/10.3758/s13421-019-01004-5

Thompson, D. (2016). Developmental psychology in the 1920s: A period of major transition. *Journal of Genetic Psychology, 177*(6), 244–251. https://doi.org/10.1080/00221325.2016.1243407

Titchener, E. B. (1921). Wilhelm Wundt. *American Journal of Psychology, 32*(2), 161–178. https://doi.org/10.2307/1413739

Titone, D., Tiv, M., & Pexman, P. M. (2018). The status of women cognitive scientists in Canada: Insights from publicly available NSERC funding data. *Canadian Journal of Experimental Psychology, 72*(2), 81–90. https://doi.org/10.1037/cep0000150

Tokumitsu, M. (2014, December). In the name of love. *Jacobin* magazine. Retrieved from https://jacobin.com/2014/01/in-the-name-of-love/

Tracy, F., & Stimpfl, J. (1909). *Psychology of the child* (7th ed.). D.C. Heath & Co.

Triandis, H. C. (1989). The self and social behavior in differing cultural contexts. *Psychological Review, 96*(3), 506–520. https://doi.org/10.1037/0033-295x.96.3.506

Tuck, E., & Yang, K. W. (2012). Decolonization is not a metaphor. *Decolonization: Indigeneity, Education & Society, 1*(1), 1–40.

Tuke, S. (1813). *Description of the Retreat, an institution near York for insane persons of the Society of Friends containing an account of its origins and progress, the modes of treatment and a statement of cases.* W. Alexander.

UNCF. (2023). K–12 disparity facts and statistics. https://uncf.org/pages/K-12-Disparity-Facts-and-Stats

Unger, R. K. (2001). Women as subjects, actors, and agents in the history of psychology. In R. K. Unger (Ed.), *Handbook of the psychology of women and gender* (pp. 3–16). John Wiley & Sons.

University and College Union. (2013). Guidance for UCU branches in relation to implementation of government immigration rules. Retrieved from www.ucu.org.uk/media/8122/Points-based-immigration-UCU-guidance-2013/pdf/pdi_guidanceforbranches_may13_1.pdf

University and College Union. (2021). Home Office Independent review of Prevent: Submission from the University and College Union. Retrieved from www.ucu.org.uk/media/12452/Prevent-review-UCU-response-May-21/pdf/UCU_Prevent_review_-_May_2021.pdf

US Department of Education CRDC. (2016). Key data highlights on equity and opportunity gaps in our nation's public schools. Retrieved from www2.ed.gov/about/offices/list/ocr/docs/2013-14-first-look.pdf

US Senate Subcommittee on Foreign Aid Expenditures of the Committee on Government Operations. (1970). *Population crisis: Hearings, 1965–1968.* Socio-Dynamics Publications.

Vaid, J., & Geraci, L. (2016). V. An examination of women's professional visibility in cognitive psychology. *Feminism & Psychology, 26*(3), 292–319. https://doi.org/10.1177/0959353516641139

van der Lee, R., & Ellemers, N. (2015). Gender contributes to personal research funding success in The Netherlands. *Proceedings of the National Academy of Sciences, 112*(40), 12349–12353. https://doi.org/10.1073/pnas.1510159112

van Rooij, I., & Baggio, G. (2021). Theory before the test: How to build high-verisimilitude explanatory theories in psychological science. *Perspectives on Psychological Science, 16*(4), 682–697. https://doi.org/10.1177/1745691620970604

Vanpée, J. (1990). Rousseau's Emile ou de l'Education: A resistance to reading. *Yale French Studies, 77*, 156–176. https://doi.org/10.2307/2930152

Varga, D. (2022). The legacy of recapitulation theory in the history of developmental psychology. In *The Oxford Encyclopedia of the History of Modern Psychology*. Oxford University Press.

von Neumann, J., & Burks, A. W. (1966). *Theory of self-reproducing automata.* University of Illinois Press.

Wagner, A. D., Shannon, B. J., Kahn, I., & Buckner, R. L. (2005). Parietal lobe contributions to episodic memory retrieval. *Trends in Cognitive Sciences, 9*(9), 445–453. https://doi.org/10.1016/j.tics.2005.07.001

Wallace, A. R. (1870). Hereditary genius, an inquiry into its laws and consequences. *Nature, 1*(20), 501–503. https://doi.org/10.1038/001501a0

Wallin, J. E. W. (1911). A practical guide for the administration of the Binet-Simon Scale for measuring intelligence. *The Psychological Clinic, 5*(7), 217–238.

Warren, E. (1909). Some statistical observations on termites, mainly based on the work of the late Mr G. D. Haviland. *Biometrika, 6*(4), 329–347. https://doi.org/10.1093/biomet/6.4.329

Washington, H. A. (2006). *Medical apartheid: The dark history of medical experimentation on black Americans from colonial times to the present.* Doubleday.

Watson, J. B. (1928). *Psychological care of infant and child.* W. W. Norton & Co.

Watson, R. I. (1963). *The great psychologists: From Aristotle to Freud.* Lippincott.

Watters, E. (2010). *Crazy like us: The globalization of the American psyche.* Free Press.

Weiss, T., Soroka, T., Gorodisky, L., Shushan, S., Snitz, K., Weissgross, R., Furman-Haran, E., Dhollander, T., & Sobel, N. (2020). Human olfaction without apparent olfactory bulbs. *Neuron, 105*(1), 35–45. https://doi.org/10.1016/j.neuron.2019.10.006

Werskey, G. (1979). *The visible college: The collective biography of British scientific socialists of the 1930s.* Holt, Rinehart, and Winston.

West, J. D., Jacquet, J., King, M. M., Correll, S. J., & Bergstrom, C. T. (2013). The role of gender in scholarly authorship. *PLoS ONE, 8*(7), e66212. https://doi.org/10.1371/journal.pone.0066212

West, J. M. (2010). Black intelligence test of cultural homogeneity (B.I.T.C.H.). In C. S. Clauss-Ehlers (Ed.), *Encyclopedia of cross-cultural school psychology* (pp. 164–165). Springer US. https://doi.org/10.1007/978-0-387-71799-9_46

Whitaker, K., & Guest, O. (2020). #bropenscience is broken science. *The Psychologist, November*, 34–37. www.bps.org.uk/psychologist/bropenscience-broken-science

Whitaker, R., & Cosgrove, L. (2015). *Psychiatry under the influence: Institutional corruption, social injury, and prescriptions for reform.* Palgrave Macmillan.

White, A. (1885). The nomad poor of London. *Contemporary Review, 47*.

White, T. L., & Gonsalves, M. A. (2021). Dignity neuroscience: Universal rights are rooted in human brain science. *Annals of the New York Academy of Sciences, 1505*(1), 40–54. https://doi.org/10.1111/nyas.14670

Williams, R. L. (1972). The BITCH-100: A culture-specific test. Paper presented at the American Psychological Association Annual Convention, Honolulu, Hawaii, September 1972. https://files.eric.ed.gov/fulltext/ED070799.pdf

Williams, R. L. (1975). *Ebonics: The true language of black folks*. Institute of Black Studies.

Wilson, R. A. (1995). *Cartesian psychology and physical minds: Individualism and the science of the mind*. Cambridge University Press. https://doi.org/10.1017/CBO9781139174374

Winn, J. (2015). The co-operative university: Labour, property and pedagogy. *Power and Education, 7*(1), 39–55. https://doi.org/10.1177/1757743814567386

Witzig, R. (1996). The medicalization of race: Scientific legitimization of a flawed social construct. *Annals of Internal Medicine, 125*(8), 675–679. https://doi.org/10.7326/0003-4819-125-8-199610150-00008

Wolf, T. H. (1973). *Alfred Binet*. The University of Chicago Press.

Wood, M. S., Scheaf, D. J., & Dwyer, S. M. (2021). Fake it 'til you make it: Hazards of a cultural norm in entrepreneurship. *Business Horizons*. https://doi.org/10.1016/j.bushor.2021.12.001

Woolley, H. T. (1910). A review of the recent literature on the psychology of sex. *Psychological Bulletin, 7*(10), 335–342.

Wright, J. R., Jr. (2022). Société Mutuelle d'Autopsie, American Anthropometric Society, and the Wilder Brain Collection. *Archives of Pathology & Laboratory Medicine, 147*(5), 611–623. https://doi.org/10.5858/arpa.2021-0623-HP

Yarkoni, T. (2011). Brain-based prediction of ADHD – now with 100% fewer brains! [Blog] Retrieved from www.talyarkoni.org/blog/2011/10/12/brain-based-prediction-of-adhd-now-with-100-fewer-brains/

Yong, E. (2017, May 4). How a frog became the first mainstream pregnancy test. *The Atlantic*. Retrieved from www.theatlantic.com/science/archive/2017/05/how-a-frog-became-the-first-mainstream-pregnancy-test/525285/

Zarkadakis, G. (2017). *In our own image: Savior or destroyer? The history and future of artificial intelligence*. Pegasus Books.

Zeilig, L. (2021). *Frantz Fanon: A political biography*. Bloomsbury Publishing.

Ziliak, S. T. (2008). Retrospectives: Guinnessometrics: The economic foundation of 'Student's' t. *Journal of Economic Perspectives, 22*(4), 199–216. https://doi.org/10.1257/jep.22.4.199

Zola, I. K. (1972). Medicine as an institution of social control. *The Sociological Review, 20*(4), 487–504. https://doi.org/10.1111/j.1467-954X.1972.tb00220.x

Zuroski, E. (2020, January 27). 'Where do you know from?': An exercise in placing ourselves together in the classroom. *MAI: Feminism and Visual Culture*. Retrieved from https://maifeminism.com/where-do-you-know-from-an-exercise-in-placing-ourselves-together-in-the-classroom/

INDEX